THE
MORAL COSMOS OF
Paradise Lost

THE

MORAL COSMOS OF

Paradise Lost

By
LAWRENCE BABB

MICHIGAN STATE UNIVERSITY PRESS

1970

FOR
Nancy and Alan

CONTENTS

FOREWORD

I HAVE WRITTEN THIS BOOK about the physical milieu of *Paradise Lost* because I felt that a short volume assembling the available pertinent material might be useful to any student of Milton, because I believed that I could add something to the information on the subject previously published and could correct a few current misinterpretations, and because I hoped to define the rather significant poetic functions of matter and space in Milton's epic. In some parts of the volume I may seem to have gone beyond the area suggested by "physical milieu." For instance, I have included Milton's ideas about human physiology and psychology. It will become clear, I believe, that the nature of man belongs in such a study as this.

I have attempted to write the book so that the uninitiated reader (for example, an intelligent college upperclassman) might use it. I hope that it will have something also for those who are better informed. The Milton scholar will find in it a great deal that he already knows, but it would not be possible to eliminate such material without sacrificing continuity. In explaining concepts familiar to those who know the field, I have tried to be brief.

Anyone who writes on Milton in the 1960's works within the context of a very large body of Milton scholarship. Absolute originality is hardly possible. Obviously a great deal of the information that I have presented comes from predecessors. I am indebted especially to studies by Denis Saurat, Francis Johnson, Grant McColley, Arnold Williams, Walter Clyde Curry, Kester Svendsen, Robert H. West, Thomas S. Kuhn, Harry F. Robins, A. B. Chambers, William B. Hunter, Jr., C. A. Patrides. In the notes I have tried to be reasonably specific in the acknowledgement of my obligations. I have not tried to add to the massive available information on Milton's sources. In the text or notes, however, I have frequently indicated, by reference either to primary documents or to modern studies, that Milton's ideas had precedents. To support what I have said concerning *Paradise Lost*, I have quoted freely from the *Christian Doctrine*. I have not assumed, however, that Milton never changed his mind. With few exceptions I have avoided controversy.

In quoting Milton's Poetry, I have used the edition of Merritt Y. Hughes (*Complete Poems and Major Prose*, New York, 1957). For Milton's prose works, I have used the Columbia edition *(The Works of John Milton,* ed. Frank A. Patterson, 18 volumes, New York, 1930-38) and its translations of the Latin treatises.

I am indebted to my fellow members of the Department of English, Michigan State University, for release from teaching so that I might work on this project. My colleague Professor Arnold Williams has kindly read the manuscript. I am grateful for his criticism and suggestions.

Lawrence Babb

East Lansing.
September 1969

Chapter I. PRELIMINARIES

THE STORY WHICH MILTON TELLS in *Paradise Lost* requires a setting of tremendous spatial stretch. He has created a setting which is vaster than that
of any other literary classic. Yet even when the story moves into remote
regions which men have never seen and which they can comprehend only
dimly, he is remarkably definite. The action always occurs in a specific
location, and every location is specifically related in space to all others.
Milton seems to see the various regions of this enormous setting with
peculiar vividness, and he recreates his vision of beauty and grandeur in the
imagination of his reader, sometimes introducing detail, more often de-
pending on broad suggestion.

He has done a good deal of thinking about physical reality and has
formulated ideas concerning it which he has incorporated in the poem. He
believes that God's physical universe is an emanation from God himself.
Every part of it, in some degree, shares in the divine nature. Every part has
kinship with every other and has a high or low function in the realization
of the divine purposes. Milton, then, has conceived the physical milieu not
only imaginatively but also intellectually. It is not merely background. It
is one of the means by which he conveys the religious and moral ideas with
which *Paradise Lost* is concerned. With the possible exception of the *Divine
Comedy,* I know of no other narrative poem in which the setting is given
so much attention or has so great significance. (What is there to say about
the setting of the *Odyssey,* the *Aeneid,* or *The Faerie Queene?*)

In this book I shall describe the various parts of Milton's cosmos in some
detail in the hope of aiding the reader of *Paradise Lost* in visualization, I shall
attempt an exposition of Milton's ideas concerning matter and its relation
to spirit, and I shall try to define the contribution which the milieu makes
to the meaning and the imaginative impact of the poem. I shall assume that
my reader knows the poem but is not acquainted with the voluminous
commentary on it. To clarify and elaborate, I have quoted from other works
of Milton's, especially often from the *Christian Doctrine,* his prose treatise
on theology.

It will be necessary to make some rather extended excursions into subjects which may not seem obviously relevant. To show the significance of
the setting, for example, it will be necessary to show that humanity and

I

physical nature, in Milton's scheme of things, are intimately related. Milton tells us emphatically that human nature and angelic nature are not very different; a discussion of human nature leads inevitably to angel nature. Just as in God's universe there is an interrelation of all things, so in *Paradise Lost* there is an integration of all its elements. This integration is so thorough that one cannot discuss any of its elements in isolation. In spite of the apparent digressions, the emphasis will remain on the physical milieu.

This study is concerned with some of Milton's meanings and some of his poetic effects. It does not try to evaluate. The poetic and dramatic excellences of *Paradise Lost* do not need defense, and it seems quite unnecessary to plaster over or explain away the occasional obscurities and inconsistencies that one finds in it. When I say that I am concerned with the poet's meanings, I refer to his conscious meanings. I have not read anything between Milton's lines. I do not know what subconscious desires and antipathies or what primeval mythic patterns have swum up from the subliminal depths to influence the form or content of his epic. I regard *Paradise Lost* as a work of art consciously planned to achieve certain purposes, and I believe that on the whole Milton has done what he set out to do.

An initial survey of Milton's universal geography and an explanation of a few terms will prevent possible confusions. The empyreal Heaven, the dwelling of God and the angels, is a flat plane at the top of everything; Hell is a flat plane at the bottom. The great space between the two is occupied by Chaos, a seething ocean of undifferentiated matter. The world, which is comparatively very small, hangs by a chain from one edge of Heaven into a pocket in the upper surface of Chaos. The *world*, as Milton uses the term, consists of the starry heavens (concentric spheres which surround the earth) and of the earth itself. He sometimes uses *universe* as an alternate term. I shall use *world* in Milton's inclusive sense. His world includes everything visible to earthbound man; when he means the planet on which we live, he uses *earth*. Because I need a term which Milton does not supply, I shall use *cosmos* for the totality (Heaven, Hell, the world, Chaos).

There is no doubt in Milton's mind that the story of *Paradise Lost* is a true story. He believes, moreover, that the setting which he provides for it was the setting in which these things really happened. Indeed he believes that the whole content of his poem is true. The sense in which this debatable statement should be understood is the subject of the next chapter.

Chapter II. KNOWLEDGE

ONLY AN INFORMED MAN can be a wise and virtuous man. It is the moral duty, therefore, of all the sons of Adam to seek knowledge, and this is a difficult duty.

Adam himself needed to acquire very little. God gave him at creation intellectual faculties far more perceptive and more clearly logical than those of his descendants. He endowed him also with a fund of innate knowledge,[1] with all that he needed to know in order to live happily and virtuously in Paradise. Adam knew something about the physical world—about the flora and fauna and about the stars and their spheres. The moral law by which he must live was "so implanted and innate in him, that he needed no precept to enforce its observance . . . the law of nature, which is sufficient of itself to teach whatever is agreeable to right reason, that is to say, whatever is intrinsically good."[2] He had an innate knowledge of God: In *Paradise Lost*, when he awakes just after his creation, he does not know just who he is "or where, or from what cause," but he knows at least that he is the creature of "some great Maker. . . . In goodness and in power preëminent" (VIII, 270-79). He knows without being told that God is "infinite; / And through all numbers absolute, though One" (VIII, 420-21).

Milton's Adam does, to be sure, receive some instruction. Just after his creation, God tells Adam who he is and the conditions of his being (VIII, 295-348). When Satan enters Paradise, God sends Raphael to instruct him further concerning his happy state and the conditions of its continuance (V, 233-45). Raphael's principal message is an emphatic reminder of something which Adam already knows: that his primary duty is obedience and that disobedience merits punishment. But Raphael, responding to Adam's natural desire to know, imparts a great deal of subsidiary information. He tells the story of the war in Heaven (which warns "*Adam* by dire example to beware / Apostasy," VII, 42-43); he describes the Creation of the world; he explains the physical and moral hierarchy of God's creatures (which Adam understands already in part); he enlightens Adam concerning his two possible destinies. Although much of it seems intended rather for the reader's instruction than for Adam's, all that Raphael tells Adam is designed to enlarge his understanding of his obligations and of his place in God's scheme. There is no irrelevancy.

3

The Original Sin brought intellectual ruin. Man lost much of his innate knowledge. His will and understanding were greatly weakened; his passions (faculties which he shares with the beasts) were greatly strengthened; and in Adam's sons, more frequently than not, the passions confuse the processes of the intellect, obscure its perceptions, overrule its decisions. Not only are our intellectual powers less capable than Adam's but we live in a world in which, as a result of his sin, we are surrounded by a multitude of beguiling evils, which we must learn to recognize. Until Satan entered, distinguishing between good and evil was no problem in Paradise, for there was no evil, only the potentiality of evil; in the postlapsarian world the drawing of this distinction is a difficult, ever-present, and painfully important task. Adam created intellectual and moral problems far more difficult than his own, which his sons must solve with their diminished and vitiated endowments.

But these problems are not beyond solution. God has given mankind a second chance; he has in some measure renewed man's "lapsed powers" (*PL*, III, 176). Man may therefore, by strenuous effort, rectify his erring reason and gain the knowledge requisite to righteous living, knowledge which was either innate in Adam or not necessary to him. To "repair the ruines of our first Parents"[3] is the object of education. The reconstruction of man's intellectual ruins is an arduous task which can never be fully accomplished yet must be undertaken.

Humanity retains at least a little innate knowledge as a basis for reconstitution. The "Deity has imprinted upon the human mind . . . many unquestionable tokens of himself";[4] and by God's grace, "a certain remnant, or imperfect illumination" of the "law of nature given originally to Adam . . . still dwells in the hearts of all mankind." Our intellectual labors should be directed toward the "renewal of its primitive brightness." The "regenerate" may daily advance in knowledge and wisdom "under the influence of the Holy Spirit."[5] But they must desire improvement and earnestly strive for it.

Nature is "the mysterious power and efficacy of that divine voice which went forth in the beginning, and to which, as to a perpetual command, all things have since paid obedience."[6] This perpetual command is "that general law which is the origin of every thing, and under which every thing acts."[7] The law of nature, then, is both a law of physical causation and a moral law. All inanimate things, all plants, all animals can do no other than to act or react according to this law. They must obey it. Men, because they are free agents, are not compelled. They may and should obey the law of nature, but they have the power of choice. They are therefore capable of evil and of disrupting the God-ordained order of things. For the inferior creatures, natural law is a statement of what is; for man it is a statement of what should be.

4

As it applies to human conduct, the law of nature is the province of moral philosophy, or ethics. The study of ethics clearly is proper for the man who desires to live the good life. The law of nature as it applies to subhuman creatures is the province of science, or as Milton would call it, natural philosophy. This also has its value. For one thing, knowledge of their natural environment enables men to increase their physical well-being. The body is less than the spirit, but Milton, being no ascetic, is nevertheless conscious of the body's legitimate, though lesser, claims. The primary value of the study of the physical world, however, lies in the support which it gives to religion; that is, the evidence which it discloses of the power and benefi- cence of the Creator. I shall return to this subject.

The knowledgeable and virtuous man must understand the principles of nature. But religious truths transcend these. "No one ... can have right thoughts of God, with nature or reason alone as his guide, independent of the word, or message of God."[8] Among classical philosophers, there were good men, men who were virtuous because they followed the law of nature, their best and only guide. Christians have also the benefit of revelation. If in humble faith they endeavor to learn the lessons which God has offered them, they will be better instructed for the righteous life than any pagan could be, and they will have a far better chance of salvation. If one under- stands the nature and extent of God's gracious kindness and if he realizes "that to obey is best, / And love with fear the only God," he has "attain'd the sum / Of wisdom":

> only add
> Deeds to thy knowledge answerable, add Faith,
> Add Virtue, Patience, Temperance, add Love,
> By name to come call'd Charity, the soul
> Of all the rest.   (*PL*, XII, 561-85)

II

Men must seek knowledge if they are to live wisely. It is not possible, however, to understand all objects of knowledge in the same degree. Some subjects, at least theoretically, may be mastered completely; for example, recorded historical fact, mathematics, grammar, natural and moral philoso- phy. None of these subjects is too abstruse for the capable human mind. If mastery is never absolute, this is because life is short and art is long. What men learn in such fields is presumed to correspond with fact and theoreti- cally may include all the facts. I shall call knowledge of this kind *literal knowledge*.

There are objects of knowledge, however, which lie beyond human experience and which the limited human mind cannot, in any literal sense, understand. During the course of their long dialogue, Adam questions Raphael on certain subjects which belong in this supra-human category, principally three: the rebellion of Satan, the creation of the world, and the structure and operation of the mundane heavens. On the first two of these Raphael is very willing to speak: "for thy good," he says, "This is dispens't" (V, 570-71); "such Commission from above / I have receiv'd" (VII, 118-19). But to explain these things to so limited a mind as Adam's will be a difficult task:

> to recount Almighty works
> What words or tongue of Seraph can suffice,
> Or heart of man suffice to comprehend?   (VII, 112-14)

Raphael's method is to express "what surmounts the reach / Of human sense ... By lik'ning spiritual to corporal forms" (V, 571-73); that is, to employ, as rough equivalents, phenomena of human experience which are remotely similar to, though much simpler than, the celestial counterparts, "Thus measuring things in Heav'n by things on Earth" (VI, 893).

So in describing the Creation and the war in Heaven, Raphael is conveying to Adam an incomplete approximation of the realities. If a four-year-old were to ask, "What is a university?" one might answer, "A place where people go to learn things." This would by no means completely express the nature of a university, but it would convey to the child an idea which was at least not inaccurate. If one's greatgrandfather spoke from the grave to ask, "What is an automobile?" one might answer, "A horseless carriage," and thereby convey a significant fraction of the truth. For some decades now we have realized that Euclid's geometry is such an approximation. A straight line is not the shortest distance between two points. Just what a straight line is and just what kind of line represents the shortest distance are concepts which elude the uninitiate. For most of us the Euclidian axiom is as close to spatial reality as we can get—and quite close enough for our practical purposes. The difference between celestial reality as Raphael knows it and celestial reality as Adam can comprehend it is much greater, however, than the difference between the Einsteinian and Euclidian concepts of space.

Milton regards a great many of God's revelations in Scripture as truths only in this limited sense. God has adapted supra-human truths to the limitations of the human mind. God wills that men should know these things, and he wills that they should know them in just the form in which he has revealed them. Angels, Milton writes, are "Endued with the greatest swiftness, which is figuratively denoted by the attribute of wings."[9] Just what physical equipment do angels have which explains their celerity? As far as human beings are concerned, the answer is: wings. Milton does not believe that angels have actual wings, yet he would not think of not believing that angels have wings. The Biblical statement that God made man in his image expresses a true relationship (a relationship involving both body and spirit, but spirit more than body[10]). Yet one cannot assume from this statement "that God is in fashion like unto man in all his parts and members."[11] God "has made as full a revelation of himself as our minds can conceive, or the weakness of our nature bear." In neither the "literal" nor the "figurative descriptions" of Scripture is God exhibited "as he really is." We should conceive of him "as he, in condescending to accommodate himself to our capacities, has shown that he desires we should conceive."[12]

There is, then, a supra-human realm of knowledge which man may enter only through supernatural revelation. What he knows of this realm which is beyond his experience and understanding he knows only in the form of rough analogies and approximations. His comprehension of what exists and what happens in this realm is highly incomplete, only relative. Borrowing a word from the traditional terminology, I shall call such knowledge *accommodated knowledge*.[13] The theory of accommodation had been current in Christian literature since patristic times. How else could God's "anger" and God's "jealousy" be explained?

Raphael tells Adam the story of the war in Heaven in accommodated language. To represent an angel as a warrior in armor is not completely to express the nature of the angel, but at least it suggests something of the embattled angelic character. To represent spiritual conflict in Heaven by means of the images of human warfare is highly incomplete communication, but partial truth is better than no truth at all. (We have to overlook the fact that Adam had had no experience with warfare. War has a meaning to all of Adam's sons, and it is to them that *Paradise Lost* is addressed.) Raphael's story of the Creation is also a relative communication. What Milton says of the physical appearances of Heaven and Hell and of the activities of the angels, loyal and rebellious, must be understood as likewise adapted to the human mind.

There is no moral reason why man should not seek knowledge of the impious defection of Satan, of the Creation, of the final Consummation, or of other such matters beyond his experience. There is no reason why he should not acquire literal and complete knowledge of these matters except that he cannot. It is a simple matter of inability, and because of this inability, his knowledge of these things must remain relative. There are truths above and beyond these, however, which not only are incomprehensible but are forbidden. "The hidden wayes of [God's] providence we adore & search not."[14] When "Scripture is silent," we should not be "concerned to inquire."[15] Scripture is silent concerning the hypostatical union, the manner in which the divine and human natures were united in Jesus; since "God has not revealed the mode in which this union is effected, it behoves us to cease from devising subtle explanations, and to be contented with remaining wisely ignorant."[16] What God has not chosen to reveal is *forbidden knowledge.*

Though they are intellectually much less narrowly restricted than men, angels also are creatures of limited knowledge. There are many things

> which th'invisible King,
> Only Omniscient, hath supprest in Night,
> To none communicable in Earth or Heaven.   (VII, 122-24)

God has "wisely" concealed some truths "From Man or Angel" (VIII, 72-73). Raphael does not know the answers to all of the questions which Adam raises. The angels "do not look into all the secret things of God ... some things indeed they know by revelation, and others by means of the excellent intelligence with which they are gifted; there is much, however, of which they are ignorant."[17] "Even the Son ... knows not all things absolutely."[18]

The endeavor to learn God's secrets, either by speculation or by scientific investigation, is the sin of *curiosity.*[19] Curious inquiry is sinful because it is presumptuous; no man has the capacity to discover or to understand the hidden truths. Curiosity is intellectual pride. Humanity is lamentably inclined to this sin—"prone to search after vain curiosities"[20]—and this inclination shows itself in the father of all men. Raphael approves of Adam's desire to know: "To ask or search I blame thee not" (VIII, 66). He has commission from God to satisfy Adam's desire "Of knowledge within bounds" (VII, 118-20). But he warns Adam against inquiry concerning things beyond the limit:

> Solicit not thy thoughts with matters hid,
> Leave them to God above.   (VIII, 167-68)

Not only are there mysteries which are "Not lawful to reveal" (V, 570), but Adam must not attempt to devise explanations of them by his "own inventions" (VII, 121). Adam confesses that the human "mind or fancy" is apt "to rove," and resolves upon intellectual humility. He will repress his curiosity concerning "things remote / From use, obscure and subtle" (VIII, 191-92), things which do not concern him or his being.

Pious Renaissance writers frequently attacked scientific investigation as a curious prying into God's arcana. Milton, at least during the first forty-five to fifty years of his life, did not share this view—quite the contrary. He denounces the curious speculations of theologians in the *Christian Doctrine,* but he has no quarrel with the natural philosophers. Yet Raphael delivers his warning against curiosity as a result of Adam's questions concerning the heavenly bodies. Astronomy is the only subject, except the loves of the angels, which Raphael refuses to discuss. It seems strange that Milton should place astronomy beyond the bounds of permitted knowledge. I shall discuss this apparently unreasonable interdiction later.

There are, then, three categories of knowledge, or truth: 1) that knowledge which men may discover and master by the use of their own faculties (including natural and moral philosophy), 2) that which is permitted and revealed to men but which they can apprehend only in adapted or relative form, 3) that which is both incomprehensible and forbidden. To seek knowledge in the first two categories is wholly commendable; to attempt to enter the final category is to commit the sin of curiosity. There is a fourth category: knowledge permitted to angels but not to men. Raphael suggests this when he refers to "The secrets of another world, perhaps / Not lawful to reveal" (V, 569-70), implying that he knows many things which he may not communicate to Adam even in accommodated form. But Milton has little occasion in *Paradise Lost* to refer to this angelic category of knowledge.

It is unlikely that, as he wrote *Paradise Lost*, Milton was sharply conscious of the lines of demarcation in this threefold, or fourfold, classification of truth. I believe, however, that it represents Milton's conscious or semiconscious ideas concerning knowability with reasonable accuracy. If one applies it in reading *Paradise Lost*, many things become clearer.

III

The Tree of Knowledge—a very significant property in Milton's story—introduces some confusion into what Milton has to say on the subject of knowledge. The phrase "forbidden knowledge" immediately and inevitably suggests the forbidden fruit, but it is hard to find any correspondency between the forbidden knowledge just discussed (knowledge of God's arcana) and the knowledge which the forbidden fruit symbolizes. There is no reference to the Tree of Knowledge in Raphael's warnings against curiosity.

God lays upon Adam a single negative injunction: he may not taste the fruit of the Tree of the Knowledge of Good and Evil. The name of the tree suggests that its fruit has a miraculous power of imparting to whoever eats it an understanding of, an insight into, the nature of good and evil and the distinction between them. The objections to this understanding of the matter are obvious. Knowledge of good and evil is moral knowledge, knowledge which is essential to wisdom and righteous living, such knowledge as God enjoins. Satan twice points out, rightly, that God's prohibition is most unreasonable (IV, 515-20; IX, 696 ff.). Adam, furthermore, does not need to eat a miraculous fruit to understand what good and evil are. He knows innately that good is loving obedience to God, that evil is disobedience.

Milton undoubtedly sees the difficulty. He makes an effort to meet it in the *Christian Doctrine.* As a test of Adam's obedience and fidelity, he says, God laid upon Adam a single negative command, forbidding "an act in its own nature indifferent." The forbidden tree was "a pledge, as it were, and memorial of obedience. It was called the tree of knowledge of good and evil from the event; for since Adam tasted it, we not only know evil, but we know good only by means of evil."[21] (In both Genesis and *Paradise Lost* the naming of the tree preceded the sin, but perhaps God's foreknowledge enabled him to name the tree "from the event.") The moral problem of postlapsarian men is different from that of Adam in the state of innocence. Adam knew good in the sense that he lived a good life in a world which was wholly good, in which evil existed only potentially. Because he sinned, his descendants live among evils and temptations to evil; they may know good through learning to distinguish it from the manifold evils with which it is intermingled and intertwined and through rigorous rejection of the evil and practice of the good. In our time, Milton writes in the *Areopagitica,* "the knowledge of good" is "involv'd and interwoven with the knowledge of evill," in "many cunning resemblances hardly to be discern'd. ... And perhaps this is that doom which *Adam* fell into of knowing good and evill, that is to say, of knowing good by evill."[22] Adam bought "Knowledge of Good ... dear by knowing ill" (*PL,* IV, 221-22; cf. IX, 1071-72). The inhabitants of Heaven, illogically, seem to know both good and evil (XI, 84-89).

Evidently *know* must be understood, in this train of reasoning, not as meaning "apprehend intellectually," but as meaning "appreciate through having experienced." In the first sense, one knows the law of gravity, or the principle of osmosis, or the Aristotelian categories, or Roberts' rules of order; in the second sense, one knows the exultation of victory, or the sting of defeat, or the ennui of inaction. Before the Fall, Adam knew good in both senses; he was forbidden to know evil in the second sense. More simply, he was forbidden to sin. The effect of eating the fruit, then, was nothing more mysterious than the engendering of a feeling of guilt.

This solution of the problem seems to have satisfied Milton. It may not satisfy all of his readers. Satan seems, like the rest of us, to take "knowledge of" to mean "information concerning" (IV, 514-27). By the eating of the fruit, Eve expects to "feed at once both Body and Mind" (IX, 779). Eve may be naive, but Satan is intellectually very sharp. The name which God has given the tree is misleading. Adam and Eve are not in the least better informed after they have eaten the fruit. Can God be deceitful?

If Genesis had referred simply to a "Tree of Knowledge," not to a "Tree of the Knowledge of Good and Evil," Milton would have been spared a good deal of mental effort. He could, moreover, have fitted the forbidden tree very readily into his intellectual scheme: the fruit might then have represented knowledge of God's prohibited mysteries rather than, as it does, knowledge which seems ethically needful. The difficulties arise simply from the fact that Genesis includes an awkward detail. If Milton has not been altogether logical, he has probably done as well as could be done.

IV

Milton's acceptance of the principle of accommodation might suggest that he did not believe that the Tree of Knowledge was an actual tree growing in the soil of an actual Garden of Eden. It might suggest, indeed, that he did not literally believe anything that he read in the first three chapters of Genesis. The story of the Temptation and Fall might be simply God's accommodated way of conveying a truth, the moral weakness and consequent degradation of man.

There is a great difference, however, between the story of the Fall and the account of the Creation which precedes it. The Creation was an event of supra-human character; Raphael must describe it to Adam in such adapted language "as earthly notion can receive" (VII, 179). But the story of the Fall requires no adaptation. The actors are a man, a woman, and a demonically possessed serpent; the setting is the earth on which we live. There is nothing in this episode beyond human understanding or imagination. Milton believes the story of the Fall very literally. This sequence of events happened to two persons from whom we are all descended; they lived in an actual Paradise, within which there stood a Tree of Knowledge and a Tree of Life. On the other hand, the narrative of the first two books of *Paradise Lost*, describing events in Hell and Chaos, is accommodated narrative. The dialog in Heaven—in which, to so many readers, God has seemed an insufferably complacent and arbitrary head-of-state—is an accommodation. Raphael's stories of the annual celestial assembly, the exaltation of the Son, the battle on the plains of Heaven, the Creation—all of these are accommodations.

The non-literal character of at least some of the supra-human episodes of *Paradise Lost* has been clearly recognized in Milton criticism, but there has been little recognition of the distinction between literal and non-literal. There has been, furthermore, some ambiguity in the critical language used in this connection. Non-literal elements in the poem, for example, have often been said to be metaphoric. The war in Heaven, according to one writer, is "a complex metaphor."[23] The statement is quite true if one adopts a sufficiently inclusive definition of *metaphor*. But this word is likely to be understood as meaning a comparison of two things which are very unlike except in one or a small number of particulars: a girl's face is metaphorically a rose; a valiant fighter is a lion; a song smooths the raven down of darkness.

The angelic battle was not unlike human battle; there was actual physical combat in Heaven, and after their defeat, the rebels suffered physical punishment.[24] *Symbol,* another term which recurs in Milton criticism, is often loosely used. *Symbol* is commonly understood to mean an object, action, or quality endowed by tradition or conventional association with a meaning —frequently a very rich and complex meaning—which the object in itself could convey only incompletely or not at all: the Cross, the Crescent, the Stars and Stripes, the crown of laurel, the flying horse.[25] There are many symbols in *Paradise Lost:* the forbidden tree, the golden chain and the golden stairway which join the world and Heaven,[26] the chariot in which the Son of God rides forth to battle,[27] the broad causeway which leads from the world to Hell, the serpentine form into which Satan is punitively changed after he returns to Hell. These would certainly have had symbolic values for seventeenth-century Christians. But Heaven, Hell, and Chaos as Milton describes them are not symbols but accommodations.

Whatever terms we may use in discussing Milton's representation of things above human apprehension, we can agree that his language is "more in intention than it is in existence and constantly points to something beyond itself," that it is a kind of language which enables a "poet or theologian to be 'articulate about an insight.' "[28] We can agree further that there is a frequent doubleness of meaning. The forbidden tree, the golden stairway, the bridge to Hell—these are both symbols and physical realities. There is also a considerable element of typology in Milton's story. Like many Christian writers before him, Milton regards various persons and events of sacred history as types, or foreshadowings, especially of Jesus and the Redemption. "No passage of Scripture," he writes, "is to be interpreted in more than one sense; in the Old Testament, however, this sense is sometimes a compound of the historical and typical."[29] In other words, the Old Testament story is both factual and figurative. *"Moses* in figure bears" the high office of the coming Mediator (*PL,* XII, 240-42); the sacrifices of bulls and goats required by the old law are "shadowy expiations weak" (XII, 291), types of the greater blood sacrifice to come. In Biblical narrative there is progression "From shadowy Types to Truth, from Flesh to Spirit" (XII, 303).[30]

V

Investigation of the exegetical and literary background reveals that there is less invention in *Paradise Lost* than one might suppose. Milton was quite familiar with a body of exegesis on the early chapters of Genesis which had been accumulating for centuries and with a considerable number of literary treatments of the Creation and the Fall of Man. He drew upon these sources freely, often choosing with an artist's discrimination among the various solutions to the puzzling problems inherent in the Biblical story.[31]

Milton nevertheless has invented many scenes and events and a great deal of dialogue. There is no close precedent for the Father's "begetting," or exaltation, of the Son in Book V (600-15).[32] The poet seems to have felt that the story needed a specific event to explain the boiling up of Satan's pride, envy, and malice, an event to serve as the immediate motivation of his rebellion and to give dramatic emphasis to the opposition between Satan and Christ. Obviously he is inventing when he tells which loyal angels met in single combat with which apostates and what defiances each warrior shouted at his opponent. In these passages he is following the traditional practice of the epic poet in supplying suitable details of action and speech. Homer attributes to Hector, Achilles, Odysseus—persons whose historicity he does not doubt—words of his own devising. Even historians, classical and Renaissance, write speeches for persons who never made them, but probably should have. There is no Biblical basis for Raphael's visit to Adam in *Paradise Lost* and their long colloquy. It would seem very likely to Milton, however, that God would not subject Adam to his test without warning; Raphael, traditionally "the sociable spirit," would seem to be God's proper messenger. Since Lot and Abraham entertained angels at dinner, what more natural than for Adam to do so? Milton could hardly know just what Adam said to Eve or Eve to Adam on the morning of the day of the Temptation—or even that they had an argument. But he writes dialogue for them such as he believes the father and mother of mankind might speak to each other under the circumstances, such dialogue as would explain their unfortunate separation on the crucial day of trial. He deals very imaginatively with the Temptation itself, supplying dialogue (including the Devil's very eloquent speech), interior monologue, and the sequence of events leading to the first quarrel. He succeeds in making the episode psychologically very plausible and very moving. All of these elaborations and additions have the obvious purpose of engendering in the reader a sense of reality and dramatic immediacy. Milton is exercising the privileges universally granted the story teller. No one would think of objecting.

If anyone feels that liberty becomes license when Milton invents speeches for the Eternal God, he should remember that most of what God says in Book III corresponds with orthodox Protestant belief and would be quite acceptable to most of Milton's English contemporaries. When God speaks on such controversial points as predestination, he expresses ideas which the poet earnestly believes to be God's truth. If God were to speak forth on predestination, this is what he would say.

Some parts of *Paradise Lost*, however, depart further from the basic narrative than any so far mentioned. Milton has added to it a few personifications. He introduces the god Chaos, borrowed from Greek mythology, to represent primitive disorder, as distinguished from the willful disorder which is evil. He does not believe or ask his reader to believe that such a person exists, but the concept is a reality to him. Sin and Death appear as characters. Milton does not believe that Sin and Death exist as persons, but sin and death, he knows, are real. Chaos, Sin, and Death seem to me inappropriate in Milton's non-allegorical story.[33] No seventeenth-century reader, however, would have been disturbed. Personification and allegory appear very frequently in Christian literature. In the Bible itself there are precedents; for example, the four horsemen of the Apocalypse. Milton's Sin-Death allegory has a basis in James i, 15. The drama on the Fall which he planned in the 1640's evidently would have been much more allegorical, proportionally speaking, than the epic is. His faith in the allegorical method seems to have diminished.

In the passage on the Paradise of Fools (III, 444-97), Milton invents very freely. Assuming the role of jeering satirist, he becomes as fantastic as Lucian. The derisive scene of the symbolic punishment of Satan and his followers in Hell is also free invention. In neither case, however, has Milton departed from moral truth as he sees it.

In spite of all addition and elaboration, *Paradise Lost* is not fiction, for there is no doubt at all in the poet's mind of the basic facts of the story. It is not in the same category as the "feigning" fables of the Greeks. He is simply writing as a narrative poet is expected to write.

VI

In representing the physical milieu, however, Milton allows himself less freedom than in his story-telling. He has not merely designed and painted a stage set for the action. He is endeavoring to tell his reader something about the nature of God's world and (in so far as they are knowable) about the realities of the more remote parts of God's cosmos. He is writing now, not like Homer, but rather like Lucretius. He no longer enjoys the privileges of the narrative poet and does not wish any such license. The truth of the narrative and dramatic parts of *Paradise Lost* is a fidelity to the moral significance. This fidelity does not preclude embroidery upon the supposedly factual narrative. But a writer who undertakes such subjects as the nature and origins of matter and space should not be fanciful. He should present simply the truth—incomplete perhaps but, in any case, unadorned.

Among the lamentable results of the Original Sin, according to Renaissance moralists, is the human tendency to rest content with *opinion*, which is defined as "a vain and easy, a crude and imperfect Judgment of Things, taken up upon slight and insufficient grounds."[34] Milton is acutely aware of the distinction between *opinion* and *knowledge*. He declares in the preamble to *The Judgment of Martin Bucer* that what he has written of divorce *"was not my opinion, but my knowledge."*[35] He is satisfied, he says in the introduction to the *Christian Doctrine,* that he has "discovered, with regard to religion, what was matter of belief, and what only matter of opinion."[36] The physical milieu which he provides for the action of *Paradise Lost* he believes likewise to be of his knowledge, not of his opinion.

Chapter III. MILTON AND SCIENCE

Paradise Lost IS AN UNUSUALLY "scientific" poem. Its author has consciously and frequently introduced his ideas concerning physical nature. It is hardly possible to demonstrate that Milton was scientifically a learned man, but there is abundant evidence of his enthusiastic interest in science.

The program of studies at Cambridge in the 1620's included very little science. Yet Milton evidently did some extra-curricular scientific reading while he was at the university. In the Third Prolusion, he invites his fellow students to join him in the study of nature (as an alternative to the "distressing logomachy" of scholastic learning). He urges them to travel with their eyes "about the whole earth as represented on the map ... to investigate and to observe the natures of all living creatures; from these to plunge the mind into the secret powers of stones and plants. Do not hesitate, my hearers, to fly even up to the skies."[1] The Seventh Prolusion recommends the sciences with some fervor, referring specifically to the fields of astronomy, meteorology, biology, mineralogy, geology, anatomy, psychology.[2] In "Ad Patrem," written probably at about the time of his departure from Cambridge,[3] young Milton thanks his father warmly and gracefully for his opportunities for study. His father has made it possible for him to acquire understanding of, among other things, "all that heaven contains and earth, our mother, beneath the sky, and the air that flows between earth and heaven, and whatever the waters and the trembling surface of the sea cover."[4] He seems to feel that there is little left for him to learn about the physical world. During his travels in Italy, he impressed at least two of his Italian friends with his knowledge of natural philosophy. In a laudatory poem, Antonio Francini writes that Milton comprehends "clearly the profoundest arcana which nature hides in heaven and earth."[5] Carlo Dati praises Milton as "one in whose memory the universal world reposes ... who, with Philosophy as his instructress, reads deeply into the significance of the marvels of nature by which the greatness of God is portrayed."[5]

The curriculum which Milton outlined in 1644 in the essay *Of Education* includes agriculture, geography, meteorology, mathematics, astronomy, physics, medicine, and anatomy. Edward Phillips' brief biography of Milton reveals that he actually taught most of these subjects to the pupils of his small school of the 1640's. He evidently believed that the well informed Christian gentleman must know something of the natural world. Before he finished *Paradise Lost* his enthusiasm for natural science underwent some qualification, but he never altogether withdrew his approval.

Milton's reasons for recommending the study of science include its contributions to man's physical well being. The sciences are useful, even essential, in the arts of medicine, metallurgy, agriculture, navigation. The treatise *Of Education* shows clearly that Milton valued the sciences for their practical uses. After study of mathematics in the abstract, he says, students "may descend . . . to the instrumental science of *Trigonometry*, and from thence to Fortification, Architecture, Enginry, or Navigation." They should be instructed in medicine "that they may know the tempers, the humours, the seasons, and how to manage a crudity." He suggests that their studies be supplemented by "the helpful experiences of . . . Gardeners, Apothecaries . . . Architects, Engineers, Mariners, Anatomists."[6] In *Paradise Lost* Raphael tells Adam that it is profitable and proper for men, by the study of the heavens, to learn of God's "Seasons, Hours, or Days, or Months, or Years" (VIII, 69); thus, men may establish a calendar and devise means of telling the time of day.

The natural world, furthermore, is the gift of a loving God to mankind. It is beautiful and exhilarating; it not only may be but should be enjoyed: "it were an injury and sullenness against nature not to go out, and see her riches, and partake in her rejoycing with Heaven and Earth."[7] Simply to behold natural beauty, however, is insufficient for the wise and inquiring mind. All matter is divine, and all material things behave according to divinely ordained principles. God has made for man, his noblest and most perfect mundane creation, a world of orderly complexity and beauty. It is possible for men to learn something of the Creator from the study of his creatures, for "The heavens declare the glory of God; and the firmament showeth his handiwork" (Psalms xix, 1). The contemplation of the cunning adaptation of God's works to their purposes, of the intricate regularity of their operation, and of their surpassing loveliness cannot fail to inspire awe and admiration for the power and glory of the transcendent God and gratitude for his loving kindness.[8]

There is abundant evidence in Milton's works that he regarded the study of physical nature as a means of knowing God. In the Seventh Prolusion he exhorts his auditors to "ponder over this entire scheme of things: the illustrious Artificer of the great work has built it for His own glory. The deeper we investigate its extraordinary plan, its remarkable structure, its wonderful variety, which, without [scientific] knowledge, we cannot do, the more do we honor the Author."[9] He writes in the *Christian Doctrine* that "traces of [God] are apparent throughout the whole of nature . . . every thing in the world, by the beauty of its order, and the evidence of a determinate and beneficial purpose which pervades it, testifies that some supreme efficient Power must have pre-existed."[10] Raphael tells Adam, in *Paradise Lost,* that the starry heavens are

> as the Book of God before thee set,
> Wherein to read his wond'rous Works. (VIII, 67-68)

Our first parents, in prayer, express their perception of God in nature:

> These are thy glorious works, Parent of good,
> Almighty, thine this universal Frame,
> Thus wondrous fair; thyself how wondrous then!
> Unspeakable, who sit'st above these Heavens
> To us invisible or dimly seen
> In these thy lowest works, yet these declare
> Thy goodness beyond thought, and Power Divine.
>   (V, 153-59)

Milton regards his blindness as a very great deprivation, for he can no longer read "the Book of knowledge fair";[11] "Nature's works" are for him

> expung'd and raz'd,
> And wisdom at one entrance quite shut out.
> So much the rather thou Celestial Light
> Shine inward.   (III, 47-52)

II

The highest function of poetry, Milton believes, is the engendering of piety in the reader through the revelation of the power, glory and goodness of God. Since nature testifies to these, it would seem reasonable to him that description of the physical world and explanation of the principles which operate in it would serve that function. A poet, then, may make laudable use of natural philosophy.

Milton and his contemporaries read classical poems of scientific content with admiration: Lucretius' *De Rerum Natura,* Manilius' *Astronomica.* One of the most popular poetic works of the period—one which exercised a considerable influence on Milton—was Du Bartas' *Les Semaines,* which includes a great deal of scientific material. Du Bartas even digresses to argue scientific questions. (The earth could not possibly be rotating; if it were, an arrow shot upward would fall far to the east.) Englishmen wrote scientifically instructive poems: John Davies of Hereford's *Microcosmos,* on psychology; Phineus Fletcher's *The Purple Island,* on physiology; Abraham Cowley's *Sex Libri Plantarum.*[12] Milton's generation saw no great differ-

ence between the functions of the poet and the natural philosopher. Both
were concerned with truth. It was in their methods of conveying truth that
they differed. Since the poet's medium was more delightful and moving
than the pedestrian prose of the philosopher, it would seem proper that the
poet should undertake the presentation of the philosopher's very significant
material.

The cleavage between science and literature was only beginning to open
in Milton's lifetime. In our time it has become so wide that it is hard for
us to accept the idea that scientific detail is proper in poetry. We are inclined
to doubt that a poet's sensitive and imaginative mind could feel at home
among the scientist's cold and prosaic data concerning salts and acids, genes
and chromosomes, subatomic particles. Indeed we sometimes seem to regard scientific incompetence as an endearing weakness in a poet. We may
be right. But we must not impose our attitudes on Milton or try to do his
critical thinking for him. A scholar who has written very competently on
Milton's use of the sciences[13] asserts that Milton's convictions were never
deeply involved in scientific questions, that he drew images suitable to his
purposes from his fund of scientific information without seriously believing
or disbelieving. Other writers remind us with wearisome iteration that
Milton was a poet, not a scientist or philosopher. The implication seems to
be that we must not expect him to be scientifically well informed or accurate (even according to the beliefs and standards of his time) or philosoph-
ically logical—and that, in any case, he was little interested in science or
philosophy. Milton would never concede that a poet should be presumed
to be inexpert in science and philosophy and should therefore be excused
for absurdity or error. I can readily agree that Milton was a much better poet
than scientist, or philosopher, or theologian, but I cannot agree that he was
indifferent to science, or philosophy, or theology.

Very early, when he was nineteen years old, he declared his intention to
write poetry of scientific content. "At a Vacation Exercise," lines composed
at the same time as the Sixth Prolusion, reviews various subjects on which
he hopes one day to write. These include "the wheeling poles ... the
Spheres of watchful fire," the "misty Regions of wide air ... hills of Snow
and lofts of piled Thunder," the stormy seas, and

> secret things that came to pass
> When Beldame Nature in her cradle was.   (Lines 34-36)

He has suggested here, roughly and incompletely, the scientific material
which years later he incorporated in *Paradise Lost.* The Seventh Prolusion
indicates that, during this period, he was engaged in studies which would
prepare him to write on natural philosophy. He would not be contented to
write ignorantly or fatuously.

But *Paradise Lost* fortunately is not an expository composition like *Nosce*

Teipsum or *The Purple Island.* It is hard to think of any poem intended primarily as scientific instruction which is successful as a poem. (*De Rerum Natura* may be the exception.) The scientific material in *Paradise Lost* is an incidental part of the poem but is nevertheless a genuinely integrated part. It shares with the story the function of conveying the moral meanings. Otherwise it would be merely a series of rather tedious digressions.

III

Milton considered himself scientifically well informed; in fact, he seems to have taken some pride in his knowledge of the natural world. Pride was hardly justified. Kester Svendsen has pointed out that most of the scientific lore which appears in Milton's works he could have found in the popular encyclopedias.[14] This does not mean that he read no further than the encyclopedias. But it is undoubtedly true that he reveals no scientific information which was not common among his educated contemporaries.

Because of the enthusiasm for the sciences which he expresses in the early works, it is fair to assume that, during his college years, Milton was reading scientific works. These would have included, surely, such standard classics as Lucretius' poem, Seneca's *Quaestiones Naturales,* Plato's *Timaeus,* and Aristotle's several scientific writings. Young Milton's contempt for the scholastics did not extend to their master. But in no early work does Milton mention any specific scientific document. It is not possible to list his early scientific readings.[15]

The course of study which he outlines in *Of Education* is designed as a progression from the concrete and particular to the abstract.[16] For "our understanding cannot in this body found it self but on sensible things, nor arrive so clearly to the knowledge of God and things invisible, as by orderly conning over the visible and inferior creature."[17] Accordingly, in the earlier stages of instruction, scientific readings predominate. Among the authors whom Milton recommends are twenty writers who might be regarded as scientific authorities.[18] Since he throws the sciences and the practical arts together without discrimination, we shall understand "scientific" very broadly. All of the natural philosophers in the list are writers of some antiquity, many of whom have, in our time, been long forgotten. For instruction in agriculture, the boys are to read Cato (second century B.C.), Varro (first century B.C.), Columella (first century A.D.), Hesiod, and "the rural part of *Virgil.* " (The context suggests that Milton is classifying Theocritus also as an agricultural writer.) For "Historical Physiology" (description of animals and plants) they will study Aristotle and Theophrastus; for architecture, Vitruvius; for meteorology, Aratus' *Diosemeia* (third century B.C.) and Seneca's *Quaestiones Naturales*; for geography, Pomponius Mela (first century A.D.), Gaius Julius Solinus (third century A.D.), and Dionysius Periegetes (third-fourth century A.D.); for medicine, Celsus (first century A.D.); for astronomy, Aratus' *Phaenomena* and Manilius' *Astronomica* (first century A.D.). Some of the authorities are hard to classify. Mineralogy is possibly represented by "Orpheus," supposed author of *Lithica*, an ancient poem concerning precious stones and their magical virtues. Nicander (second century B.C.), who wrote poems on venomous animals and on poisons, may perhaps be considered a medical writer. Oppian's *Cynegetica* and *Halieutica* (second century A.D.), poems on hunting and fishing, are possibly regarded as natural history. Lucretius' *De Rerum Natura* and Pliny's *Historia Naturalis* are included, the first perhaps for its basic physical principles, the latter for its instruction in several fields. Milton recommends the study of mathematics without naming specific authors. Although Celsus is on the list, he suggests that "the Institution of Physick" be given the boys through reading to them from "some not tedious Writer."

Milton seems to have been more interested in geography than in any other science with the possible exception of astronomy. Every reader of *Paradise Lost* becomes conscious of the richness of the author's geographical information. The three geographical writings mentioned in *Of Education* are all ancient works, but the boys are "to learn in any modern Author, the use of the Globes, and all the Maps; first with the old names, and then with the new." *Modern* as it is used by Renaissance authors is sometimes a misleading word. Yet Milton's knowledge of geography—at least at the time when he wrote *Paradise Lost*—was up to date.[19] Geography was to Milton not merely cartography and was not a physical science; it was the study of countries, climates, topography, peoples and their ways of life, governments, religions, natural resources, etc.[20]

The boys whom Milton taught in his home in the 1640's seem to have followed a course of study very similar to that which he outlines in *Of Education* and not much less rigorous. In his biography of Milton, Edward Phillips is fairly specific in naming the works that he and his fellow pupils studied with his uncle[21] ("from ten to fifteen or sixteen years of age"), though the list is doubtless incomplete. The scientific readings which Phillips names correspond fairly closely with those listed in *Of Education*, although there are omissions and additions. Milton's pupils read the agricultural works of Cato, Varro, Columella, Palladius (fourth century A.D.?), and Hesiod;[22] they read Vitruvius' work on architecture; *De Situ Orbis* by Dionysius Periegetes on geography; the medical work of Cornelius Celsus, "an ancient physician of the Romans"; "Oppian's *Cynegetics* and *Halieutics*" (hunting and fishing); "Aratus his *Phaenomena*, and *Diosemeia*" (astronomy and meteorology); astronomical works by Geminus (Greek, first century B.C.) and Manilius; "a great part of Pliny's *Natural History*"; and Lucretius' *De Rerum Natura*. These are all ancient works, but the list includes some of more recent date: "Urstisius his *Arithmetic*, Riff's *Geometry*, Petiscus his *Trigonometry*, Johannes de Sacro Bosco *De Sphaera.*" The first three of these were originally published respectively in 1565, 1610, and 1595. The *De Sphaera* of Sacrobosco (John of Hollywood) is a rather brief elementary textbook of astronomy, written early in the thirteenth century, which was widely read during the Renaissance. The numerous Renaissance editions normally included elaborating commentary by later writers.[23] The boys also read "in French a great part of Pierre Davity, the famous geographer of France in his time." Davity's geography was first published in 1614.

Phillips remarks that, "by teaching," his uncle "in some measure increased his own knowledge, having the reading of all these authors as it were by proxy." Phillips surely means, not "all," but "some of these authors." Milton would not have been contented with a secondhand knowledge of the moral and historical works that Phillips mentions. Yet many interests and duties were competing for his time and energies; he was, says Phillips, "perpetually busied in his own laborious undertakings of the book and pen" to the detriment of his eyesight. It is conceivable that he skimmed or neglected to read some of the scientific and military works on the list.[24] It is not conceivable, however, that he did not read—or had not read—such authors as Hesiod, Pliny, and Lucretius.

In choosing works on natural philosophy for students' reading, Milton evidently was considering language and style as well as content. Eleven of the scientific works listed in *Of Education* are placed in the curriculum at an early stage devoted both to the study of natural philosophy and to the mastery of languages. All of these are in prose. All of them, with the possible exception of Solinus' geography, are in classical Latin or Greek. It seems likely that Milton picked Celsus' *De Medicina* for the reason, among others, that Celsus was regarded as "Cicero medicorum." Nine scientific poets are introduced a little later, at a time when, because of proper preparation, "those Poets which are now counted most hard, will be both facil and pleasant." Nine poets among twenty writers seems a high percentage of poets in a scientific reading list, even in a seventeenth-century list. But poetry is beautiful as well as informative. Phillips' account of his studies suggests that, in teaching natural philosophy, Milton found occasion to impart enthusiasm for literary excellences as well as for scientific information. Phillips remembers Cato, Varro, Columella, and Palladius as "the four grand authors *De Re Rustica*"; Lucretius and Manilius are "two egregious poets"; Hesiod is "a poet equal with Homer." In using *De Sphaera* as a textbook, Milton must have felt that he was making a great concession to pedigogical expediency. Sacrobosco is no "Cicero astronomorum."

What one learns principally from those parts of the treatise on education and of Phillips' life which concern scientific instruction is that Milton was very much out of date. He seems to have been well informed in the geogra-

22

phy and mathematics of his time, but he knew the other sciences in virtually the form in which the Greeks had left them. Of the scientific writers listed in the treatise, all but three (Oppian, Dionysius, and Solinus) wrote earlier than 100 A.D. and none later than 350. Evidently in the mid-1640's Milton saw no reason to consider the ancient writers inadequate. Except for mathematics and geography, it was classical science that he taught his scholars. Sacrobosco's astronomy is not really an exception; *De Sphaera* teaches Greek theory (modified by the medieval Arabians).

This indifference to scientific development seems strange in a man who had professed such warm interest in science and who had undertaken to teach science to young scholars. It seems especially strange in a man who was so intellectually alive and so widely read as Milton. During the three-quarters of a century before his birth and during his lifetime, scientific development was rapid, in some sciences spectacular. In the sixteenth century, after hundreds of years of relative stasis, science came alive. Renaissance men of science progressively adopted the ideas of the inductive study of nature and of scientific progress; a "new science" developed and competed more and more successfully with tradition; modern science had begun. When Milton was born, the new science had already achieved a great deal, especially in astronomy, and was gaining rapidly in its contest with the older, authoritarian science. By the time of his death, the issue was definitely settled, at least in the view of men of scientific competence. He lived, then, in a period of transition, a period of exciting scientific developments and of spirited debate.

Milton would have heard little of this during his university days. In the early seventeenth century, Cambridge was still a scholastic ivory tower; the concepts which it offered its students concerning the natural world consisted principally of Aristotelian and scholastic physics and metaphysics; the faculty was indifferent to experimental science, and even to mathematics.[25] Jeremiah Horrox, a minor luminary in the seventeenth-century history of astronomy, entered Cambridge in 1632, the year of Milton's departure. This young man was interested in mathematics and astronomy. Finding no adequate instruction in these subjects at the university and no sympathy for his interest in them, he determined to read astronomy without a master. "By the advice of a Manchester draper, William Crabtree, he studied the works of Kepler, and with such good results that he was able to show how Kepler's Laws must be modified in order to fit the motion of the moon."[26] Young Milton also was discontented with the scholastic studies required of him ("sowthistles and brambles") and seems, like Horrox, to have turned to extra-curricular scientific reading. In the passages in the *Prolusions* in which he expresses his enthusiasm for the study of the physical world, however, he shows no acquaintanceship with any but classical scientific concepts. He had no Manchester draper to guide him.

There is no evidence that Milton ever read such major scientific works as Vesalius' *De Fabrica Humani Corporis*, Gesner's *Historia Animalium*, Gilbert's *De Magnete*, or Harvey's *De Motu Cordis*. References in the prose writings of the 1640's show that he admired Sir Francis Bacon and that he was acquainted with some of Bacon's writings on church polity.[27] In *An Apology for Smectymnuus*, he compares Jospeh Hall's "wretched" *Mundus Alter et Idem* with More's *Utopia* and Bacon's *The New Atlantis*. More and Bacon "display the largenesse of their spirits by teaching this our world better and exacter things, then were yet known."[28] It is hard to say to what extent he perceives the implications of Bacon's scientifically oriented ideal society. In the *Logic* Milton quotes a statement on the subject of induction from Bacon's *De Augmentis Scientiarum* (5, 4).[29] But there is no indication, here or elsewhere, that he understood Bacon's scientific method or its philosophical or social significance. Evidently he never realized that Bacon was the Moses of science, as Cowley calls him in the ode "To the Royal Society," or that there was any scientific Promised Land. Although he eventually waked up to the meaning of the new discoveries in astronomy, he remained, on the whole, unaware or unconcerned while one of the most consequential developments in intellectual history was in rapid progress.

Milton's scientific thinking is not scientific at all as the twentieth century understands "scientific." His thinking about natural phenomena seems fuzzy, unintegrated, and careless of obvious fact. Adam's sin, he believes, brought death into the world for the inferior creatures as well as for man. If Adam had not fallen, then, life would have strangled itself. How could the earth have supported the myriads of plants, animals, and human beings that would have been born to live everlastingly? Why are the fires of Hell not luminous? What are the primary qualities of the fifth element? Of what element or elements do the vital and animal spirits in the human body consist? Such problems do not trouble him.

In spite of his professions of interest in the natural world, furthermore, he seems to have no desire to observe natural phenomena for himself. It would not occur to him that one should have sensuous evidence of the humor melancholy or the humor choler to have a true knowledge of its existence. He has no apparent interest in experimentation or collection of data and has apparently no idea of the value of these processes. He sees clearly the possibilities of the moral improvement of mankind and of the political improvement of society, and he endeavors to contribute all that he can toward moral and social progress. But he does not think of science as a changing, improving, and expanding body of knowledge. He seems to think that most of what is knowable about the physical world has long been known. A static science, to the modern mind, is a contradiction in terms, but not to Milton. In the Third Prolusion, he advises his fellow students to "Let that famous man, Aristotle, be your teacher in all these [scientific] subjects, who possesses so much charm, who indeed has left to us almost all those things, which ought to be learned, written in a learned manner and with much pains."[30] His respect for Aristotle as a scientist remains with him at least as late as 1651.

In other words, Milton's science is bookish and authoritarian. His habit √ of mind is deductive. He is accustomed to reasoning from propositions which he regards as needing no proof. He shares with the more conservative of his contemporaries a deep respect for the wisdom and perceptiveness of the great minds of the distant past. He is more medieval than modern.

He is not conscious, I am sure, of being an authoritarian conservative, and he does not always seem so. He does not insist on the accuracy of Strabo's *Geography.* In the note on tragedy which precedes *Samson Agonistes,* he seems to approve of the relatively new homeopathic medicine.[31] He would undoubtedly welcome any discovery which would improve the methods of medicine, or agriculture, or metallurgy, or navigation. But he does not seem to realize that a great many such discoveries could yet be made or to give any thought to how they might be made. He has no real scientific curiosity.

The preceding, of course, is not a belittlement of Milton. Everything that I have said of him might be said of a great many of his contemporaries, including some who regarded themselves as natural philosophers. I mean merely to say that Milton was not so much of a scientist as he thought he was—not scientific at all in the modern sense—and not so much of a scientist as he could have been. His authoritarian assumptions, as we see it, have misdirected his scientific thinking sadly. But he is much less concerned with science than with ethics and religion, in which fields deductive thought is surely normal and right. Faith, not evidence, is the point of departure for religion, and for the Christian (the Christian in the strict sense) this means faith in divine revelation.

For Milton the Bible is the principal and indispensable source of knowledge.[32] Because it is the word of God himself, he regards its authority as absolute (except for passages which he suspects have suffered corruption[33]). The Scriptures, furthermore, are "plain and perspicuous in all things necessary to salvation, and adapted to the instruction even of the most unlearned."[34] The Bible means what it says. Every man has the right—and duty —to seek truth in the Bible for himself. The seeker should examine scriptural texts closely, not to test their validity but to determine precisely what they mean. The Bible supplies the premises for a great deal of Milton's thinking, sometimes even for his scientific thinking. With the aid of his very considerable linguistic learning, he carefully determines the meaning of a Biblical text and then makes argumentative use of its consequences. This kind of logical exercise occupies page after page of the *Christian Doctrine.*

He is also likely to accept as axiomatic ideas whose authority is Christian tradition rather than the Bible. It is never easy to keep a sharp line drawn between the actual wording of a well known document (for instance, the preamble to the American Constitution) and the common interpretation. Even so thoroughly Protestant a mind as Milton's might have trouble in maintaining a clear distinction between what the Bible said and what it was traditionally supposed to mean. It would not occur to him to doubt that Lucifer raised impious war in Heaven. Yet he tried, not always successfully, to distinguish between the earlier and later origins of religious ideas. The true Christianity, he believed, was that of the primitive Church; this was religion in "its original purity."[35]

Authoritarianism and deductive intellectual habits may disqualify Milton as a scientist, but they do not disqualify him as a religious thinker. If the Bible is truly the word of God (certainly a proper Christian assumption), then religious thought must be deductive. Milton's authoritarianism, moreover, does not disqualify him as a poet. Obviously Cowley's *Plantarum* and *Davideis* are not, because their author was abreast of the times scientifically, superior to *Paradise Lost*. Indeed Milton's deficiencies in scientific thought and learning may have been no disadvantage. Incorporation of the newest ideas in chemistry or physiology would have made little difference. If he had abandoned the old astronomy for the new, he might have confused his contemporaries more than he inspired them. The new scientific ideas were absorbed only slowly by the lay public. Most laymen of Milton's time were probably worse informed than he was.

Most of the ideas from which Milton has formed his conceptions of the earth and the supra-terrene world had, in his time, been current for centuries. He has derived nothing from the new experimental science, and he introduces no novelties. His representation of the vast regions beyond the world, however, differs greatly from what his contemporaries would have expected. His cosmos is just like nothing conceived before. Yet its original features are due, not to any new basic ideas, but to Milton's very independent deduction from familiar premises, derived usually from a Greek source, from the Bible, or from Christian tradition. Nothing can be created in a place which does not exist; when Hell was created the earth did not exist; therefore Hell could not have been placed in the center of the earth (*PL*, I, argument). The action of *Paradise Lost* is laid in a deductive cosmos which is humanistic-Christian rather than scientific.

IV

The principal subjects of the next chapter are the earth (with its atmosphere) and the nature of man. What Milton has to say of these belongs in the category of natural philosophy and therefore in the category of literal knowledge. None of it takes the reader beyond the realm of human understanding; it is not necessary to regard it as accommodation or symbolism. Astronomy also, at least in the earlier decades of his life, he regarded as factually knowable. Everything sensible, everything within the range of human vision, was a legitimate object of inquiry and might be literally understood.

To say that Milton believes everything that he writes concerning terrestrial nature would be to overstate the matter. It is hard to know whether or not he believes that Scandinavian mariners sometimes mistake sleeping whales for islands and fix their anchors in the "scaly rind" (*PL*, I, 206). The island-like whale, at any rate, is an apt simile. Although he uses the phoenix as an image (V, 272), he probably does not believe that there is or ever was a phoenix. But undoubtedly he believes that, upon such a height as that of the Tower of Babel, the atmosphere would be too thin to support human life (XII, 76-78); that metals and gems are created within the earth by penetrating solar rays (III, 608-12); that the body of an old man is literally dry (XI, 542-46). What he has to say about matter and about the scale of being is to him knowledge, not opinion; and because understanding of natural philosophy leads to perception of the power, glory, and beneficence of God, he considers it significant knowledge. He presents it in all seriousness, not with indifferent half-belief. Indeed for him it is related to religious doctrine.

Chapter IV. EARTH, MEN, AND ANGELS

THE NATURAL PHILOSOPHY of the Renaissance perpetuates the ancient Greek theory that the matter of the earth and of all things on it and immediately above it is analyzable into four elements: earth, water, air, and fire. By infinitely diverse combination, these produce an infinite variety of terrestrial forms. Each one has two primary qualities: earth is cold and dry, water is cold and moist, air is warm and moist, fire is hot and dry. The elements differ also in relative rarity and density, earth being the heaviest, water the next heaviest, air the next, and fire the lightest. A fifth element, the quintessence, is the substance of the heavens.

In the sublunar world, according to traditional ideas derived from Aristotle (*De Mundo, Meteorologica*), Seneca (*Quaestiones Naturales*), and other ancient writers, the four terrestrial elements, by seeking levels proper to their relative levity or weight, have formed themselves into concentric spherical zones. At the center of the world is the round, solid core of earth. The earth-orb is largely covered by water, which, if it were not for the irregularities of the earth's surface, would surround it as an unbroken sphere. Above the earth and water is a region of air many tens of thousands of miles thick. Outside this is a sphere of fire (the "element of fire" which, according to John Donne, the new philosophy has quite put out). This sphere is the outermost of terrestrial phenomena. Just above it is the lunar sphere, the lowest of the celestial spheres, about 200,000 miles from the surface of the earth. The sublunar regions are subject to constant change and to decay; the celestial regions, says Aristotle (*De Caelo*) are immutable and everlasting.

The enormously deep envelop of air is divided into three concentric zones.[1] Meteors—that is, winds, clouds, rain, snow, rainbows, thunder, lightning, comets, falling stars, etc.—are located in or originate in the three-fold region of air and are, in general, explained by the action of cold or heat upon "exhalations" (evaporations) drawn from the earth by the sun. Some of these exhalations are dry (earthy) and some moist (aqueous). The relatively dense air of the inner layer—in which we move and breathe—is warmed by the sun's rays reflected from the earth. The winds are motions of this inner air. In the "middle air," which is extremely cold, aqueous vapors condense and form clouds; rain (sometimes accompanied by thunder

28

and lightning), snow, and hail originate here. St. Paul speaks of the Devil as "the prince of the power of the air" (Ephesians ii, 2); later Christians specifically assign to him the middle zone as his habitation. The outer layer of air is heated by the sun and by proximity to the sphere of fire. This is the region of comets, falling stars, and other fiery phenomena.

Although one finds minor deviations from the conventional, this brief sketch represents fairly well the conception of the sublunar regions that was in Milton's mind as he wrote *Paradise Lost*.[2] The four elements were "the eldest birth / Of Nature's Womb" (V, 180-81). At the time of the Creation, each one rose or sank, according to the Creator's plan, to its appointed station:

> Swift to thir several Quarters hasted then
> The cumbrous Elements, Earth, Flood, Air, Fire,
> And this Ethereal quintessence of Heav'n
> Flew upward. (III, 714-17)

The "quintessence," which corresponds remotely with Aristotle's fifth element, or *ether*,[3] formed itself into the heavenly bodies.

There is no sphere of fire in the world of *Paradise Lost*.[4] In tracing the step-by-step sublimation of matter, Milton says that the air feeds "those Fires / Ethereal, and as lowest first the Moon" (V, 417-18). This disregarding of the sphere of sublunar fire destroys the traditional boundary between terrestrial and celestial. The upper region of air seems, in *Paradise Lost*, to extend outward to the limits of the world (see Chap. V, Sec. ii), becoming presumably more and more rarefied as the distance from the earth increases. One would expect a sphere of fire in this basically Aristotelian world, yet belief in the sphere of fire was not universal even among men of traditional opinions.[5]

Milton is vague about the outer zone of air, but he makes some definite statements concerning the middle region. When Adam hears Michael's prediction of Nimrod's building of the Tower of Babel, he is appalled not only by Nimrod's impiety but by his foolishness:

> thin Air
> Above the Clouds will pine his entrails gross,
> And famish him of breath. (XII, 76-78)

Babel, then, is to reach up into the middle air. Since their entrance into the world as a result of Satan's enterprise and of Adam's sin, the fallen angels, or devils, have dwelt in and dominated the middle zone.[6] By God's sufferance Satan has become "Prince of the Air" (X, 185; XII, 454). In their day, the Greek gods (demons)

> on the Snowy top
> Of cold *Olympus* rul'd the middle Air,
> Thir highest Heav'n.   (I, 515-17)

On and in the earth itself and in its waters, matter appears in a multitude of forms, including living creatures. The elements are not by their own nature capable of assuming form, much less of assuming life. God gave to matter the capabilities of form and animation when, at the time of the Creation, he breathed into it an infusion of divine virtue (see Chap. V, sec. iv). Since the Creation, terrestrial nature has required the light and warmth of the sun, which is "both Eye and Soul" of the world (V, 171). The creative energy which first formed and activated the world now resides in the sun.[7] Its masculine "fervid Rays" warm "Earth's inmost womb" (V, 301-02); "in the fruitful Earth . . . His beams, unactive else, thir vigor find" (VIII, 96-97), stimulating growth on the earth and effecting transmutations within it. The stars and planets, in ways not clearly explained, help to support life on earth and influence its character. Their light is for the most part reflected sunlight, but each has its "small peculiar" (VII, 368). These "soft fires"

> with kindly heat
> Of various influence foment and warm,
> Temper or nourish, or in part shed down
> Thir stellar virtue on all kinds that grow
> On Earth, made hereby apter to receive
> Perfection from the Sun's more potent Ray.
>   (IV, 667-73)

The earth receives beneficial rays from all the heavenly bodies, and their

> virtue appears
> Productive in Herb, Plant, and nobler birth
> Of Creatures animate.   (IX, 110-12)

Before the Fall the influence of the stars was wholly beneficent. Just after the Fall, angels taught the planets their

> motions and aspects
> In *Sextile, Square,* and *Trine,* and *Opposite,*
> Of noxious efficacy, and when to join
> In Synod unbenign, and taught the fixt
> Thir influence malignant when to show'r.   (X, 658-62)

Apparently Milton believed in astrology.[8] His horoscope exists. In the *Logic* he gives, as examples of evidence that is relatively dependable, "signs of physiognomy, and the prognostics of astrologers and physicians."[9] Apparently he believed, as many of his contemporaries did, that the planets influenced the physical constitutions of men and consequently their personalities. He is much less likely to have believed that specific events could be predicted astrologically. (Yet in *Paradise Regained*, IV, 382-93, the Devil accurately reads Jesus' destiny in the heavens.)

The rays of the sun are the efficient cause of life and growth on the earth. They exercise also a potency within the earth.[10] The sun's "Magnetic beam,"

> With gentle penetration, though unseen,
> Shoots invisible virtue even to the deep.   (III, 583-86)

The virtuous warmth of the sun produces "exhalations" (sublimations) from the various elements confined underground. Dry exhalations are engendered from earth or fire or from the two in combination; moist exhalations from water or air or from the two in combination. The dry exhalations are sulphurous, the moist mercurial. These exhalations, when they are imprisoned within the earth, form various combinations. A union of dry and moist exhalations, if it brings together all four elements, produces a metal. The particular metal produced depends upon the proportion in which the four elements are combined. A perfectly balanced combination becomes gold. Silver comes of a slightly less perfect mixture. Precious stones are generated within dry exhalations.

Milton's mineralogy shows the influence of alchemy.[11] He seems to accept the alchemical theory of transmutation; that is, he apparently believes in the theoretical possibility of turning lead or iron into gold (of rendering perfect an imperfect metallic combination). He is sceptical, however, of the alchemists' ability to achieve this. "Philosophers" by their "powerful Art," he says, have succeeded in controlling "Volatile *Hermes*" and "old *Proteus*" (III, 601-04). Hermes and Proteus are "metaphorical names for 'the mercury of the philosophers,' the proximate material of the philosopher's stone or transmuting elixir"[12]—the substance which, by catalytic action upon or by union with baser metals, would produce the golden balance. Yet, although their art is powerful, human philosophers have never quite succeeded in producing the transmuting agent; they have long sought "That stone . . . in vain." "Th'Arch-chemic Sun," incomparably more capable than human adepts, produces upon its own surface gems and precious metals, fields which "Breathe forth *Elixir* pure" and rivers which "run / Potable Gold." The "virtuous touch" of the sun produces, even in the dark and remote depths of the earth, "many precious things / Of color glorious" and rare effect (III, 600-12). Elsewhere in the poem Milton refers disparagingly to the human practitioner and his pretensions:

by fire
Of sooty coal the Empiric Alchemist
Can turn, or holds it possible to turn
Metals of drossiest Ore to perfet Gold.   (V, 439-42)

"Empiric" is derogatory.

But Milton is much less interested in transmutation of metals than in transmutation of elements (not the same thing at all in seventeenth-century thought). This he believes to be a normal process of nature. At one point he seems to be thinking of this elemental interchange as cyclic: "ye Elements ... that in quaternion run / Perpetual Circle ..." (V, 180-82).[13] All other pertinent passages suggest that it is a progression from the heavier and denser to the rarer and lighter, or as Milton would say it, from the "grosser" to the "purer."[14] The purer substances are "sustain'd and fed" by "The grosser." Earth is sustenance for water (is the raw material from which water is engendered), earth and water sustain air, water and air sustain "those Fires / Ethereal,"

lowest first the Moon;
Whence in her visage round those spots, unpurg'd
Vapors not yet into her substance turn'd.

The spots on the Moon are undigested water or air. The moon exhales nourishment "to higher Orbs." The sun receives

From all his alimental recompense
In humid exhalations, and at Even
Sups with the Ocean.   (V, 414-26)

The substance of the sun is the purest quintessence. There are grades of excellence, then, among the elements (the simple substances) from grossest earth to rarest quintessence, and there is a constant movement upward on the scale of excellence.

There are degrees of excellence also among living creatures. Each higher form of life possesses all of the abilities of the forms below it. In the Aristotelian language[15] of the Renaissance psychologists: a plant has a *vegetable soul*, whose powers are nutrition, growth, and reproduction; an animal has a *sensible soul*, whose faculties are those of sensation and movement (the imagination and the memory are internal sensory faculties; the emotions are internal motions); a man has a *rational soul.* The sensitive soul includes a vegetable soul; the rational soul includes a vegetable soul and a sensitive soul. Satan, as he looks at God's terrestrial handiwork in wonder and admiration, sees

32

> Herb, Plant, and nobler birth
> Of Creatures animate with gradual life
> Of Growth, Sense, Reason, all summ'd up in Man.
> (IX, 111-13)

Every living creature comprises a variety of substances. Among these constituent substances also there are different degrees of excellence, or purity. Within an animate creature, as among the elements, the evolutionary progression of matter occurs:

> from the root
> Springs lighter the green stalk, from thence the leaves
> More aery, last the bright consummate flow'r
> Spirits odorous breathes. (V, 479-82)

The perfume, the final product, is a very tenuous substance—therefore a very pure substance—, here called "spirits." Raphael uses the progressive rarefaction of matter in the plant as an illustrative parallel in explaining similar processes in the human body, of which more a little later.

God's creation is a hierarchy[16] of

> various forms, various degrees
> Of substance, and in things that live, of life;
> But more refin'd, more spiritous, and pure,
> As nearer to him plac't or nearer tending. (V, 473-76)

There is an aspiration in all matter which motivates an upward effort, a striving to rise to higher station and to rejoin finally the source of the one "one first matter" (V, 472) from which all matter, in its infinite variety of forms, is derived. Nature is a scale

> From centre to circumference, whereon
> In contemplation of created things
> By steps we may ascend to God.[17] (V, 510-12)

From God, the center, "All things proceed"; all things, "If not deprav'd from good," may "up to him return" (V, 470-71).

II

The earth which God has given man to dwell in is beautiful and delightful. Nature was even more benignant in the pristine earth than it is now, and most of all in the Garden of Eden.[18] In his opulent description of

Paradise, Milton elaborates generously on the scanty information in Genesis, drawing upon tradition and filling in with details which, although they have no authoritative source, do not violate poetic truth.

God "planted" Paradise (that is, a garden) "in the East / Of *Eden*" (IV, 209-10), a land which Milton, like many Christian writers before him, identifies with Mesopotamia. Before the Fall this region lay on the equator. Paradise, as Milton imagines it, was a level area on the top of a high hill, whose sides were overgrown with tall trees and dense thickets (IV, 133-37, 174-77). There was a single gate, facing eastward (IV, 178). Beneath and through this hill a river (the Tigris, IX, 71) flowed southward;

> through veins
> Of porous Earth with kindly thirst up-drawn,
> Rose a fresh Fountain, and with many a rill
> Water'd the Garden.   (IV, 227-30)

The fountain rose, apparently in the center of the plateau, by the Tree of Life,[19] which bore "Ambrosial Fruit / Of vegetable Gold." The Tree of Knowledge grew "fast by" (IV, 218-21). Diverging

> from that Sapphire Fount the crisped Brooks,
> Rolling on Orient Pearl and sands of Gold . . .
> Ran Nectar.   (IV, 237-40)

As the river emerged from underground on the south side of the hill, it divided "into four main Streams" (IV, 233). This dividing of the river may seem geologically unlikely, but Milton is following Genesis ii, 10.

Paradise was well protected from invasion of evil. As Satan first approached it from the direction of Mount Niphates, he saw a "steep savage Hill" (IV, 172) whose protective thickets were impenetrable. Later we learn more about the eastern side. The gate was a rock "Of Alabaster, pil'd up to the Clouds . . . The rest was craggy cliff, that overhung / Still as it rose" (IV, 543-48). The gate was guarded by a band of angels under the command of Gabriel.

Nature was profusely bountiful in this uncultivated garden. Here stood

> Groves whose rich Trees wept odorous Gums and Balm,
> Others whose fruit burnisht with Golden Rind
> Hung amiable, *Hesperian* Fables true,
> If true, here only, and of delicious taste:
> Betwixt them Lawns . . . .
> Flow'rs of all hue.   (IV, 248-56)

There were cool grottoes, brooks, a myrtle-fringed lake like a "crystal mirror" (IV, 263), singing birds. Gentle breezes bore "Native perfumes" (IV, 158), "flow'ring Odors, Cassia, Nard, and Balm" (V, 293). Here in this "Wilderness of sweets" where Nature "Wanton'd as in her prime" (V, 294-95), all the human senses were continually delighted, and here

> Universal *Pan*
> Knit with the *Graces* and the *Hours* in dance
> Led on th'Eternal Spring.   (IV, 266-68)

No other garden of legend or history "might with this Paradise / Of *Eden* strive" (IV, 274-75). Satan, during his surreptitious roamings through the Garden, envies man's dwelling place deeply: "O Earth, how like to Heav'n, if not preferr'd" (IX, 99).

To Milton variety is essential to beauty and to pleasure.[20] Paradise, as he pictures it, was "A happy rural seat of various view" (IV, 247), where God had

> Varied his bounty so with new delights,
> As [might] compare with Heaven.   (V, 431-32)

The landscape was hilly. Shortly before the Expulsion, Michael showed Adam a prophetic vision from the summit of "A hill, / Of Paradise the highest," as high as that on which, in time to come, Satan would set

> Our second *Adam* in the Wilderness,
> To show him all Earth's Kingdoms and thir Glory.
> (XI, 377-84)

(This high hill in Paradise is a topographical curiosity. A mountain on a mountain?) Indeed, all the earth had its heights and hollows, its "pleasure situate in Hill and Dale," a "variety" imitated "from Heav'n" (VI, 640-41). According to a theory current in Milton's day, the earth, when God created it, was a perfect sphere, that is, perfectly smooth.[21] It is evident that Milton has rejected this theory.

Adam and Eve lived in the Garden fully conscious of its delightfulness and of its superlative loveliness. Because of the mild and even climate— "th'Eternal Spring"—they needed no clothing. Life was an uneventful rhythm of pleasant days.[22] The only work required of them was to dress the Garden and keep it, a "sweet" labor only strenuous enough "To recommend cool *Zephyr*" and make "ease / More easy" (IV, 328-30). With "tender hand" Eve cultivated flowers which would never "in other Climate grow" (XI, 274-76). The happy couple had a bower, a "Sylvan Lodge . . . that like

Pomona's Arbor smil'd / With flow'rets deck't" (V, 377-79). Eve adorned this dwelling "With what to sight or smell was sweet" (XI, 281). They ate the abundant fruits and drank the water of the brooks. They were surrounded by affectionate and playful animals (IV, 340-52), all vegetarians like themselves. Before the Fall, the animals had no noxious or predatory impulses. The rose had no thorns (IV, 256). Animals and plants as well as human beings were immortal.

Milton gives only hints concerning the character of the prelapsarian earth outside Paradise. Evidently it was somewhat less delightful than Paradise, for although the air outside was "pure," the air of Paradise was "purer" (IV, 153; XI, 284-85). It seems to have been inhabited by animals (IX, 82-84). Even though the rest of the earth was inferior to Paradise, the whole of it, except presumably the polar regions, would have furnished a pleasant environment for human life; that is, for the numerous descendants of Adam and Eve who were to people the earth. Certainly the whole of the earth was more luxuriant, more beautiful, climatically more temperate than it is now. There were no seasons, no storms.

Before the Fall man lived in perfect harmony with the natural environment created for his happiness. This harmony was so close that, when Eve bit into the apple,

> Earth felt the wound, and Nature from her seat
> Sighing through all her Works gave signs of woe.
> (IX, 782-83)

And when Adam joined Eve in transgression,

> Earth trembl'd from her entrails, as again
> In pangs, and Nature gave a second groan,
> Sky low'r'd, and muttering Thunder, some sad drops
> Wept at completing of the mortal Sin
> Original. (IX, 1000-04)

In "Lycidas" the mourning of nature is figurative, an example of the pathetic fallacy; in *Paradise Lost* it is literal. The Original Sin broke the pristine harmony. Many of the animals immediately developed carnivorous instincts and attacked the milder beasts (X, 710-12). The animals developed fear of man or hostility toward him (X, 712-14). Men, animals, and plants became subject to death (X, 267-69, 603-13). At God's command, angels made changes in the celestial mechanics to produce harsh weather (see Chap. V, sec. v). Since the Fall there has been discord in nature, discord between man and nature, and discord among men.

After the Expulsion, Paradise remained uninhabited for generations and was finally destroyed by the Flood. The mountain on which it was located was devasted by waters and was carried down the Tigris to the Persian Gulf; there it took "root an Island Salt and bare, / The haunt of Seals and Orcs, and Sea-mews clang" (XI, 834-35).

III

Although man was the "Master work" of the Creation, "the end / Of all yet done" (VII, 505-06), he is nevertheless a material creation like all other things in God's world. He is not set apart from physical nature; he is the apex of the terrestrial scale of life. Human nature, then, is a proper subject for the student of the natural sciences. Even psychology is within the realm of the natural philosopher, for it is not altogether distinguishable from physiology.

Milton has acquired considerable information concerning the human body and mind as they were understood in his day. He is evidently somewhat interested in medical science. Several medical figures appear in the prose works.[23] In *Paradise Lost*, however, there is little reference to medical ideas, for the poem concerns man in the state of innocence, when disease was not yet a part of human experience. Disease is an aspect of the physical and moral degeneration which followed sin into the world. Adam learns of disease only when, in the vision of the future which Michael shows him, he sees a hospital, "sad, noisome, dark," in which lie "Numbers of all diseas'd, all maladies." There follows a list of painful ailments (XI, 477-90). After the publication of *Paradise Lost*, Milton must have felt that he had neglected the mental diseases, for in the second edition he adds the three psychopathological conditions most frequently and most voluminously described in the psychiatric sections of Renaissance medical works: "Daemoniac Frenzy, moping Melancholy / And Moon-struck madness" (XI, 485-86). Michael explains that the diseases of the future will be due to "Intemperance ... In Meats and Drinks" (XI, 472-73); the patients of the vision will have perverted "Nature's healthful rules" (XI, 523) and will have defaced God's image by their sinful self-indulgence. They will deserve their suffering. The temperate man will live much more happily (XI, 530-46), but even he, because of Adam's sin, must grow old and die. Milton is not prepared to say, however, that disease is always due to self-indulgence. He asserts in the *Second Defense of the English People* that his own blindness resulted from his cruel straining of his eyes in preparation of the first *Defense*. He has sacrificed his eyesight, he believes, in the service of his country and his God.

Milton's ideas concerning human physiology are those that one would expect of a seventeenth-century man whose scientific information was not quite up to date. He accepts without serious question the ancient Greek conception of a human body containing four *humors,* or fluids: melancholy, phlegm, blood, choler. These elements in the microcosm are analogous respectively to the earth, water, air, and fire of the macrocosm. Various physiological functions are assigned to the several humors. Disease is explained by plethora, disporportion, or corruption of humors. A man's personality is believed to be strongly influenced by his *complexion,* or *temperament;* that is, by the relative proportions in which the humors are present in his body.

Although the familiar ideas concerning the humors and temperaments appear somewhat frequently in Milton's works as a whole, there is very little reference to them in *Paradise Lost.* Before the Fall, Adam's temperament was undoubtedly the golden temperament—the complexion of the Golden Mean, of perfect balance among the humors—, but Milton does not say so. He makes somewhat more obvious use, however, of certain other ideas derived from the physiology of the Greeks.

Among these is a theory of aging. The qualities of life are heat and moisture.[24] Each living creature is endowed at birth with a certain amount of *natural heat* and *natural moisture.* These two physiological qualities or entities seem to be regarded as a single substance; a certain writer describes natural heat as "a substance moist and very vaporous."[25] Natural heat and moisture are not renewable and are slowly expended by the activities of living. Aging is a cooling and drying. Since cold and dryness are qualities inimical to life, the old man must suffer various degenerative debilities; and in the end his life will flicker out like the flame of a lamp which has burned up its oil. Even though one avoids disease by righteous and temperate living, he cannot, because of Adam's sin, escape death and the slow decline which precedes it. He will outlive his youth, strength, and beauty and will grow "wither'd weak and gray" (XI, 540). Michael tells Adam:

> for the Air of youth
> Hopeful and cheerful, in thy blood will reign
> A melancholy damp of cold and dry
> To weigh thy Spirits down, and last consume
> The Balm of Life.   (XI, 542-46)

In old age, melancholy, the cold and dry humor, increases at the expense of blood, the warm and moist humor. From melancholy arises a "damp," a dry, noxious vapor. "The Balm of Life" is the natural heat-moisture which resides in the blood.

The concept of "spirits," to which Milton makes incidental reference here, has considerable importance in his thinking concerning man's place in the hierarchy of creatures. The term *spirit,* or *spirits* (sometimes the singular form appears; sometimes the plural form with a singular meaning), refers to a substance in the human body which is described as either a very subtle fluid or a vapor. Renaissance physiologists and psychologists usually distinguish three kinds of spirit: *natural spirit, vital spirit,* and *animal spirit,* and assign certain functions to each. These kinds of spirit are produced by successive stages of rarefaction.

The progressive refinement begins with the digestion of food in the stomach. The product of this is a fluid known as *chyle.* In the liver the chyle undergoes a second digestion. During this process a small part of it becomes natural spirit, whose function is to stimulate and direct the natural operations of the body, those which are involuntary or subconscious. (Milton never mentions the natural spirit.) From the rest of the chyle, the liver produces the four humors. Of these blood is the most abundant. In the heart a portion of the blood is still further refined, is endowed with natural heat, and thus becomes vital spirit. The vital spirit ("flammula," a little flame[26]) flows with the arterial blood and serves as the vehicle of natural heat and moisture. The "spirits" which in old age are neutralized by the cold and dryness of the melancholy humor are vital spirits. Some of the vital spirit is conveyed to the brain, and there it undergoes another rarefaction. The crude nourishment received by the stomach has now, by four successive refinements, become a substance which is extremely tenuous. This is the animal spirit (from Latin *anima,* mind, soul). It flows through the nerves ("velut lumen," like a light[26]) and serves as medium of communication between mind and body, bearing the commands of the mind to the physical members and sensory impressions back to the brain. The animal spirit, as John Donne phrases it, is "That subtle knot which makes us man." It is, furthermore, the physical medium of all operations of the brain itself: ratiocination, revery, memory, imagination.

If the mind is to operate clearly, surely, and swiftly, the animal and vital spirits must be pure, delicate, and nimble. Their quality depends upon one's emotional and physical state. When "the heart is in good temper, so that it is not troubled either with anger, or sadnesse, or any other euill affection, it is manifest that the spirits are a great deale the better in the braine."[27] Ill chosen diet makes the spirits less delicate and the mind less capable: "those nourishmentes that are moyst, grosse, and not firmely compacted ... maketh the conceit blunt, and disableth much the faculties of the minde: which a thinner, drier, and more subtle foode doth entertaine."[28] Any disaffection of the body, by vitiating the humors and spirits, may impair the reason and thwart its natural inclination to virtue: "a fulness and repletion of infected and malignant humors" will taint and even corrupt "the clear Crystalline and rarified Spirits" and disturb "their noblest actions. These Spirits the more attenuated and purified they be, the more ... our reason ... doth bear dominion."[29] Milton himself knows the mental benefits of physical health: in a healthy body, "the blood is fresh, the spirits pure and vigorous, not only to vital, but to rationall faculties, and those in the acutest, and the pertest operations of wit and suttlety."[30]

There are five clear references to the spirits in *Paradise Lost.* Michael explains to Adam, in the passage already quoted, the decline of the vital spirits in old age. In creating Eve, God takes from Adam's left side "a Rib, with cordial [vital] spirits warm" (VIII, 466). Squatting at Eve's ear in the form of a toad, Satan tampers with her normally tranquil mental processes; he endeavors "to reach / The Organs of her Fancy" (her imagination) and to forge with them "Illusions . . . Phantasms and Dreams" or to taint with venom

> Th'animal spirits that from pure blood arise
> Like gentle breaths from Rivers pure, thence raise
> At least distemper'd, discontented thoughts.
>
> (IV, 802-07)

Right thinking requires purity of spirit. (Milton is a little confusing in this passage; animal spirit does not arise directly from blood.) After she eats of the forbidden fruit, Eve feels among its effects "dilated Spirits" (IX, 876). The fruit is intoxicating; Eve is feeling effects like those of wine. Renaissance physicians often recommend wine to quicken and dilate sluggish spirits.

When Raphael is explaining to Adam the successive purifications through which matter passes in a living creature to become progressively more excellent, he uses a flowering plant as illustration. From the root grows the "lighter" green stalk; from the stalk, the "More aery" leaves; then "the bright consummate flow'r," which breathes "Spirits odorous" (V, 479-82). The perfume is the final product of the progressive rarefaction in the flower. Raphael now speaks of processes in man which are both analogous to this sublimation and a continuation of it:

> flow'rs and their fruit
> Man's nourishment, by gradual scale sublim'd,
> To vital spirits aspire, to animal,
> To intellectual. (V, 482-85)

The passage is elliptical; the full statement would read: "To vital spirits aspire, then to animal spirits, then to intellectual spirits." So it seems that in man there is a form of spirit even higher on the scale than animal spirit, an *intellectual spirit,* and the flower analogy suggests that it is a refinement of animal spirit. It is the product of the final rarefaction in a series of five, evidently a very rare vapor, incomparably purer than the gross materials from which it has been produced. This is the subtlest and noblest component of the human body. It is a kind of matter which allies man with the angels. Speaking very loosely, one might call it the human soul.[31]

A fundamental doctrine of Milton's is the materiality of every created thing. An angel, a celestial spirit, has substance, and so does man's most elevated spirit. Flesh and spirit do not differ in kind; they are simply different degrees in a continuum from grossest matter up to God. This philosophic materialism was not original with Milton; there are several sources from which he could have derived it.[32] But he has linked body and spirit with a specificness which is at least highly unusual. He has done so by understanding *spirit* (meaning such a being as an angel) and *spirit* (referring to the greatly rarefied substances in the human body) as, not two terms, but one. He has assumed—or deduced—the existence of a material intellectual spirit which is the substance of the angels and which man alone among earthly creatures possesses, and thus he bridges the gap between man and angel. In the rather numerous medical and psychological works (classical, medieval, and Renaissance) which I have consulted at one time or another,[33] I have never found mention of more than three kinds of physiological spirit, and the animal spirit is always the highest kind. In these works I have never met the phrase *intellectual spirit* (or *spiritus intellectualis*) used in a physiological sense. To most men of the Middle Ages or the Renaissance, the phrase would have meant "angel."[34] If one accepts Milton's materialistic meaning, the expression is still applicable to an angel, but it is applicable also to a man, at least to the noblest part of him. Milton has thus erased the distinction between material and spiritual. Man's intelligence, his psyche, is a high degree of matter produced by natural processes, one of the steps (nearly the last) by which matter rises to God.

The link which Milton establishes between corporal and spiritual is somewhat tenuous, and he seems not very confident in proposing it. The concept of intellectual spirit appears nowhere in his works except in this one passage in *Paradise Lost,* and here its unconventionality is disguised by the use of a conventional phrase which most readers would take to mean something else. Yet he consistently regards the human spirit as a material substance, the same as the total substance of the angels.

In adopting this theory of spirit, Milton has not departed from his deductive habit of thought. He has deduced from scriptural texts that all forms of existence in time and space are material and has found confirmation in authoritative Christian authors. The spirit which relates man to God must therefore be a substance. It would be convenient to identify this divine spirit with the animal spirit. But they cannot be the same, for beasts as well as men have animal spirit, though a beast does not have all of man's animal faculties. There is reason to believe, then, that there is a nobler form of spirit in man, a substance purer and subtler than any appearing in the lower creatures.

Raphael has more to say about spirit. After naming the successive grades of spirit, he explains that these

41

> give both life and sense,
> Fancy and understanding, whence the Soul
> Reason receives, and reason is her being,
> Discursive, or Intuitive.   (V, 485-88)

It is the vital spirit, bearer of the natural heat and moisture, that gives life; heat and moisture are the qualities of a living creature. The animal spirit is the instrument of sensation, imagination ("Fancy"), understanding, and other faculties. Though Milton elsewhere uses *understanding* in a different sense, he seems here to be referring to the "estimative faculty," the ability to recognize the potential benefit or noxiousness of an object, to see that "the wolf is to be avoided and the child to be loved."[35] This is the highest degree of abstraction possible to an animal. Sensation, imagination, and the estimative faculty serve the reason, the noblest of the faculties. Reason is the "being" of the soul in the sense that it is man's—or angel's—distinctive faculty. According to the conventional psychology, the animal spirit is the physical instrument of reason as well as of sense and motion. In Milton's psychology, the animal spirit evidently serves only the faculties of sense and motion; the physical instrument of reason is the intellectual spirit. This is logical: Man is distinguished from all other earthly creatures by the possession of reason; he is distinguished also by the possession of the fourth spirit. It is possible to conclude, then, that this spirit is the means by which man reasons.

But it appears that there are two kinds of reasoning, "Discursive, or Intuitive." *Discourse* is ratiocination, the putting together of evidence, the following of a logical train of thought, the drawing of conclusions. Intuition is immediate perception.[36] Raphael continues: "discourse / Is oftest yours, the latter most is ours" (V, 488-89). Men normally think discursively but sometimes have flashes of intuition. Angels, spiritually more perfect, normally think intuitively but must sometimes resort to discourse, step-by-step reasoning. These two thought processes, however, differ only in "degree, of kind the same" (V, 490).

In fact Raphael makes it clear to Adam that there is much less difference between man and angel than he might be inclined to suppose.[37] When Adam apologetically offers him human food—"unsavory food perhaps / To spiritual Natures" (V, 401-02)—, Raphael assures him that whatever God gives

> to man in part
> Spiritual, may of purest Spirits be found
> No ingrateful food: and food alike those pure
> Intelligential substances require
> As doth your Rational.   (V, 405-09)

There is semantic confusion here. Both Adam and the angel are "rational substances" (both reasoning creatures). The angel is obviously a "pure intelligential substance," but Adam also is in part such a substance. Milton evidently means simply to distinguish two ranks in the hierarchy. It is clear at least that angels are "purest Spirits," that is, pure intelligence. Yet angels eat, "concoct, digest, assimilate" (V, 412). At Adam's table,[38] Raphael eats

> with keen dispatch
> Of real hunger, and concoctive heat
> To transubstantiate.   (V, 436-38)

One learns elsewhere that angels require sleep (V, 644 ff.). Angels have both the physical needs of men and their sensory capabilities. They have also emotions: they love God and they love one another; Lucifer's pride and envy motivate rebellion. Each higher living substance has every capability that the less noble forms have. The intelligential substances of both angel and man contain

> Within them every lower faculty
> Of sense, whereby they hear, see, smell, touch, taste,
> Tasting concoct, digest, assimilate,
> And corporeal to incorporeal turn.   (V, 410-13)

"For spirit being the more excellent substance," as compared with flesh, "contains within itself the inferior one; as the spiritual and rational faculty contains the corporeal, that is, the sentient and vegetative faculty."[39] An angel, then, has every capability of feeling or action that a man has. But he has additional and nobler capabilities.

Angels differ from men also in their homogeneity. Man's spirit (vital, animal, and intellectual) constitutes only a very small fraction of his substance. His body consists mainly of matter, or a variety of matters, of much grosser nature. Angels are all spirit; Raphael is a "pure / Intelligence of Heav'n" (VIII, 180-81). Because the angel is homogeneously spiritual, he has no solidity, and in his body there is no diversification, no specialization of function, as there is in the human body. When they embrace, angels find no obstacle

> Of membrane, joint, or limb, exclusive bars:
> Easier than Air with Air, if Spirits embrace,
> Total they mix, Union of Pure with Pure.   (VIII, 625-27)

This seems to imply that any function may be performed by any part of the angelic body or by the angel's total substance.

The pure intelligential substance is capable of actions and experiences that a man can hardly conceive; nevertheless an angel requires food; he experiences sensation and emotion; he imagines and remembers; on occasion he thinks discursively like a man. The difference between angel and man is one of degree, not one of kind; essentially an angel is a man plus something.

Furthermore men may become like angels. It is possible that the flesh may "up to spirit work" (V, 478). Raphael tells Adam that, if they are obedient, men's

> bodies may at last turn all to spirit,
> Improv'd by tract of time, and wing'd ascend
> Ethereal.   (V, 498-500)

Thus humanity may rise on "the scale of Nature" which leads up "to God" (V, 509-12). Mankind may become a tenth order of angels. By his sin Adam forfeited this bright but conditional future both for himself and for his descendants, but in his graciousness God has given man a second chance. Through virtuous effort, he may still ascend. The refinement of flesh into spirit, if it has been earned, will occur after the Second Coming of the Son and the Last Judgment.

Those of God's creatures who sin heinously suffer a permanent degeneration. In *Comus* Milton expresses this idea figuratively by means of the rout of beasts who were once self-indulgent men. In *Paradise Lost* the degeneration is literal and material. The rebel angels, once "Spirits of purest light, Purest at first," have grown "gross by sinning" (VI, 660-61). They have become heavier and denser, and they are now capable of feeling pain. Even at the time of the celestial battle, the apostate angels had developed such solidity that

> Thir armour help'd thir harm, crush't in and bruis'd
> Into thir substance pent, which wrought them pain.
>   (VI, 656-57)

When Michael struck Satan on the first day of the battle, "then *Satan* first knew pain" (VI, 327).[40] The loyal angels meanwhile remained "unobnoxious to be pain'd / By wound" (VI, 404-05). In Eden Satan is conscious of the unfallen Adam's superiority to himself:

> Foe not informidable, exempt from wound,
> I not; so much hath Hell debas'd, and pain
> Infeebl'd me, to what I was in Heav'n. (IX, 486-88)

Satan has descended to the very bottom of the scale of being. When Adam sins, he suffers a degeneration which makes him for the first time capable of pain.

IV

Although the Renaissance did not have the word *psychology* in its vocabulary, it had a body of lore concerning the senses, the emotions, and the mind. Like the Galenic physiology, this science had a history stretching back to classical sources. This was the only psychology current in the earlier seventeenth century; there was no "new psychology." Every educated man of the period knew its principles. Students of sixteenth and seventeenth century literature become very familiar with it.

Renaissance psychology recognizes, perhaps as clearly as modern psychology, the close relationship between body and mind. The theory of the four temperaments explains character as the effect of physical causes. The human mind operates by physical means, principally the spirits. The emotions are physical states or processes. The Renaissance regards its psychology as a branch of natural philosophy.

But because psychology furnishes guidance for conduct, it is regarded also as a branch of moral philosophy. The psychological writers of the period, most of them moralists, repeat again and again the ancient exhortation: *nosce teipsum*, know thyself.[41] Self-knowledge is prerequisite to self-control and to virtuous living and happiness. Every man should understand the organization and proper operation of the mind. Most particularly he should be aware of the dangers inherent in the passions and should know how to curb and direct them. Because of its ethical value, there is an even more specific reason for the study of psychology than for the study of the other branches of natural philosophy.

In his warm recommendation of the sciences in the Third Prolusion, young Milton tells his auditors that it is the "most important matter" that the mind "learn thoroughly to know itself."[42] Psychology, then, is a part of the program of scientific study which he is urging. He himself seems to have mastered the subject, and he makes good use of his psychological lore in *Paradise Lost*.

He departs from the standard opinion concerning the nature of the psyche. In Renaissance psychologies one reads frequently that there is an immaterial element in man, the *soul*, or the *rational soul*. This, the psychologists say, is incorruptible, although its instruments may be injured and vitated; and it is immortal. Milton has adopted the Aristotelian concept of *soul*: The soul is the form of man; that is, the complete man, body and spirit. To inquire whether soul and body are separable, says Aristotle, is as meaningless "as to ask whether the wax and the shape given to it by the stamp are one."[43] In terms of the Aristotelian causes, a variety of matter—in which Milton would include the spirit—is the material cause of man; the soul is the formal cause. In Milton's thinking, the intellectual spirit is the nearest thing to the common conception of the soul; but the spirit, he believes, is definitely corruptible and, in fact, mortal (see below, sec. v). He recognizes the fact that *soul* and *spirit* are very often used synonymously; and he tries, not always successfully, to keep them distinct. Aside from his somewhat uncommon use of these terms, his psychology is conventional.

The psychologists of the Renaissance characterize the faculties of the soul somewhat elaborately. They place four faculties in the brain: the *common sense,* the *imagination,* the *reason,* and the *memory.* The first two are located in a cell in the forward part of the head; reason occupies a middle cell; memory is placed in the rearmost cell. The common sense assembles sensory images, which it retains only momentarily. The imagination receives these images and presents them to the reason. In dreams and reverie, it often forms fantastic combinations of images. The imagination is often called the *fancy,* and this is the term which Milton uses. He never refers to the common sense, apparently assigning its function to the imagination. The common sense, the imagination, and the memory are known as the *internal senses;* that is, they are sensory, not rational faculties. Beasts as well as men possess them.

The reason operates upon the sensory data which reach it through the imagination (it has no other means of perceiving the world outside) and draws upon the memory for images and information previously acquired and stored there. It is divided into two subfaculties: *understanding* (or *reason* proper) and *will.* The function of the understanding is *discourse,* the step-by-step process by which the mind reaches conclusions. The function of the will is, of course, *volition,* choice. The understanding forms ideas, opinions, and convictions. When it concludes that a course of action is good or evil, the will, unless it is feeble or corrupted, desires this course if it is good, abhors it if it is evil; and it commands the lower faculties to perform or avoid the action.

Seventeenth-century thinkers regard reason (understanding plus will) "as the godlike principle in man . . . the principle of moral control rather than of intellectual enlightenment."[44] To Milton "conscience [is] right reason";[45] "Virtue . . . is reason" (*PL,* XII, 98). If reason functions as it should, it invariably sees which is the righteous course and chooses it. "Reason is choice" (*PL,* III, 108); a reasonable being is a moral being. Among God's creatures only men and angels can choose, and they, therefore, are the only creatures who have moral responsibility and who are capable of good and evil.

The reasonable will commands the emotions, the immediate motivating agents of action. Renaissance psychologists regard the emotions as physiological processes which can be keenly felt. (When Adam learned of Eve's sin, "horror chill / Ran through his veins, and all his joints relax'd," IX, 890-91.) In seventeenth-century language, the emotions are *affections,* or *internal motions.* The *concupiscible* (desiring) affections are sometimes called *appetites.* An emotion of unusual violence is a *passion,* or a *perturbation.* In a psychologically healthy man, the affections are strong, but not too strong. Either excess or defect is morbid, but excess is much more frequent than defect.

Animals are governed by imagination and affections. But in man the affections are, or should be, the servants of reason, which is the proper mistress of the soul. A man who allows his emotions to overrule his reasonable will sacrifices his freedom and his virtue. His actions, like those of a beast, become simply reactions to stimuli; he has forfeited his humanity and has descended on the scale of being. He has become the slave of his passions, enthralled to his bestial self.

As God originally constituted human nature in Adam, the understanding perceived clearly, never doubtfully or erroneously; the will unhesitantly chose the good and abhorred the evil; the affections obediently performed their subordinate functions. Adam was a virtuous man and a calmly happy man, completely master of himself and free of all emotional turmoil. If mankind had remained so, all men would understand and agree upon all significant truths, and all would invariably follow the clearly perceived laws of nature and of God. But by the Original Sin human understanding has been darkened; the will has been vitiated; the affections have become passions, turbulent and insubordinate. Virture is much more difficult for Adam's sons than it was before the Fall for Adam.

The Adam of *Paradise Lost* has some innate knowledge of psychology and of its ethical uses. When Eve tells him of her disturbing dream, he can explain: "Fancy," receiving images of the external world through the senses,

> forms Imaginations [images], Aery shapes,
> Which Reason joining or disjoining, frames
> All what we affirm or what deny, and call
> Our knowledge or opinion; then retires
> Into her private Cell while Nature rests.
> Oft in her absence mimic Fancy wakes
> To imitate her; but misjoining shapes,
> Wild work produces oft, and most in dreams,
> Ill matching words and deeds long past or late.
>
> (V, 105-13)

Eve's dream, as it happens, arises not from the spontaneous playfulness of the imagination, but from Satan's interferring with "The Organs of her Fancy" (IV, 802). But Adam's explanation accurately follows Renaissance theory.[46] Later Adam lectures Eve on the moral functions of reason (understanding) and will: "Against his will" a man or woman cannot be harmed by evil:

> God left free the Will, for what obeys
> Reason, is free, and Reason he made right,
> But bid her well beware, and still erect,
> Lest by some fair appearing good surpris'd
> She dictate false, and misinform the Will
> To do what God expressly hath forbid.   (IX, 350-56)

Adam knows that moderate emotion is normal and right but that passion, emotion of abnormal strength, threatens the government of reason. He tells Raphael of his feeling for Eve:

> here passion first I felt,
> Commotion strange, in all enjoyments else
> Superior and unmov'd, here only weak.   (VIII, 530-32)

Adam has allowed love to become excessive, to become a passion; and at the same time, as Raphael points out, he is guilty of defect of pride in yielding his priority to Eve:

> weigh with her thyself;
> Then value: Oft-times nothing profits more
> Than self-esteem, grounded on just and right.
> (VIII, 570-72)

In spite of his understanding of himself, Adam needs the warning which Raphael gives in parting:

> take heed lest Passion sway
> Thy Judgment to do aught, which else free Will
> Would not admit.   (VIII, 635-37)

The moral function of the reason and the evil of insubordinate passion are basic ideas in Milton's political thinking. In explaining to Adam the tyrannies which are to appear in future societies, Michael says that "true Liberty . . . always with right Reason dwells / Twinn'd"; if "upstart Passions catch the Government / From Reason," men lose both their inner and their outer (political) freedom (XII, 83-90).[47] A nation gets the kind of government that it deserves.

The story of the Fall can be told in psychological-ethical terms.[48] Raphael's last word to Adam as he leaves him is a warning against his emotional weakness. On the following day Adam is tested first when Eve asks to do the morning's work alone and, when Adam hesitates, insists somewhat tartly on having her way. Adam knows that Eve is not completely dependable; he knows better than to do what he does. Yet he lets her go. In both an internal and an external sense, he has violated the God-ordained scheme of subordinations: he has allowed the lower faculty (affection or passion) to rule the higher, and he has allowed the inferior creature (woman) to govern her superior. So it happens that Satan is able to shun Adam's "higher intellectual" (IX, 483) and deal with credulous Eve alone.

When Eve reveals to Adam that she has eaten of the forbidden fruit, he sees immediately that this is disaster. He solves his fearful dilemma with the unhesitating decision to share in Eve's sin, even though this means death. "How can I live without thee .. ?" (IX, 908). He eats the fruit

> Against his better knowledge, not deceiv'd,
> But fondly [unwisely] overcome with Female charm.
> (IX, 998-99)

The poet makes it very clear that Adam's sin is due, not to failure of understanding, but to failure of will. Adam has allowed emotion, his lower nature, to govern him.

A. J. A. Waldock has horrified Milton's more obstinate admirers by pointing out that Adam acts as all of us would wish him to act. If he turned his back on Eve and left her alone to face a vaguely understood but frightening fate called "death," he would seem to us a self-righteous coward and weakling. His eating of the fruit seems not a sin but a courageous act of "selflessness in love."[49] Waldock, I believe, is right. But this, of course, is not Milton's view of the matter. Adam is guilty of "foul distrust, and breach / Disloyal," of "revolt, / And disobedience" (IX, 6-8). Milton might tell us, if he could, that our reaction is evidence of the corruption of the human faculties by the Original Sin. Our thinking is emotional, not rational. If we had the clarity of mind and the emotional control that Adam had before the Fall, we should understand the matter properly—as Adam himself understood it. The difficulty nevertheless remains. Milton is writing the epic, not for Adam, but for us, who are postlapsarians. He should clarify our degenerate minds for us, check and correct our erring emotions.

The degree of Eve's responsibility for the Original Sin is hard to determine. She is, after all, a second class human being. Adam understands (innately) that Nature

> on her bestowed
> Too much of Ornament, in outward show
> Elaborate [painstaking], of inward less exact.

She is "th'inferior, in the mind / And inward Faculties" and even resembles less than Adam "His Image who made both" (VIII, 537-44). She is not endowed with clarity of understanding or strength of will in the same degree that Adam is. Even before the Fall she fails to control her pride. When she insists on going out alone, she is guilty of pride in that she is impatient with subordination to her superior; when she listens to Satan's flatteries, she is guilty of pride in her physical beauty; when she too readily accepts his reasoning, she becomes guilty of curiosity (intellectual pride) and of desire for a proud station in the hierarchy. Yet Eve does not see clearly what is happening. She never suspects the serpent's duplicity. (Which of us, if he met a talking serpent who argued so plausibly would do better than Eve?) Her eating of the fruit, then, is due to a failure of understanding, not a failure of will. The will, not the understanding, is the faculty which is capable of sin. The primary responsibility is Adam's, and he is the greater sinner. Indeed it seems doubtful that, in the terms of Milton's psychological ethics, Eve's eating of the apple is a sin. Her sin, if she is guilty of any, occurs earlier at the time when she willfully overrules her husband and goes out alone.

When they have eaten of the fruit, Adam and Eve become mirthfully drunk and then lustful. After sexual pleasure and drunken slumber, they wake miserably—"destitute and bare / Of all thir virtue" (IX, 1062-63)—to feel fully the psychological changes which their disobedience has made in them. With the veil of innocence gone, their eyes are open to their shame, but "thir minds / How dark'n'd" (IX, 1053-54). High "Winds" of passion rise —"Anger, Hate, / Mistrust"—and sorely shake the tranquility of their minds, hitherto calm "And full of Peace, now toss't and turbulent." For understanding is no longer in control; the will does not hear "her lore"; both are now in subjection "To sensual Appetite," which has usurped the office of "sovran Reason" (IX, 1122-31). At this point our first parents have sunk to the level of the beasts. But for the grace of God, there we should all be.

The story of the fall of Lucifer can also be told in psychological language. Since angels have reason, free will, and affections, they have the same opportunities of virtue and vice that men have and the same problem of moral self-control. The angels serve God "freely," says Raphael, because they "freely love"; but "some are fall'n, to disobedience fall'n" (V, 538-41). Lucifer's primary sin is his yielding to passionate pride, as Adam's is his yielding to passionate love. Lucifer and his followers refuse "reason for thir Law ... Right reason" (VI, 41-42). Lucifer's uncontrolled pride engenders other passions: "Envy and Revenge" (I, 35), "steadfast hate" (I, 58). Abdiel tells him that he is "not free, but to [himself] enthrall'd" (VI, 181). The soliloquy which he delivers early in Book IV suggests that he can no longer choose a course of action; he must persevere in evil. Unlike Eve and Adam, he is "Self-tempted, Self-deprav'd" (III, 130), and he therefore gets no second chance.

V

When Adam sinned he became subject not only to pain but to death, and this, materially speaking, was the gravest of the consequences of the Fall. As punishment for man's first disobedience, all men must die, for all men sinned with Adam. But God so loved his erring creatures that he gave his only begotten Son to expiate the sin by his own death on the Cross. The Redemption did not reverse the sentence of death (obviously all men die), but it gave men the opportunity to live again. Those who believe and who match their faith with deeds will be saved, for Christ's "obedience / Imputed becomes theirs by Faith" (*PL*, XII, 408-09).

In the *Christian Doctrine* Milton distinguishes four kinds of death, the last two of which are relevant. One of these is *"the death of the body.... All nature is likewise subject to mortality and a curse on account of man."*[50] The other is *"death eternal, the punishment of the damned,"*[51] that is, of both sinful men and apostate angels. By dying the death of the body, Christ has saved from the eternal death all men who deserve salvation.

But all men, nevertheless, must die the death of the body. Their powers of motion, feeling, and thought will cease; they will have no consciousness. Their bodies will decay, and the substance of their bodies will in the course of the years be dispersed. At the end of time, the angel's trumpet will summon all men to judgment. The substances which constituted their bodies during life—"the smallest particles ... sometimes most widely dispersed throughout different countries"[52]—will reassemble, and they will rise, body and spirit, to face their Maker. Both good men and evil men will be spirit-bodies, material beings, when they come to judgment. Evil men will be sentenced to the death everlasting, to physical and mental torment in Hell. The chosen will enter heaven with their substance purified, sublimated presumably to such a degree that they will be fleshly no longer, that they will be all spirit. It is not incredible, Milton writes, that "what is spiritual should arise from body; which ... we believe will be the case with our own bodies at the resurrection."[53] Thus at least some men will attain the spiritual state which Raphael conditionally promises to Adam. Enoch and Elijah must have undergone this spiritualization at the time when, without suffering death, they were translated to Heaven (*PL*, XI, 705-09).

The reconstitution of the body at the time of the Resurrection is a venerable Christian doctrine.[54] It is based on I Corinthians xv, 42-55, and appears in the Apostles' Creed. Milton's conception of death and resurrection is on the whole quite conventional. It is unorthodox, however, in that he insists somewhat emphatically that the soul dies—and is subsequently revived—with the body. For spirit, body, and soul are the same entity: "Man is a living being, intrinsically and properly one and individual [undividable], not compound or separable, not, according to the common opinion, made up and framed of two distinct and different natures, as of soul and body . . . . the whole man is soul, and the soul man, that is to say, a body, or substance individual, animated, sensitive, and rational."[55] His belief in the total death of body-spirit-soul places Milton among a hazily defined class of heretics known as mortalists.[56]

The mortalist heresy was an old one. Eusebius tells that, in the reign of the Emperor Philip (244-49 A.D.), "a new group appeared on the Arabian scene, originators of a doctrine far removed from the truth, namely, that at the end of our life here the human soul dies for a time along with our bodies and perishes with them; later, when one day the resurrection comes, it will return with them to life."[57] At a synod convoked to deal with this doctrinal crisis, no less a person than Origen persuaded them of their error. Among Renaissance Protestants, especially in the minor sects, mortalism was very active in the form known as *psychopannychism*, the belief that the soul sleeps between death and the Last Judgment.[58] The principal alternative belief, embraced by most Catholics and many Protestants,[59] was that the soul at death goes immediately to its reward or punishment (or purgation), though it will not be reunited with its body until the time of the Judgment. Thus the soul is judged twice, once at the time of death and once at the end of time. The Last Judgment is reduced to a formality.

In the chapter "Of the Death of the Body" in the *Christian Doctrine*, Milton argues that death is a total, though temporary, annihilation, not simply a suspension of consciousness as in sleep. He quotes St. Paul's references to the dead as those who "are asleep" and those "which sleep in Jesus" (I Thessalonians iv, 13-14); he uses these texts, however, to demonstrate that there could be no conscious intermediate state between death and resurrection. Evidently he understands St. Paul's use of "sleep" as metaphoric. The principal points in the chapter are, first, "that the whole man dies, and, secondly, that each component part suffers privation of life."[60] Because he regards the soul as the form of man, he could hardly admit that the soul survives death and dissolution. After his death a man obviously cannot exist—not until the body, glorified, is reunited with the spirit at the end of the world. Because the spirit is, like the body, a material thing, like the body it is subject to dissipation and subsequent reconstitution. It would not be reasonable, furthermore, that God should punish the body with death and spare the spirit, for it is mind or spirit which has sinned. In the *Christian Doctrine* Milton's rigorous logic leads him to an uncompromising mortalism.

In *Paradise Lost* he says nothing about the after-life which would disturb even the most orthodox. Aside from the passage in which Adam, in his ignorance, speculates on the meaning of death (X, 775-820), I have been able to find only two passages, both very brief, which clearly refer to the condition of man between carnal death and resurrection: the Trump of Doom "shall rouse" the dead from "thir sleep" (III, 329); because of the Redemption, "temporal death" for the blessed will be "like sleep, / A gentle wafting to immortal Life" (XII, 433-35). These lines are very indefinite. If they support any doctrine, it is the idea of a suspended consciousness, not of temporary nothingness. Milton's mortalism, however, is a necessary consequence of the materialism which permeates the poem. Although no single passage clearly betrays the author's heresy, *Paradise Lost* is mortalistic.

VI

Many of the passages in *Paradise Lost* which concern physical nature and human psychology seem prosaically expository. Although Milton is likely to excel at any kind of poetry that he attempts, he sometimes does not rise very far above Sylvester and John Davies of Hereford when he undertakes to write scientific verse.

His scientific and ontological poetry, furthermore, is intellectually unsatisfactory—at least to a twentieth century reader. His explanation of the physical nature of being invites unkind questions. How can an angel digest food with his whole body? Could an angel eat and digest fire? If a sinning creature moves down the rarity-density scale, then Adam must have become heavier after the Fall. Did he? As a result of his apostasy, Satan fell to the bottom of the scale. How dense is Satan? Logically his specific gravity is incredibly high. If angels must eat, then devils also need food. What do devils eat? The monsters of Hell? Is it curiosity to inquire about such matters?

It is easy to ridicule. But Milton's scientific deficiencies do not greatly mar the poem. They would have been apparent to very few of his contemporaries. They are, moreover, much less interesting and significant than the purposes for which Milton presents this pseudo-scientific universal scheme. He is endeavoring to support certain moral and ontological generalizations which, however weak the support may be, have dignity and value. "Entity is good,"[61] for all being emanates from God. All forms of existence which we know are material, derived from the one first matter which in the beginning came from God. All existences, therefore, are by nature good. God's creatures (inanimate and animate) form a graded sequence, a chain of being, from grossest to rarest, from the meanest to the noblest. Among them there are no distinctions of kind, only of degree; there is no significant difference between carnal and spiritual. All creatures share in the divine nature and all strive to return to the divine source. Milton's philosophy is an "essentially theistic form of monism. ... The insistent demand of his mature ethics was for a view of man and his life which gave no foothold for more asceticism, yet preserved a clearly marked and inviolable hierarchy of values."[62]

Chapter V. THE SUPRALUNAR WORLD

Except for ideas confined to a few lines of *Paradise Lost* (of which more later), Milton's astronomical thinking was based on concepts which had originated among the ancient Greeks, which, with modifications and accretions, had survived through the centuries, and were still regarded as valid by most astronomers of the sixteenth century. The supraterrestrial world of *Paradise Lost* cannot be adequately explained without at least a sketchy review of some early astronomical theories.[1]

I

If an intelligent but completely uninformed observer undertook to study the heavens, his first conclusion might reasonably be that the earth (obviously static) was surrounded by a huge hollow sphere to which the heavenly bodies were attached, a sphere revolving around the earth once in twenty-four hours. Even superficial observation over a brief period, however, would reveal that the motion of the moon does not correspond with that of the sun and the stars. Careful observation over a year would reveal that the fixed stars completed their daily revolution a little faster than the sun and that five troublesomely erratic stars (the visible planets) moved about each in its own independent way. To explain these various movements, the ingenious observer might decide that, instead of a single sphere, there were eight hollow spheres, one inside the other, with the earth at their common center. The sun would be attached to, or imbedded in, one of these, the moon in another, the five planets in five others, the fixed stars in another (the outermost). If one assigned to each of these spheres a different rate of revolution, he could, very roughly, account for the motions of the heavenly bodies. Of necessity all of these spheres, except perhaps the outermost, would be transparent. If one supposed that they had actual substance, he would imagine them as consisting of glass, crystal, or a like material.

Some such explanation of celestial movements was devised very early among the Greeks, possibly first by Parmenides of Elea (early fifth century B.C.). But accumulating observational data revealed apparent irregularities in the movements of the seven planets which could not be explained by a set of eight simple spheres. (Early astronomers classified the sun and moon as planets.) All of the planets appear to move along the great circle of constellations known as the zodiac, but they move at very different speeds. The moon completes its circuit of the sky in twenty-seven days; Saturn in twenty-nine years. Their velocities, moreover, are not constant; and some of them at times seem to stop, then move backward (retrograde motion), then resume their motion in the original direction.

Eudoxus of Knidus (fourth century) attempted to account for everything by devising a set of seven compound spheres. This means that some spheres are turning upon axes which are fixed in other moving spheres; there are as many as four in a set. An eighth sphere, outside the others, bears the fixed stars. According to Eudoxus' theory, there are twenty-seven spheres al- together. Eudoxus seems to have come fairly close to an adequate explana- tion of celestial movements in so far as they had been observed. His pupil Kalippus refined upon the system by adding seven more spheres. Aristotle attempted still further improvement. There are fifty-five spheres in Aristot- le's system (*Metaphysica*, 1073-74).

As Greek astronomers accumulated new data and corrected the old, it became more and more evident that compound spheres could never explain the phenomena no matter how many spheres were added. In the course of the two or three centuries after Aristotle, they devised another astronomical theory, one which had a very long life before it. This was the Ptolemaic system, so called because it was expounded in its latest classical form by the Greco-Egyptian astronomer Claudius Ptolemy, of the second century A.D., in his great work the *Syntaxis*. This book represented the cumulative results of at least five centuries of observation and speculation. The predecessor to whom Ptolemy owed most was Hipparchus of Nicea, of the second century B.C.

To explain the planetary movements, the Ptolemaic astronomy superim- posed three principal features upon the basic idea of the eight primary spheres. These were the eccentric orbit, the epicycle, and the equant. An eccentric is a planetary orbit which encircles the earth but whose center is a point other than the earth. An epicycle is an orbit whose center travels along a much larger orbit (called the deferent) which encircles the earth. The planet moves around the circumference of the epicycle, while the center of the epicycle moves around the deferent. Ptolemaic theory imposes epicycles on eccentrics and minor epicycles on major epicycles. An equant is a point within a planetary orbit other than its center; the center of the planet's epicycle moves around the deferent (larger orbit) at such a varying rate that a line drawn from the equant to the center of the epicycle moves through equal angles in equal times. Equants are sometimes used within epicycles as well as within deferents. Epicycles explain retrograde motion; equants explain variations of orbital speed. Until the time of Kepler, all orbits were assumed to be circular.

The foregoing hardly does justice to the ingenious intricacy of the Ptolemaic astronomy. Theorists of this school found it necessary to devise "complicated combinations of epicycles within epicycles, equants, and eccentric motions." After successive modifications, the Ptolemaic astronomy, in the sixteenth century, distinguished "over 70 simultaneous different motions."[2] In spite of its frustrating complexity, however, it could predict celestial movements with reasonable accuracy, and it provided the basis for useful astronomical tables and almanacs.

Not all ancient theorists assumed a stationary earth. Philolaus, a Pythagorean of the fifth century B.C., proposed that the earth was circling around a great central fire with its face (that side of the earth which was inhabited) turned always outward toward the heavenly bodies. These, he believed, moved much more slowly about the same center. A century later Herakleides of Pontus offered the hypothesis that the earth was rotating.[3] In the early years of the third century B.C., Aristarchus of Samos went even further, proposing, not only that the earth was spinning upon an axis, but that the earth and the other five planets were revolving around the sun. It is hard to explain why this hypothesis, which solved so many problems, made so little impression upon astronomical thought until Copernicus proposed it once more eighteen centuries later. Perhaps the reason was the apparent absurdity of the proposition that the earth is revolving and moving through space. Greek theorists in general devoted themselves to explaining the celestial motions under the assumption that the heavenly bodies were carried around a stationary earth by a nest of concentric spheres.

Greek astronomy reached the furthest point of its development with Ptolemy. For the next several centuries there were no significant developments in astronomy anywhere. After the Islamic conquests, however, Arabian scholars adopted the Greek astronomy, as well as other Greek sciences, and refined and perpetuated it. The list of notable Arabian astronomers includes men of periods as early as the ninth century and as late as the fifteenth. Their observatories ranged from Samarkand on the east to Castile on the west. Many of them were astrologers rather than astronomers. Those who concerned themselves with celestial mechanics did not perceptibly improve the Ptolemaic system, but they made some rather significant modifications.

Developing certain implications of Ptolemaic theory, the Arabian astronomers, in the ninth and tenth centuries, added two primary spheres to the Ptolemaic set of eight: the *primum mobile,* a sphere surrounding all the others, and the *crystalline sphere,* placed between the fixed stars and the *primum mobile.* Neither one of these bears any heavenly body. There are now ten spheres.

The *primum mobile* was introduced to explain the simultaneous diurnal movement of all the heavenly bodies. The phrase means "first movable" and is translated into English as "first mover" or "first moved." Either translation fits the function well enough. God or his agents whirl the *primum mobile* about, with great velocity, so that it completes one revolution from east to west every twenty-four hours, carrying the interior spheres along with it. Yet the other spheres, revolving on axes tilted at an angle of 23½ degrees from the axis of the *primum mobile,* have their own (much slower) motions from west to east. These peculiar motions ("proper" motions) are largely neutralized by the first mover, but the inner spheres nevertheless accomplish sufficient slow motion of their own to account for the planets' relative changes of position within the zodiacal zone. The outer spheres feel the influence of the *primum mobile* more directly and more forcefully than the inner spheres; the more distant planets, therefore, accomplish their sidereal revolutions much more slowly than those which are nearer the earth. The contrary motions of the *primum mobile* and the planetary spheres furnish John Donne with the basic conceit of his "Good Friday."

The crystalline sphere was invented as a result of certain misapprehensions concerning the precession of the equinoxes. Precession is the small annual westward shift of the sun in relation to the stars. A given constellation rises a little later each year on a given date; and thus, through the centuries, the stars seem to wheel slowly eastward. The sidereal revolution is completed in about 25,800 years. Some Greek theorists believed that the stars' change of position in relation to the sun was an oscillation, an alternating forward and backward motion of the stellar sphere with a slowing down before and a speeding up after each reversal. After some centuries, precession would become recession. The Arabians, adopting and elaborating this theory, introduced the crystalline sphere. The poles of the stellar (the eighth) sphere, they supposed, were joined to the inner surface of the crystalline sphere, each pole very slowly describing a small circle on this surface, thus accounting for the supposed reversals of direction and the variations of speed. A slow eastward drift of the ninth sphere explained completion of the cycle. This imagined stellar oscillation was called *trepidation.* Donne's "A Valediction: Forbidding Mourning" has made "trepidation of the spheres" a familiar phrase.

The spheres are not always regarded as mechanical realities. Ptolemy himself undertakes only to describe the celestial movements in such fashion that they may be predicted and to supply data which will make it possible to calculate position by the stars. The spheres are a convenient supposition. To a genuine Ptolemaist, astronomical theorizing is largely a mathematical and geometric exercise. Theory must respect observational data—must "save the appearances"—, but it need not pretend to be a statement of celestial reality.

Many of Ptolemy's predecessors, however, thought of the spheres as having material substance. Plato's description of the cosmos in Book X of the *Republic,* for example, implies substantial heavens, although the nature of the substance is not clear. Aristotle's world is a construction of material wheels within wheels. The stars, the fifty-five spheres, and the numerous pivots on which these turn consist of ether, the fifth element.[4] The astronomy of Ptolemy's Arabian successors is, as regards basic principles, Ptolemy's astronomy. But they were interested, as Ptolemy was not, in describing the physical constitution and organization of the heavens. With Aristotle as their example, they worked out a construction of contiguous crystal spheres. To accommodate epicycles and eccentrics in a set of rigid spheres requires spacious and ingenious engineering, for no planetary orbit may intersect any other. The Arabian heavens are a colossal machine, constructed of crystal, amazingly intricate and operating at incredible speed.

It was natural for men who believed in planetary spheres to suppose that the heavenly motions—the motions of such tremendous bodies as the stars and planets and of the spheres that bore them—would produce a sound; and the beauty and regularity of the cosmos would suggest harmonious sound. The idea of musical heavens goes back to the sixth century B.C. In the mathematical world of the Pythagoreans, the planetary spheres were separated by intervals corresponding to those of the musical scale; the cosmos was a huge musical instrument. Cicero's account in the *Republic* of the dream of Scipio includes a passage based on this ancient concept: The beautiful sound which Scipio hears in his dream "is produced ... by the onward rush and motion of the spheres ... for such mighty motions cannot be carried on so swiftly in silence; and Nature has provided that one extreme shall produce low tones while the other gives forth high. Therefore this uppermost sphere of heaven, which bears the stars, as it revolves more rapidly, produces a high, shrill tone, whereas the lowest revolving sphere, that of the Moon, gives forth the lowest tone ... [The] eight spheres, two of which move with the same velocity, produce seven different sounds,— a number which is the key of almost everything.... Men's ears, ever filled with this sound, have become deaf to it."[5] Only the keenest sensitivity can pierce the film of familiarity; those who can hear the celestial harmony are very few. Milton attributes to unfallen man the ability to hear it (*PL*, V, 178).

A student of Renaissance literature meets innumerable references to the music of the spheres. He may get the impression that Renaissance poets in general believed, as the Arabian astronomers did, that the spheres were of solid crystal. Milton himself seems to have thought so when he wrote "On the Morning of Christ's Nativity":

> Ring out ye Crystal spheres,
> Once bless our human ears. ...

59

And with your ninefold harmony
Make up full consort to th'Angelic symphony.
(Lines 125-32)

Probably most poets never troubled to make up their minds on the question of the composition of the heavens, but they found the heavenly harmony an appealingly beautiful idea.

The Ptolemaic cosmos was not a tight little world. It consisted principally of vast emptiness, or if one assumes contiguous material spheres, of colossal solid objects. Eccentrics and epicycles would require great spaces to prevent interference of one planetary orbit with another. The early astronomers made some purely theoretical efforts to determine the distances of the planets from the earth. The figures which they arrived at for the more distant planets were much smaller than the actual distances, yet large enough to be impressive. They disagreed among themselves, but not very greatly.[6] For illustration I shall take a figure given by Al Fargani, an Arabian of the ninth century, who enjoyed great respect during the Renaissance. According to him, the outer surface of the sphere of Saturn, which is contiguous with the inner surface of the stellar sphere, is about 65 million miles from the earth. (The actual mean distance between Saturn and the sun is about 886 million miles.) The circumference formed by these contiguous surfaces, then, measures about 410 million miles. The closed universe of the classical astronomy is insignificant in comparison with the open cosmos which superseded it, yet it is almost inconceivably huge.

In the geocentric cosmos, all of the heavenly bodies, in addition to other slower movements, sweep around the earth once in twenty-four hours. What speed did Al Fargani have to assume for the stellar sphere—its inner surface at the equator—in its diurnal sweep of 410 million miles? My computation gives about seventeen million miles an hour, about 285,000 miles a minute, about 4,750 miles a second. (The actual mean orbital speed of Saturn is about 21,600 miles an hour; that of the earth is about 66,600 miles an hour.) The outer spheres would move even faster. Number does not fail in the computation of these velocities, as Milton's Adam says it does (*PL*, VIII, 38), but it astonishes: "what fury is that, saith Dr. *Gilbert* . . . that shall drive the Heavens about with such incomprehensible celerity . . . an arrow out of a bow must go seven times about the earth whilst a man can say an *Ave Maria*, if it keep the same pace, or compass the earth 1,884 times an hour. . . . A man could not ride so much ground, going 40 miles a day, in 2,904 years, as the Firmament goes in 24 hours; or so much in 203 years, as the said Firmament in one minute."[7]

Renaissance Europe inherited from the Greeks and the Arabs such a conception of the world as the foregoing has superficially suggested: a geocentric cosmos, unimaginably vast yet closed, consisting of a set of concentric spheres whirling swiftly around a comparatively very small earth. Those who wished to know about these matters could learn from the original Greek documents (in Greek or in Latin translation); from Latin translations of Arabic works; from a great many astronomical works of their own period, in Latin, which expounded and elaborated Greek and Arabic astronomy; or from popular vernacular works which also presented the traditional ideas. Through the sixteenth century most men were contented with the Arabic-Ptolemaic astronomy and with the Aristotelian concept of the sublunar spaces.

Many sixteenth century Englishmen were curious about the heavens[8] and other scientific subjects. Very few had the competence in mathematics to follow Ptolemy or Al Fargani. A layman who knew a little Latin, however, might turn to such works as the popular *De Sphaera* of Sacrobosco, which presents a simplified version of Arabic astronomy. Through the first half of the century, the lay inquirer who had no Latin would have had to depend on the popular encyclopedias. But in the later sixteenth century he would have had a much larger choice of astronomical material in his own language, including not only translations but works in English by Englishmen of considerable scientific ability, notably Leonard Digges' *Prognostication* (1553) and Robert Recorde's *The Castle of Knowledge* (1556), both of which expound the classical astronomy.

In the late sixteenth century and the very early seventeenth century, a seeker for astronomical knowledge might become somewhat confused. He would find the same basic ideas in all astronomical works of the old school: the swiftly revolving spheres, the contrary motions of the *primum mobile* and the inner spheres, etc. Yet in spite of basic agreement, there were many points in dispute among the traditionalists. The relatively new Copernican hypothesis, moreover, had furnished new issues for debate and had provoked a variety of theories, like those of Tycho Brahe, Ramerus, and Origanus, which attempted compromise between the old and new. "*Maginus* makes eleven Heavens, subdivided into their orbs & circles, and all too little to serve those particular appearances: *Fracastorius* 72 homocentricks; *Tycho Brahe, Nicholas Ramerus, Helisaeus Roeslin,* have peculiar hypotheses of their own inventions."[9] Within a few decades, Copernicanism would quiet the clamor of contention by demonstrating its own validity, but for a while it compounded the confusion.

II

Astronomy makes a more important contribution to *Paradise Lost* than any other science. Satan, Raphael, and other persons journey through the heavens above the earth, Adam and Raphael discuss them, and there are

many incidental references to them. They constitute a spacious and beautifully luminous background which the reader is seldom allowed to forget.

The supralunar world which Milton constructs in *Paradise Lost* is
thoroughly Ptolemaic. The poet's clearest statement of the structure of the
heavens is his account of a journey upward through the spheres. After death,
the souls of certain Roman Catholic friars rise hopefully but vainly toward
the empyreal Heaven:

> They pass the Planets seven, and pass the fixt,
> And that Crystalline Sphere whose balance weighs
> The Trepidation talkt, and that first mov'd.   (III, 481-83)

Here are the traditional seven planetary spheres, the sphere of the fixed
stars, the crystalline sphere, and the *primum mobile*. "Trepidation talkt"
suggests that Milton has his doubts concerning the theory of trepidation,
perhaps even concerning the existence of the crystalline sphere. Neither is
mentioned elsewhere in *Paradise Lost*.

The entire world is encased in a hard, opaque shell, a "firm opacous
Globe," which divides and protects "The luminous inferior Orbs . . . From
Chaos and th'inroad of Darkness old" (III, 418-21). The protective orb evidently is motionless; there is an opening in it which remains directly below
the gate of Heaven and directly above a certain spot on the stationary earth
(III, 501-28). This shell could not be the *primum mobile*, for the first mover
in Milton's heavens is in rapid motion; the daily rotation of the "prime Orb"
is "Incredible how swift" (IV, 592-93). So there seem to be eleven spheres.[10]
Although most Renaissance astronomers (of the old school) distinguished
ten spheres and only ten, there was some disagreement about the number
of spheres. It is hardly necessary, however, to look for authoritative support
for Milton's eleventh sphere. Milton has added it because in his cosmos the
world is half embedded in the disruptive turmoil of Chaos and must be
protected. It has no astronomical function and differs from the spheres that
move the stars and planets in its solidity, its fixity, and its opaqueness. It is,
in fact, quite another kind of sphere. There is no necessity, on the other
hand, to search out authority for the idea of a motionless *primum mobile* in
order to preserve the expected number of ten.[11] Only a system like Dante's,
which identifies the uttermost orb with the empyreal Heaven, might require an unmoving outer sphere.[12] In Milton's cosmos, God's Heaven is
separated by some distance from the world. In *Paradise Lost*, then, the
world consists of the earth, ten transparent rotating spheres, and the
opaque, motionless protective shell which encloses the whole.

It is this outer casing which Satan, after his difficult journey up through
Chaos, sees as he approaches the "pendant world" hanging just beneath
Heaven "in a golden Chain" (II, 1051-52). After Satan has alighted on the

shell-of-the-world, he sees it as "a boundless Continent, / Dark, waste, and wild . . . Starless expos'd" to "the frown of Night" and to the "ever-threat'n-ing storms / Of *Chaos* blust'ring round" (III, 423-26).

He finds an opening at the highest point of the incasing sphere, the point nearest the empyreal Heaven and "Just o'er the blissful seat of Paradise" (III, 527). This passage between Heaven and the yet sinless earth is wide, far wider than the later opening above Mount Zion and the Promised Land (III, 528-31). Above the aperture is a splendid golden stairway leading to the gate of Heaven, "such as whereon *Jacob* saw / Angels ascending and descending" (III, 510-11). Each step of the stairway has a symbolic meaning ("mysteriously was meant," III, 516), but the poet does not explain further. The stairway is sometimes lowered to give access to the world, sometimes is drawn up to Heaven. When Satan comes upon it, it is let down, either "to dare / The Fiend by easy ascent, or aggravate" his sense of exclusion from the bliss of Heaven (III, 523-25). Beneath the stairway, Satan sees a flowing crystalline sea. Later, just after Adam's disobedience, Sin and Death build a bridge of incredible length over and through Chaos, connecting Hell gate

> to the outside bare
> Of this round World: with pins of Adamant
> And Chains they made all fast, too fast.   (X, 317-19)

From this time forward, three ways meet at the uppermost point of the world, one leading to Heaven, another to the earth, "and on the left hand Hell" (X, 322). The broad and easy road to Hell will remain in place until the Second Coming.

How literally should one take these various details? It is hard to picture both the golden chain and the golden stairway simultaneously in place as links between Heaven and the world. Perhaps the stairway is merely a symbolic image[13] inspired by the story of Jacob's dream of the ladder, introduced for its moral meaning and its visual splendor without regard to its suitability in the physical construction. No creature ascends or descends the stairway in the poem. Symbols, however, can be real objects in *Paradise Lost*. Are the golden chain and the bridge to Hell to be taken as physical realities? I think that Milton certainly means them so. The chain has a mechanical as well as a symbolic function. The bridge serves a purpose in the story, is actually trodden upon: Satan goes "down / The Causey to Hell Gate" (X, 414-15). Milton knows very well, however, that he is using his imagination in representing these extra-mundane regions, and surely he may do so legitimately if his inventions have some basis in revelation or if they express a spiritual truth.

The world within the protecting orb is a little less puzzling. Satan, still on the outer shell, looks down through the opening in it. From this spot "So high above the circling Canopy / Of Night's extended shade" (III, 556-57), the view is magnificent. He is looking downward on the zodiac, turned edgewise to him, and he sees the half of it which happens to be uppermost:

> from Eastern Point
> Of *Libra* to the fleecy Star [Aries] that bears
> *Andromeda.*   (III, 557-59)

Satan is standing just above the celestial equator. In the original world the celestial equator and the zodiac coincide.

After brief and envious admiration, the Devil plunges downward,

> and winds with ease
> Through the pure marble [luminous] Air his oblique way
> Amongst innumerable Stars.   (III, 563-65)

The account of the friars' journey upward through the heavens, though not detailed, is quite definite concerning the spheres. The account of Satan's journey downward is vaguer. The route is evidently not a direct line; Satan "winds" an "oblique way." Attracted by the splendor of the sun, he travels toward it

> Through the calm Firmament; but up or down
> By centre, or eccentric, hard to tell,
> Or Longitude.   (III, 574-76)

Amid the complexities of the possible routes through the spheres, certainly it would be hard to tell exactly which one Satan follows, and the poet declines to be specific. After his pause on the sun, "Down from th'Ecliptic" Satan "Throws his steep flight in many an Aery wheel" (III, 740-41). Reaching the earth, he alights on Mount Niphates.

"Firmament" in the lines quoted above means simply the sky above us. This is the usual meaning of *firmament* in Milton's poetry. A common Renaissance meaning is "eighth sphere"; but Milton, possibly remembering Genesis i, 8—"And God called the firmament Heaven"—, uses the word to refer to everything from the lunar sphere to the outer shell.

Still a third passage through the firmament is described in *Paradise Lost*, Raphael's precipitant journey from the empyreal Heaven to earth:

> Down thither prone in flight
> He speeds, and through the vast Ethereal Sky
> Sails between worlds and worlds, with steady wing
> Now on the polar winds, then with quick Fan
> Winnows the buxom Air.   (V, 266-70)

64

Once more Milton is vague about celestial geography. His intention is to express the angel's swiftness and beauty rather than to trace a route.

The celestial travelers of *Paradise Lost* meet no solid impediments. Yet the firmament consists of actual spheres which revolve daily around the earth. There are several specific references to them in the poem: God's Heaven is "above the starry Sphere" (III, 416); the stars are "fixt" in an "Orb" (V, 176); Adam and Eve call upon the morning star to praise God "in thy Sphere" (V, 169); Satan refers to the "Sphere" of the sun (IV, 39); etc. Milton sometimes calls the spheres "heavens": there was a time when "this World was not, and *Chaos* wild / Reign'd where these Heav'ns now roll" (V, 577-78). Sometimes the spheres are collectively "heaven": when the Creation was nearly complete

> Heav'n in all her Glory shone, and roll'd
> Her motions, as the great first-Mover's hand
> First wheel'd thir course.   (VII, 499-501)

God's empyreal Heaven, of course, is a different heaven.

Unlike Ptolemy, Milton does not regard the spheres merely as a convenient hypothesis. His spheres have material reality. The path which a celestial traveler takes is somehow determined by their shape and motion. Like the courses of the planets, it must wind intricately by "centre, or eccentric . . . Or Longitude" and follow "many an Aery wheel." Of what material do the spheres consist? After Satan has entered the world through the aperture in the outer shell, he moves easily "Through the pure marble Air." He discovers a little later that the "Air" is "Nowhere so clear" as on the sun (III, 619-20). The adjectives "pure," "marble," and "clear" distinguish the celestial atmosphere from the sublunar air. Whether the distinction is one of degree or one of kind is not clear, but it does not seem likely that Milton would repeatedly use the word *air* for two distinct forms of matter. In his world, moreover, there is no sphere of fire to separate sublunary from celestial. The celestial atmosphere appears to be continuous with the terrestrial atmosphere and to be the same in kind, although in the outer spaces it becomes purer and more tenuous than the earthly air. Adam, who seems to have a considerable knowledge of natural philosophy, says that "the ambient Air" which embraces "round this florid Earth" fills "All space" (VII, 89-91). On the first day of the Creation, God (the Spirit) joined like things with like, separated unlikes, "and between spun out the Air" (VII, 241). On the second day God (the Son) made

> The Firmament, expanse of liquid, pure,
> Transparent, Elemental Air, diffus'd

> In circuit to the uttermost convex
> Of this great Round.   (VII, 264-67)

Milton's belief that the planetary spaces were filled with air was not unusual: The terrestrial air and the heavens, according to *"Christopher Rotman, John Pena, Jordanus Brunus,* with many other late Mathematicians, . . . is the same and one matter throughout, saving that the higher the purer it is, and more subtile." The substance of the heavens "is not hard and impenetrable, as *Peripateticks* hold, transparent, of a *quinta essentia, but . . . penetrable & soft . . . the Planets move in it, as Birds in the Air, Fishes in the Sea.*"[14]

The matter of the planets and stars in Milton's world is *quintessence.* At the time of the Creation, according to Uriel, the four "cumbrous Elements" hastened to their appointed places,

> And this Ethereal quintessence of Heav'n
> Flew upward, spirited with various forms,
> That roll'd orbicular, and turn'd to Stars
> Numberless . . . .
> The rest in circuit walls this Universe.   (III, 715-21)

Milton sometimes speaks of the stars and planets as the "fires" of Heaven: "those Fires / Ethereal" (V, 417-18). This seems to mean that the quintessence is luminous like fire, though undoubtedly purer and subtler and not necessarily hot. The shell-of-the-world, although it is hard and apparently non-luminous, also consists, inexplicably, of quintessence.

It is very likely that Milton's fifth element was suggested by Aristotle's *ether,*[15] but it does not serve just the same purposes. According to Aristotle, ether is the matter of both the heavenly bodies and the spheres. In Milton's world only the stars, the planets, and the outer shell consist of quintessence; the spheres are of air. But like Aristotle's ether, Milton's quintessence is weightless (it is distinguished from the "cumbrous Elements") and seems not to be qualified by heat, cold, moisture, or dryness. The word *ether* does not occur in Milton's English poetry.[16]

Milton thinks of the regular movements of the planets as a stately dance accompanied by music, a dance performed in celebration of God's glory.[17] The completion of a single figure in this celestial dance along the band of the zodiac would require many centuries. The sun occupies the central point in the figure; the other heavenly bodies "keep distance due" and "Turn swift thir various motions, or are turn'd / By his Magnetic beam" (III, 578-83). Adam and Eve, in their evening prayer, call successively upon the heavenly bodies to join them in praising God, the sun, the moon,

66

And yee five other wand'ring Fires that move
In mystic Dance not without Song.   (V, 177-78)

This is not metaphor. When Raphael describes a dance of the angels before
the throne of God, he uses the planetary and stellar motions as analogy:

Mystical dance, which yonder starry Sphere
Of Planets and of fixt in all her Wheels
Resembles nearest, mazes intricate,
Eccentric, intervolv'd, yet regular
Then most, when most irregular they seem:
And in thir motions harmony Divine
So smooths her charming tones, that God's own ear
Listens delighted.   (V, 620-27)

In the "Nativity Ode" crystal spheres furnish accompaniment for the "angelic symphony." The spheres of *Paradise Lost* are concentric zones of air.
They nevertheless have sufficient substance to constitute a musical instrument to glorify God and to give him pleasure.

To follow in imagination through Milton's world, one must conceive of
the earth as a

Terrestrial Heav'n, danc't round by other Heav'ns
That shine, yet bear thir bright officious Lamps,
Light above light, for [man] alone.   (IX, 103-05)

The earth is surrounded by successive layers, which have no visible lines of
separation, which are completely transparent and readily penetrable, but
which have actual substance. There are three sublunar layers of air, and
above these there are eight revolving spheres in which the celestial bodies
are embedded or enveloped. The seven spheres bearing the planets are
complicated by internal mechanisms which explain the motions of the
heavenly bodies in relation to one another. Milton is vague—intentionally,
I think—about the mechanics and the patterns of these motions. But he is
aware of their unfailing regularity; and like many of his contemporaries, he
regards the intricate movements of the planets as a luminous and majestic
dance, with musical accompaniment, testifying to the glory of God. The
eighth sphere bears the fixed stars, which form a background for the planetary dance. Beyond the starry sphere there are a starless crystalline sphere
and finally the *primum mobile,* which gives motion to all the spheres inside
it. This Chinese nest of spheres is inclosed by a hard opaque shell, which
protects the world from the seething turmoil of Chaos.

God created the earth as a beautiful and pleasant dwelling place for man.
He made the tremendous and complex system of spheres to shed upon the

earth light, heat, and other influences not specifically explained. The earth and all the heavens around it, then, exist for man. Adam wonders why such colossal machinery is necessary for man's service:

> When I behold this goodly Frame, this World
> Of Heav'n and Earth consisting, and compute
> Thir magnitudes, this Earth a spot, a grain,
> An Atom, with the Firmament compar'd
> . . . . . . reasoning I oft admire,
> How Nature wise and frugal could commit
> Such disproportions.　　(VIII, 15-27)

The distances traversed by the outer spheres, he says, are "sumless"; rotation through such distances in twenty-four hours would require "Speed, to describe whose swiftness Number fails" (VIII, 36-38). Many of Adam's seventeenth-century descendants had the same doubts.

III

In those periods in which the Bible was recognized as absolute authority, any Christian who attempted to formulate a conception of the world had to accept as true, in one sense or another, every scriptural statement with a bearing on cosmology. He would find such statements in Genesis i, in Job xxvi and xxxviii, in Psalms civ, 1-15, in Proverbs viii, 22-31, and in various briefer passages.

The men who wrote the Bible incorporated in it the cosmology and cosmogony which they had learned from an ancient mythology. There is diversity and confusion among these Hebrew myths, but there is an area of agreement: Originally there was nothing but darkness and waters. God called forth light, divided the waters into upper and lower, and created earth and the heavens. The earth is "a plain or hill . . . swimming in water. Over this is arched the solid vault of heaven. To this vault are fastened the lights, the stars."[18] There are supporting pillars beneath the earth; the mountains support the heavens. The firmament, an invisible crystalline vault, is placed just below the heavens; it "is not more than three fingers thick, nevertheless, it divides two such heavy bodies as the waters below, which are the foundations for the nether world, and the waters above, which are the foundations for the seven heavens."[19]

In Hebrew myth the universe is commonly conceived as being multilayered. According to one concept, there are seven earths lying one on another. The uppermost is the home of men; the lower earths are hells. The seven-storied earth is supported by huge pillars. "The pillars stand on water;

the water rests upon mountains; the mountains rest upon wind; the wind rests upon the storm; and the storm is suspended upon the mighty arm of God." Arched over the uppermost earth are seven heavens. (The idea of multiple heavens appears in Deuteronomy x, 14, and Psalms cxlviii, 4.) The lowest "is a curtain which covers the face of the sun in the evening and withdraws at daybreak. The second heaven is the dwelling place of the sun, the moon and the stars. . . . In the seventh heaven reside the souls of the unborn. There, also, are the ministering angels, called the *Seraphim*, who surround the two Thrones of Glory."[20]

The cosmological feature which a reader of the Bible is most likely to remember is the waters. There are many references to them; for example: God is He "that stretched out the earth above the waters" (Psalms cxxxvi, 6); God "strengthened the fountains of the deep" (Proverbs viii, 28); beneath the earth are "the springs of the sea" (Job xxxviii, 16). There are references also to the waters above: "Praise him, ye heavens of heavens, and ye waters that be above the heavens" (Psalms cxlviii, 4). Genesis i, 7, refers to both.

The Hebrew cosmology and the Ptolemaic astronomy are obviously incompatible. Biblical references to cosmology, however, are fortunately few; they include rather little detail; and to readers of a period which knew nothing of the mythology on which they are based, the incompatibility would not always be evident. An uninformed person might not see the significance of God's stretching "out the heavens like a curtain" (Psalms civ, 2; Isaiah xl, 22). Fitting scriptural ideas of the heavens and earth into a Ptolemaic world seems never to have been too difficult. One could always regard the Biblical phraseology as metaphoric; for example, "He stretched out the north over the empty place," "The pillars of heaven tremble" (Job xxvi, 7, 11). Or one could resort to the principle of accommodation: Men of authority, says Robert Burton, believe that "those places of Scripture which oppugn" the science of the learned were written "*ad captum vulgi*, and if rightly understood, and favourably interpreted, not at all against it."[21] Or one might simply overlook a troublesome text.

But the waters of Genesis i, 7, can neither be overlooked nor explained away: "God made the firmament, and divided the waters which were under the firmament from the waters which were above the firmament." The context permits identification of the lower waters with the water on the surface of the earth. There is no difficulty here. But the upper waters (the celestial waters of Hebrew myth) are not so readily explained. To the Ptolemaic Christian, waters above the firmament are waters above the sky, and he must find such waters. The crystalline sphere, although crystal and water have nothing in common except transparency, seemed to some writers to supply a convenient solution: "*Patricius* & the Schoolmen" argue for "a crystalline watery heaven," though the waters in question are certainly those "in the middle region" of air; "for otherwise, if at *Noah's* flood the water came from" the ninth heaven, "it must be above an hundred years falling down to us, as some calculate."[22] There were more reasonable solutions to the problem than identification of the upper waters with the crystalline sphere.[23] Milton's solution is ingenious.

When God created the World, one reads in *Paradise Lost*, he walled it round with an outer shell,

> the uttermost convex
> Of this great Round: partition firm and sure,
> The Waters underneath from those above
> Dividing: for as Earth, so hee the World
> Built on circumfluous Waters calm, in wide
> Crystalline Ocean, and the loud misrule
> Of *Chaos* far remov'd, lest fierce extremes
> Contiguous might distemper the whole frame.   (VII, 266-73)

So Milton places the waters above the heavens completely outside the world. Like the containing sphere, these waters serve as protection for the world from Chaos. Whereas apparently the shell gives merely mechanical protection, the waters provide insulation from extremes of temperature. They also serve as a means of approach to the empyreal Heaven. When Satan, exploring the shell-of-the-world, comes upon the golden stairway reaching to Heaven, he sees "the waters above the Firmament that flow about it" (III, argument);

> underneath a bright Sea flow'd
> Of Jasper, or of liquid Pearl, whereon
> Who after came from Earth, sailing arriv'd,
> Wafted by Angels, or flew o'er the Lake
> Rapt in a Chariot drawn by fiery Steeds.   (III, 518-22)

The world that God created is

> another Heav'n
> From Heaven Gate not far, founded in view
> On the clear *Hyaline*, the Glassy Sea.   (VII, 617-19)

Within the world is "Earth with her nether Ocean circumfus'd" (VII, 624). By the word *hyaline* ("glassy"), Milton associates his waters above the heavens with the "sea of glass like unto crystal" which, according to Revelation iv, 6, lies before the throne of God.[24]

The crystalline waters are hard to fit into Milton's scheme of things. He does not mention them when he describes the outer surface of the shell as "a boundless Continent / Dark, waste, and wild." Yet the phrase "circum-fluous Waters" seems to mean that they envelop the world. Perhaps they do not surround it entirely, for the waters which "circumfuse" the earth do not entirely cover the earth. It is difficult also to see how the souls of the elect could sail *on* such a sea or fly *over* it on the way *upward* to Heaven. But at the outer limit of the world, we reach the point at which we pass beyond human comprehension (see Chap. VII, sec. ii).

Another feature of scriptural cosmology which Milton evidently feels he cannot ignore is the foundations of the earth. There are several references to these in the Bible; for example, "Where wast thou when I laid the foundations of the earth? . . . Whereupon are the foundations thereof fashioned? Or who laid the corner stone thereof?" (Job xxxviii, 4-6); "have ye not understood from the foundations of the earth?" (Isaiah xl, 21). Sometimes they are called the foundations of the world (e.g., II Samuel xxii, 16; Psalms xviii, 15). Finding no distinction between *earth* and *world* in the Bible, Milton assigns the foundations to the world. There is really no place in or on the spherical Ptolemaic world for watery foundations, but Milton makes one. He equates "founded on" with "enveloped by and suspended in." His world is "built on circumfluous Waters" and "founded in view" of Heaven on the "Glassy Sea." Thus the waters above the heavens become the foundations of the world, and Milton solves two difficulties raised by scriptural phrases simply by the supposition that the waters above the heavens are outside the world and that they surround it in some such fashion as the terrestrial waters surround the earth. I shall say more about these apparent illogicalities.

There seems to be inconsistency between the foundations and Raphael's statement that "Earth self-balanc't on her Centre hung" (VII, 242). But there is scriptural warrant for what Raphael says in Job xxvi, 7. One wonders what Milton made of the rather numerous scriptural references to pillars supporting earth and the heavens (e.g., I Samuel ii, 8; Job xxvi, 11).[25] It is clear that he could introduce no pillars into the cosmos of *Paradise Lost.*

IV

In his account of the Creation,[26] Milton reminds his reader that the story is, at least in some degree, an accommodation:

> Immediate are the Acts of God, more swift
> Than time or motion, but to human ears
> Cannot without process of speech be told,
> So told as earthly notion can receive. (VII, 176-79)

What God performed "in a moment" (VII, 154) must be presented as a series of separate processes extending through a period of time, six days. Milton follows the six-day schedule of Genesis, for this is the way in which God wishes man to understand his creative miracle. His account of the individual acts of creation is more descriptive than explanatory, for men cannot fully understand God's ways. He is specific and detailed, however, in listing what things God successively created. All of these were mundane phenomena, things perceptible by the human senses and literally comprehensible by the human mind.

Milton's story, like many earlier hexamera, is a greatly expanded retelling of the simple narrative of Genesis. Milton prefaces the Biblical story with the Almighty God's pronouncement of his reasons for creating a world, and at the end he adds an account of the Son's reascension after performing his Father's will and of his reception in Heaven. In the intervening narrative of the six days, the several acts of creation, briefly enumerated in Genesis, are greatly elaborated with details, most of which are traditional ideas that the poet has derived from his reading in Biblical commentary and hexameral literature.[27]

In obedience to the Father's command, God the Son rode gloriously forth into Chaos, "Girt with Omnipotence, with Radiance crown'd" (VII, 194). He was accompanied by the Father's "overshadowing Spirit and might" (VII, 165), the assisting Holy Spirit (see Chap. VIII, sec. v). After quieting the seething and cacaphonous mass by a command, God outlined the world with golden compasses[28] ("he set a compass upon the face of the depth," Proverbs viii, 27), thus fixing its spatial limits and separating out from Chaos the "Matter unform'd and void" (VII, 233) which was to be shaped into the world. God's compasses were apparently capable of describing a sphere. As Genesis tells it, "the Spirit of God moved upon the face of the waters"; in Milton's version:

> on the wat'ry calm
> His brooding wings the Spirit of God outspread,
> And vital virtue infus'd, and vital warmth
> Throughout the fluid Mass.   (VII, 234-37)

The image of the nesting bird which is suggested by "brooding wings" reveals that Milton knows the patristic commentary on the Hebrew verb which the Authorized Version renders as "moved" (sometimes translated *incubabat* in Latin versions).[29] The Holy Spirit, however, was not merely warming; he was impregnating (see also VII, 278-82), infusing into characterless and neutral matter the capability of life and form. Meanwhile he "downward purg'd" that portion of matter which could not be so informed, "the black tartareous cold Infernal dregs / Adverse to life" (VII, 237-39). After the infusion of life-potential into the inert mass, the Spirit

> then founded, then conglob'd
> Like things to like, the rest to several place
> Disparted, and between spun out the Air,
> And Earth self-balanc't on her Centre hung.[30]
>   (VII, 239-42)

This seems to mean that under the influence of God's quickening Spirit, matter began to organize itself, thus taking the first steps toward the achievement of forms (see Chap. VIII, sec. ii). It is reasonable to suppose that these first steps were the formation and stabilization of the elements ("the eldest birth / Of Nature's Womb") and then the separation of the elements into their proper spherical zones according to their relative rarity and density. At this point the world had assumed its general global shape corresponding with the outline traced by the divine compasses; and within the spherical limits, the matter of which the world was to consist, now impregnated with potentialities, was roughly organized and was ready to assume specific forms.

The sequence of events in Uriel's very brief account of the Creation in Book III does not altogether agree with that in Raphael's story, and Uriel does not mention the assistance of the Spirit. The disagreements, however, are not really important, and Uriel supplies some additional information. As the elements hastened "to their several Quarters," the "Ethereal quintessence . . . Flew upward, spirited with various forms . . . and turn'd to Stars" (III, 714-18); that is, the quintessential substance was endowed with the potentiality of the astral forms which it subsequently assumed (on the fourth day, according to Genesis and Raphael). Presumably not only the quintessence but all matter within the sphere described by the golden compasses was "spirited" with the potentiality of forms when the brooding Spirit infused "vital virtue" into it; it was thus endowed with the power to realize one or another of the numberless potentialities of entity or identity in the mind of God.

After the initial rough organization of the world's material, God commanded, "Let there be Light," and the profound darkness which covered the abyss was dispelled by "Light / Ethereal, first of things, quintessence pure" (VII, 243-44). Now the adornment of the world, the actualization of innumerable forms, proceeded. The last form to become actual was man, the crowning work, "the Image of God / Express" (VII, 527-28).

The work was now complete, and the Son ascended to the empyreal Heaven while angels sang hymns of praise. On the seventh day he rested from his labors, having actualized the "great Idea" of his Father (VII, 557), a geocentric and homocentric world.

As Satan, a short time later, emerges from Chaos into the light of Heaven and approaches the new creation, he discovers that "here Nature first begins / Her fardest verge, and *Chaos* to retire" (II, 1037-38). In this context *nature* means "order." The creation was a process of ordering—of organizing, forming, illuminating, and harmonizing the tumultuous matter of Chaos. Light superseded darkness, and harmony succeeded furious dissonance. The Creation, in fact, was performed to musical accompaniment. It began and ended in music (VII, 206-07, 557-74), and while it was in progress, the angels expressed their wonder and enthusiasm in song:

> with joy and shout
> The hollow Universal Orb they fill'd,
> And touch't thir Golden Harps, and hymning prais'd
> God and his works.   (VII, 256-59)

The mundane spheres ever since have produced a music which expresses the essential character of God's ordered nature.

V

Among the amenities of the Earth before the Fall were the mildness of its climate and the tranquility of its weather. The daily path of the sun was always identical with the celestial equator. Eden lay directly upon the terrene equator. In every latitude the sun followed the same path every day, and every day it passed directly over Paradise:

> the Spring
> Perpetual smil'd on Earth with vernant Flow'rs,
> Equal in Days and Nights, except to those
> Beyond the Polar Circles.   (X, 678-81)

In regions north and south of Eden, the course of the sun was lower in the sky; the sunshine was less brilliant. Near the poles, the sun journeyed clear around the sky just above the horizon without ever setting (X, 681-84). The air became cooler as one moved away from the equator, but between Estotiland (Labrador) in the north and a point somewhere south of the Straits of Magellan, there was never any snow (X, 685-87). Nearly all of the earth would be pleasantly habitable.

By the Original Sin our first parents forfeited, for themselves and for all of us, the pleasant tranquility of the pristine Earth. After the Fall, climatic severities were produced by alterations in the mechanics of the world. Milton offers alternative explanations: At God's command, angels tilted either the axis of the earth or the axes of the spheres:

> Some say [God] bid his Angels turn askance
> The Poles of Earth twice ten degrees and more
> From the Sun's Axle; they with labor push'd
> Oblique the Centric Globe: Some say the Sun
> Was bid turn Reins from the Equinoctial Road
> Like distant breadth.   (X, 668-73)

In either case, the equator was now 23½ degrees to the south of Eden; there were seasonal variations; the path of the sun was higher in summer than in winter. The angels directed the sun

> so to move, so shine,
> As might affect the Earth with cold and heat
> Scarce tolerable, and from the North to call
> Decrepit Winter, from the South to bring
> Solstitial summer's heat.   (X, 653-56)

The planets, hitherto invariably benign, now became capable of noxious influence. As Sin and Death entered the World just after the Fall, they moved rapidly "through thickest Constellations" and spread "thir bane; the blasted Stars lookt wan, / And Planets, Planet-strook" suffered "real Eclipse" (X, 411-13). Thus man's self-corruption corrupted the natural world which God had given him. Also angels assigned to the winds their "corners" and instructed them

> when with bluster to confound
> Sea, Air, and Shore, the Thunder when to roll
> With terror through the dark Aereal Hall.   (X, 665-67)

The earth now experienced "pinching cold and scorching heat" (X, 691):

> These changes in the Heav'ns, though slow, produc'd
> Like change on Sea and Land, sideral blast,
> Vapor, and Mist, and Exhalation hot,
> Corrupt and Pestilent.   (X, 692-95)

The poet elaborates on the snows and storms which were to afflict wretched humanity in specific regions.

VI

If man had not corrupted his world with sin, it would have endured everlastingly in its original perfection. This is the implication of Raphael's conditional predictions to Adam (V, 497 ff.). After Adam sinned, the world degenerated greatly in a very short period, and there was a corresponding deterioration of Adam's powers and faculties.

According to a medieval belief which persisted into the seventeenth century, the deterioration of the world and of man had continued at a slower rate ever since the initial, relatively rapid decline.[31] The flora and fauna of the earth had become progressively less and less vigorous and beautiful. The men born into the later, enfeebled world were smaller, weaker, shorter-lived, intellectually less capable than men of the early days (for example, Methuselah, Moses). The "new stars" (*novae*) of 1572 and 1604 engendered the suspicion that even the supposedly immutable heavens had suffered corruption. The world was aging as a man ages. It would die in about the year 2000. The Second Coming was not far in the future.

The idea of the senescence of the world was vigorously alive in Milton's lifetime. Sir Francis Bacon, defending the doctrine of progress in the *Novum Organum,* felt it necessary to attack this belief. It was the major issue in the verbose Hakewill-Goodman controversy.[32] It was a principal theme in two of the literary masterpieces of the period, John Donne's *First Anniversary* and Sir Thomas Browne's *Hydriotaphia.*

Because it was so widely discussed and credited in his time, Milton could hardly have ignored the idea of senescence. He seems to have been somewhat interested in it.[33] In 1628, at Cambridge, he wrote "Naturam Non Pati Senium" to refute it. The fact that he took the negative, however, means nothing; since he prepared this poem as an exercise for another student,[34] it is unlikely that he chose either the topic or the position to be defended. "At a Vacation Exercise," also written in 1628, contains a semi-serious reference to the early time "When Beldam Nature in her cradle was" (line 46). A passage in the Seventh Prolusion (probably 1632) sounds as if Milton half believes that the world is senile: "we, in the decadent old age of the world, we, by the speedy destruction of all things, are to be overwhelmed. ... our name is to abide but a short time, for hardly may any posterity succeed to its memory; vain is it now to produce so many books and eminent monuments of ability. ... I do not deny that this can very likely take place."[35]

The idea of decay reappears in two later works. Milton writes in *The Reason of Church Government* (1642) that if "there be nothing advers in our climat, or the fate of this age," it might be "no rashnesse" to give epic treatment to England's "ancient stories."[36] In one of the personal passages of *Paradise Lost,* he enumerates reasons why he might fail in his great undertaking: "an age too late, or cold / Climate, or Years" (IX, 44-45). He seems prudently non-committal.

Milton certainly believed that just after the Fall man had lost much of his original physical, intellectual, and moral endowment. He could see also that the human life-span, "from Adam to David, gradually became more and more contracted."[37] Yet, except in the Seventh Prolusion, he has said nothing in any of his works that might indicate serious belief in a general and continuing deterioration of nature and man. He obviously did not, like Donne, consider himself a physically and mentally feeble member of a degenerate race. He evidently did not believe, as Browne did, that it was too late to be ambitious. When he published *Paradise Lost* in 1667, he undoubtedly expected a longer life for it than two and one-third centuries.

He was convinced nevertheless that the lifetime of the world was limited. If Adam had remained obedient, the world would have endured everlastingly *(PL,* V, 499-501); but because Adam's sin tainted all mundane things, the "perverted World," like every human being, must die (XII, 545-49). It will burn when the Son of God returns to judge mankind. (Like the faithful man, it will be purified and renewed.) In the *Christian Doctrine* Milton paraphrases Matthew xxiv, 36: "The day and the hour of Christ's coming are known to the Father only."[38] He never speculates on the time of the Second Coming, and he is never either troubled or gladdened by the thought of its imminence. Yet the world was created, he believes, for an existence of "a few thousand years."[39] For him the future does not extend forward indefinitely.

Chapter VI. THE NEW ASTRONOMY

MILTON WAS BORN in a period of intense excitement among astronomical theorists. Copernicus' heliocentric hypothesis, published in *De Revolutionibus Orbis*, 1543, had provoked fervid debate. Dispute concerning astronomical fundamentals continued, although the issues changed, throughout Milton's lifetime.

Copernicus' astronomy was not wholly revolutionary. His universe, like the Ptolemaic world, was inclosed by the sphere of the fixed stars, though he removed this inclosing sphere to a much greater distance than that which earlier astronomers had supposed. Because he retained the traditional assumption that the planets must follow circular paths, he was compelled to employ the epicycles and eccentrics of Ptolemaic theory. In assuming motion of the earth, he had not very greatly simplified "the old theories, for though the objectionable equants had disappeared, the system was still bristling with auxiliary circles."[1] We use *Copernican* loosely as a general term for the heliocentric astronomy in its early phases, yet the heliocentric world of the post-Kepler astronomers was not much like the world of Copernicus. Whatever its shortcomings, his system was more coherent and more logical than the beliefs prevailing in the mid-sixteenth century.

Although Copernicus had left many problems unsolved, it became more and more evident, in the later sixteenth century, that the Ptolemaic astronomy was no longer tenable. Various non-Ptolemaic hypotheses were propounded which were not so radical as the Copernican. Some theorists granted rotation of the earth but denied its annual motion around the sun. Tycho Brahe, the greatest astronomer of his generation, devised the theory that the five lesser planets revolved around the sun while the sun and moon revolved around a stationary earth.

According to Grant McColley,[2] there were four competing schools of astronomical thought in early seventeenth-century Europe: there were the Ptolemaists (wrangling among themselves over details), there were the adherents of the theory that the earth rotates without orbiting (a much subdivided school), there were the supporters of Tycho, and there were the Copernicans. This classification seems to cover the field adequately. Yet to anyone living in the early Stuart period, deciding what to believe about the heavens would not have seemed so simple as a choice among four possibilities. "*Nicholas Ramerus* will have the Earth the Center of the World, but moveable, and the eighth sphere immoveable, the five upper Planets to move above the Sun, the Sun and Moon about the Earth. Of which Orbs, *Tycho Brahe* puts the Earth the center immoveable, the stars immoveable, the rest with *Ramerus*, the Planets without Orbs. ... *Helisaeus Roeslin* censureth both, with *Copernicus*. ... *Johannes Lansbergius*, 1633, hath ... defended his [Copernicanism] against all the cavils and calumnies of *Fromundus* his *Anti-Aristarchus, Baptista Morinus*, and *Petrus Bartholinus: Fromundus*, 1634, hath written against him again, *J. Rosseus of Aberdeen, &c.* (sound Drums and Trumpets), whilst *Roeslin* (I say) censures all, and *Ptolemaeus* himself as unsufficient. ... In the mean time the World is tossed in a blanket amongst them, they hoise the Earth up and down like a ball, make it stand and go at their pleasures."[3] But the Copernicans were gaining.

Early in the century Tycho's celebrated disciple Johann Kepler, with Tycho's very numerous and accurate observational data to work from, formulated his three laws of planetary motion. The first two of these, published in 1609 in *Astronomia Nova*, state that a planet follows an elliptical orbit, with the sun at one of the two foci, the velocity diminishing as the planet recedes from the sun and increasing as it approaches the sun. Kepler's laws would soon eliminate eccentrics and epicycles from astronomical theory. In 1609 Galileo began his observations with a telescope.[4] In 1610 he published his *Sidereus Nuncius*, which included announcement of his discovery of the moons of Jupiter and an account of his observations of the surface of the moon. His *Letters*, concerning sunspots, the phases of Venus, and other discoveries, appeared in 1613. His *Dialogue Concerning the Two Chief World Systems* (i.e., the Ptolemaic and the Copernican), which Milton is said to have read, was published in 1632. Although both Kepler and Galileo were Copernicans, their discoveries fit just as well into the Tychonic framework as into the Copernican. It was difficult to defend any theory which assumed a stationary earth, however, after the publication of Gilbert's *De Magnete* in 1600. Gilbert's experiments in the field of magnetism showed that the earth might be a spinning magnet.

Galileo's demonstration that, even after telescopic magnification, the fixed stars appeared as points of light rather than as measurable discs seemed to validate Copernicus' supposition that the stars were enormously distant. Thus the existence of a stellar sphere began to seem unlikely, the idea of an open universe very plausible. Although he never subscribed to it, Galileo in this way gave considerable encouragement to the revival of the ancient theory of plural inhabited worlds—or, according to some cosmologists, infinite worlds.[5] This theory was a subject of lively speculation and argument in the early seventeenth century. The moon seemed especially likely to be another inhabited planet.[6] Those who believed it likely that there were other worlds than ours included Bruno, Gilbert, Kepler, and Campanella.

79

The theory raised some difficult and rather painful problems. Robert Burton asks: "where's our glory?" What of the pre-eminence and dignity of man? If there are dwellers on other planets, are they *"rational creatures? . . . have they souls to be saved? or do they inhabit a better part of the World* [mundi] *than we do? Are we or they Lords of the World? And how are all things made for man?"* [7] The idea of plural inhabited worlds has been revived in our own century by writers of science fiction, and still more recently it has been proposed by astronomers as a mathematical probability.

Through the early decades of the seventeenth century, according to Francis R. Johnson, the Copernican and the Tychonic were the two principal competing astronomical systems. [8] Yet the other two hung on. Galileo's *Dialogue* is an earnest and detailed attempt to demonstrate the superiority of the Copernican system to the Ptolemaic. It is clear that in 1632 such a demonstration was still timely. The Ptolemaic astronomy had become the official doctrine of the Roman Catholic Church. The *Dialogue* was the immediate reason for Galileo's trial before the Inquisition in 1633. One finds evidence of diverse opinions also in English documents. In the late 1620's and early 1630's, Robert Burton, who was probably as well read in astronomy as any layman, was greatly perplexed. Somewhat uncertainly he chose, as the most reasonable of the rival systems, that of Origanus, which represents the earth as rotating but remaining in its central position. In the third edition of the *Anatomy* (1628), Burton inserted the opinion that Origanus' theory of the single motion of the earth was "most probable." In the fifth edition (1638), after further reading, he changed the phrasing to "more probable." [9] Bishop Francis Godwin seems likewise to have read Origanus or some other authority of similar views. In Godwin's *The Man in the Moone,* the earth spins, but the author is sceptical about annual revolution. [10] In *The New Planet No Planet* (1646), Alexander Ross, a partisan of Moses and Ptolemy, fervidly attacked John Wilkins for his advocacy of new theories. Ross's book doubtless had many sympathetic readers. Copernicanism, however, was steadily winning believers; and the intriguing idea of other inhabited worlds, which was generally associated in men's minds with Copernicanism, was much discussed. The geocentric conception of the world did not have long to live.

II

The world of *Paradise Lost* is obviously Ptolemaic. Yet among the very ancient concepts and images of the poem, one finds some astronomical ideas which were quite modern when the poem was written.

In his long dialogue with Raphael, Adam raises the question of the physical disproportion between the colossal spheres and the tiny earth—comparatively "a spot, a grain, / An Atom" (VIII, 17-18)—which they were created to light and warm. He wonders also at the inconceivable velocity —a "swiftness" which is "numberless ... Speed almost Spiritual" (VIII, 107-10)—required of the spheres in their daily revolution. Adam is inclined to think that "the sedentary Earth ... better might with far less compass move" (VIII, 32-33). Raphael replies somewhat evasively but ventures a suggestion:

> What if the Sun
> Be Centre to the World, and other Stars
> By his attractive virtue and their own
> Incited, dance about him various rounds?
> . . . . . . and what if sev'nth to these
> The Planet Earth, so steadfast though she seem
> Insensibly three different Motions move?   (VIII, 122-30)

Having sketched the heliocentric theory, the angel points out its superiorities. Unless one assumes diurnal and annual motions of the earth, the apparent motions in the heavens must be ascribed "to several Spheres ... Mov'd contrary with thwart obliquities." A moving earth would

> save the Sun his labor, and that swift
> Nocturnal and Diurnal Rhomb suppos'd,
> Invisible else above all Stars, the Wheel
> Of Day and Night: which needs not thy belief,
> If Earth industrious of herself fetch Day
> Travelling East.   (VIII, 131-38)

Raphael seems quite ready to give up the intricate Ptolemaic machinery. In fact, his phrase "Rhomb suppos'd" suggests disbelief in the *primum mobile.*

The third motion of the earth to which Raphael refers is a motion which Copernicus had postulated because he had not freed himself from traditional concepts. The earth, he supposed, orbited the sun embedded in a sphere. If the axis of the earth maintained a constant angle in relation to the axis of the sun (as he knew it did), then its angle in relation to the axis of the enveloping sphere must change constantly. To a Ptolemaist, this would be motion. In Milton's day astronomers had long ago seen that Copernicus' third motion was an unnecessary assumption. Yet Milton's reference to it does not show, as some commentators have said, that what he knew of heliocentric astronomy was quite out of date. Galileo, in his *Dialogue* (1632), defends Copernicus, explaining that "motion" is a misleading word for what he meant.[11] The astronomy which Raphael outlines is like Kepler's and Galileo's rather than like Copernicus'. There are no epicycles.

The angel has a further suggestion: It may be that the moon has soil and moisture to support intelligent life;

> and other Suns perhaps
> With thir attendant Moons thou wilt descry . . .
> Stor'd in each Orb perhaps with some that live.
> (VIII, 148-52)

Here is the popular theory of plural worlds. There are other passages in *Paradise Lost* which show that Milton has thought seriously of the possibility of worlds beyond the moon: the battling semi-elements of Chaos may become God's "dark materials to create more Worlds" (II, 916); God's wisdom has ordained the diffusion of "His good to Worlds and Ages infinite" (VII, 191); every star of the new Creation is "perhaps a World / Of destin'd habitation" (VII, 621-22).

In his dialogue with Adam, Raphael is non-committal. He offers both the heliocentric concept and the theory of plurality as conjectures, not assertions. He does not wish to encourage speculation either on the structure of the world or on any corollary problems:

> God to remove his ways from human sense,
> Plac'd Heav'n from Earth so far, that earthly sight,
> If it presume, might err in things too high. (VIII, 119-21)

It is not important that man should know "whether Heav'n move or Earth" (VIII, 70). It is possible and permissible to learn enough of celestial motions so that one may compute time; that is, descriptive astronomy is approved. But theoretical astronomy is forbidden. The "great Architect" has wisely concealed his cosmological secrets "From Man or Angel." The mechanism of the world is not "to be scann'd by them who ought / Rather admire [wonder]" (VIII, 72-75). For angels as well as for men, inquiry is impious curiosity. Astronomical truth apparently is among those

> Things not reveal'd, which th'invisible King,
> Only Omniscient, hath supprest in Night,
> To none communicable in Earth or Heaven. (VII, 122-24)

Raphael firmly shuts off discussion:

> Solicit not thy thoughts with matters hid
> . . . . be lowly wise:
> Think only what concerns thee and thy being;
> Dream not of other Worlds. (VIII, 167-75)

Adam probably never would have dreamed of other worlds if Raphael had not suggested the idea. It is the angel, if either of them, who is guilty of curiosity. But Adam has at least suggested the possibility that the earth rather than the heavens might move. He accepts Raphael's admonitions gracefuly and humbly. He now realizes, he says, the frivolity of "wand'ring thoughts," and he deplores the inclination of the human "Mind or Fancy" to "rove" (VIII, 187-88).

Milton evidently has learned something of the new philosophy, and it seems likely that, as a consequence, his mind and fancy have been roving a little. The passage reveals no more than an elementary knowledge of Copernican astronomy. Yet he seems to consider the new hypotheses significant, for he has introduced them quite unnecessarily into a poem into which they do not fit.

III

In the dialogue on astronomy Milton says things that, for him, are new. He presents, as possible truth, astronomical concepts which have not appeared in his earlier works. He asserts, as he never has before, that celestial phenomena are not altogether comprehensible. In this passage, furthermore, he passes a judgment on astronomical theorizing for which nothing that he has hitherto written has prepared us. Raphael says here that astronomy is beyond human (and angelic) understanding and that God disapproves of inquiry into this subject or speculation about it. So astronomy belongs in the third category of knowledge, knowledge which men neither may nor can acquire. It is fair to assume that Milton agrees with the angel.

In his youth he evidently had felt as free to seek knowledge of astronomy as to study any other branch of natural philosophy. "Ad Patrem" gives a prominent place to astronomy among the knowledges which Milton, thanks to his father's generosity, has acquired during his Cambridge years. In recommending scientific studies to his fellow students in the Third Prolusion, he speaks with especial warmth of astronomy: "Do not hesitate, my hearers, to fly even up to the skies, there to behold those multiform aspects of the clouds . . . nor let the most minute little stars be hidden from you. . . . Yea, follow as companion the wandering sun. . . . Nay, let not your mind suffer itself to be hemmed in and bounded by the same limits as the earth, but let it wander also outside the boundaries of the world."[12] This is confident and ambitious. In the Seventh Prolusion he asks a rhetorical question: "Will you believe, my auditors, that the great spaces of the enormous firmament, illuminated and adorned by the everlasting fires, sustain so many tremendously rapid motions, travel over such great paths of revolution, for this one reason: that they may furnish light for ignorant and stooping men?"[13] The answer is that an understanding of astronomy inspires reverence for the glorious Artificer.

There is no suggestion in the *Prolusions* or in "Ad Patrem" that astronomical principles are beyond human capacity. The heavenly bodies can be observed with human eyes; their movements have been described and measured; the principles of their behavior have been deduced. Young Milton seems to feel that these principles are quite well known. There is no hint that astronomical knowledge is knowledge out of bounds; on the contrary, this is knowledge which the pious should seek because of its revelation of the power and glory of God. The phraseology of the references to astronomy in these early works is altogether Ptolemaic. There was little chance of becoming acquainted with Copernicanism at Cambridge.

There is evidence that Milton discussed astronomy with his Florentine friends during the continental journey. Antonio Francini writes that Milton comprehends "clearly the profoundest arcana which nature hides in heaven and earth"; in Milton's memory, says Carlo Dati, "the universal world [totus orbis] reposes ... with the guidance of Astronomy [he] hears the harmonious music of the celestial spheres."[14]

At about the time when he was impressing the young Florentines with his knowledge of the harmonious spheres (in the late summer of 1638 or the early spring of 1639), Milton called upon the most famous of living astronomers, "*Galileo* grown old, a prisner to the Inquisition." Galileo was in his mid-seventies, was a sick man, and had recently gone blind. This visit evidently made a deep impression on Milton. In *Paradise Lost* there are six references to Galileo and his observations. But there is no reason to suppose that in 1638-39 he had any genuine understanding of Galileo's discoveries. His brief account of the visit in the *Areopagitica*[15] says nothing of what he talked about with the old man—if, indeed, he had any opportunity to talk with him. It is not likely that they talked of astronomy. In the *Areopagitica* Milton presents Galileo's case as an illustration of the intellectual repression that has "dampt the glory of Italian wits." He seems to be thinking of Galileo as a victim of papal tyranny rather than as a scientific pioneer. He knows that Galileo has suffered "for thinking in Astronomy otherwise than the Franciscan and Dominican licencers thought," but there is no evidence in what he says that he is interested in knowing just how Galileo has disagreed with the orthodox censors.

There are many astronomical references in the poems which Milton wrote before 1650.[16] Some of these are images involving stars, constellations, and celestial motions such as rising and setting. Some of them concern revolving heavens: "the Prime Wheel [rota prima] of the universe turns in daily rotations and transmits its movement to its enclosed spheres" ("Naturam Non Pati Senium," 1628, lines 37-38);[17] "vast ages have rolled under the revolving heaven [redeunte caelo]" ("Ad Ioannem Rouse," 1647, lines 22-23).

Some of them follow the Biblical cosmology; God hung "the well-balanc't world on hinges. . . . And cast the dark foundations deep" ("Nativity Ode," lines 122-23). None of them show any influence of the new astronomical concepts.

The prose pamphlets of 1640 to 1650 contain a very few astronomical metaphors and analogies. (These are greatly outnumbered by the medical and physiological figures.) In the *Areopagitica,* for example, Milton is writing of the difficulties of perceiving the whole truth: "We boast our light; but if we look not wisely on the Sun it self, it smites us into darknes. Who can discern those planets that are oft *Combust* [close to the Sun], and those stars of brightest magnitude that rise and set with the Sun, untill the opposite motion of their orbs bring them to such a place in the firmament, where they may be seen evning or morning?"[18] The "opposite motion" is the west-to-east motion of the planetary spheres assumed by the old astronomy. From *Tetrachordon* : "For Nature hath her *Zodiac* also, keepes her great annual circuit over human things as truly as the Sun and Planets in the firmament; hath her *anomalies,* hath her obliquities in ascensions and declensions, accesses and recesses."[19] From *Eikonoklastes* : When "Great Worthies" have disobeyed the law in order to save the commonwealth, "the Law afterward by firme Decree hath approv'd that planetary motion, that unblamable exorbitancy in them."[20]

The traditional astronomical language in Milton's earlier verse and prose proves nothing in itself. Poets are much inclined to use images which have become familiar in poetry; reference to the elliptical orbits of the planets or to the Medicean stars would hardly be appropriate. In the images from the prose also, Milton may simply be using conventional language which does not represent his real belief. We speak of the sun's rising and of the stars' wheeling across the sky, although we know well enough that they do no such thing. The significant fact is that, in the very considerable body of verse and prose which Milton wrote before 1650, there is no indication at all of acquaintanceship with the new astronomy.

There is one doubtful exception to this generalization. In the *Doctrine and Discipline of Divorce* (1645), Milton writes that he plans "to perfet such *Prutenick* tables as shall mend the *Astronomy* of our wide expositors."[21] Erasmus Reinhold's *Prutenic Tables,* when they were published in 1551, replaced the less accurate *Alphonsine Tables.* In computing them, Reinhold had used Copernican methods. Milton seems to have known that the *Prutenic Tables* were superior to earlier tables, but this does not mean that he knew how they had been computed. Reinhold himself, incidently, was not a Copernican. Recognition of the superiority of Copernicus' mathematical methods did not imply belief in the Copernican hypothesis.[22] The *Prutenic Tables* were superseded in 1627 by Kepler's *Rudolphine Tables,* of which apparently Milton knew nothing.

Among the works which Milton recommends for study in the treatise *Of Education* (1644), there are poems on astronomy by Aratus and Manilius and three other works, by Lucretius, Seneca, and Pliny, which contain a good deal of astronomical material. Manilius, Seneca, and Pliny lived and wrote in the first century A.D., Lucretius in the first century B.C., Aratus in the third century B.C. Evidently Milton still believed in 1644, as he had believed in his Cambridge days, that astronomy was a proper study for the wise and the pious and that a well informed man must have some knowledge of the heavens. Yet he seems not to have updated his own information. *Of Education* was published between five and six years after his visit to Galileo in Florence.

Milton wrote this treatise during the period when he was actually teaching. According to Edward Phillips, his boys read four astronomical authors —Aratus, Manilius, Geminus (an ancient Greek), and Sacrobosco (a thirteenth century Englishman)—and works by Lucretius, Pliny, Vitruvius, and the pseudo-Plutarch containing astronomical material. The primary textbook for instruction in astronomy seems to have been Sacrobosco's *De Sphaera*, a simplified exposition of the Greco-Arabic astronomy. Milton probably used an edition in which the basic text was accompanied by the commentary of later writers. These would all have been Ptolemaists. He was, then, teaching the centuries-old Ptolemaic astronomy (with medieval modifications) to his boys in the mid-1640's. It is hard to believe that he was misinforming them deliberately. The reason must have been that he knew no better.

What was the state of his astronomical knowledge and belief in the early 1650's? One finds pertinent evidence in the *Defense of the English People* (1651). Milton scolds at Salmasius for officious meddling: "You [are] altogether ignorant in astronomy and physic, yet are always reviling astronomers and physicians who should be trusted in their own faculties."[23] Many pages farther on he reveals which school of astronomers he has in mind: He accuses Salmasius of having "quite forgot the heaven of Moses and the heaven of Aristotle; for you have denied that in Moses's heaven 'there was any light before the sun'; and in Aristotle's you have exhibited three temperate zones."[24] (Milton himself is a little inaccurate here; Aristotle's temperate zone is a zone of air, not a part of the heavens.) There are no other significant astronomical references in the prose works of this decade.

In 1651 Milton evidently still believed, as he had always believed, that the heavens were constructed as astronomical tradition represented them. One gets the impression that he was a little complacent about his understanding of astronomy. In none of his works earlier than *Paradise Lost* (with the one doubtful exception noted) is there any evidence that he had ever looked into an astronomical work which had not been available for centuries, that he had ever heard of Copernicus, Brahe, or Kepler, or that he had any appreciation of the meaning of Galileo's discoveries.

The new astronomy appears abruptly in *Paradise Lost* in lines which have attracted far more attention than their number seems to warrant. Counting lines shows that the new theories have been given scanty space. The dialogue on astronomy, with the consequent discussion of the limitations of human knowledge, occupies 156 lines (VIII, 15-38, 66-197). One other passage refers to the possibility of the rotation of the earth:

> the Sun [had] now fall'n
> Beneath th'*Azores*; whither the prime Orb,
> Incredible how swift, had thither roll'd
> Diurnal, or this less volubil Earth,
> By shorter flight to th'East, had left him there.
> (IV, 591-95)

There are five references, totaling fifteen lines, to Galileo and his telescopic observations: to the *"Tuscan* artist" who looks "Through Optic Glass" at the geographic features of the moon's "spotty Globe" (I, 288-91);[25] to the astronomer who sees the sun spots "Through his glaz'd Optic Tube" (III, 588-90); to "the Glass / Of *Galileo,"* through which he "observes / Imagin'd Lands and Regions in the Moon" (V, 261-63); to the phases of Venus (VII, 366), which were among Galileo's discoveries; to the fact that the Milky Way is a "Zone ... Powder'd with Stars" (VII, 578-81), which fact had been revealed by Galileo's telescope.[26] There are six brief and scattered passages, totaling eleven lines, concerning the possibility of other inhabited worlds than ours.[27] I am including these even though they could have been inspired by Lucretius just as well as by any seventeenth century theorist. There are, then, 187 lines in the poem (a poem of 10,565 lines) which concern the new astronomy—if one interprets the term "new astronomy" rather liberally. If these 187 lines were blotted out, there would be no remaining trace of the new hypotheses in *Paradise Lost.* In fact (with the one doubtful exception) there would be no remaining trace of them in Milton's total work.

It is somewhat strange to find even this much about the new astronomy in a poem by a man who, a few years earlier, had been defending the authority of astronomers who knew their Moses and their Aristotle. What is really surprising, however, is his totally changed attitude toward astronomy. This is the man who once was so confident that the principles governing the celestial bodies had long been known and could be learned and who once was so enthusiastic about the study of the heavens because he found in them such beautiful and abundant evidence of the glory of God. Now in *Paradise Lost* we are told by God's angelic messenger that the structure and operation of the world are subjects not only incomprehensible but forbidden. The mechanism of the world is to be examined by neither men nor angels; they should be content merely to wonder. Speculation about the heavens can only demonstrate the inadequacies of the human (and angelic?) intellect and the presumptuousness of all attempts to penetrate God's mysteries. If in the future, Raphael says, men attempt "Conjecture" concerning God's celestial organization,

> he his Fabric of the Heav'ns
> Hath left to their disputes, perhaps to move
> His laughter at thir quaint Opinions wide
> Hereafter, when they come to model Heav'n
> And calculate the Stars, how they will wield
> The mighty frame, how build, unbuild, contrive
> To save appearances, how gird the Sphere
> With Centric and Eccentric scribbl'd o'er,
> Cycle and Epicycle, Orb in Orb.   (VIII, 76-84)

Astronomical theories are "opinions," not knowledge, and they are "wide" of the truth.

If anyone objects to God's laughter as un-God-like, let him remember the accommodations of Scripture. If it is permissible to speak of a wrathful God or of a pitying God, why not of a laughing God? Yet it is hard to justify God's mirth. Inadvertently Milton has made it appear that God has deliberately misled men with appearances—with a very elaborate deception—for his own amusement.[28]

The most notable thing about God's derision is that it falls more heavily on some theorizers than on others. It is directed, not at astronomers who attribute motion to the earth, but at those who scribble the sphere over "With Centric and Eccentric ... Cycle and Epicycle, Orb in Orb." This might conceivably apply to Copernicus, for his heavens are filled with the traditional intricacies. It is not at all likely, however, that Milton has any acquaintance with Copernicus' highly technical treatise or with his solutions of specific astronomical problems. Milton knows the heliocentric hypothesis in a later and much simpler form. It is much more likely that he is thinking of the classical astronomy. God finds the Ptolemaic efforts to save appearances more amusing than the sun-centered construction. If one can assume that Milton agrees with God, then he is scoffing at the very writers from whom, in earlier years, he learned his astronomy and whose theories he taught to his boys in the 1640's. He seems, in his disillusionment with their lessons, to be turning upon his formerly respected preceptors with resentful irritation. He is not taking the discovery that he has been misled at all lightly.[29]

There is little novelty in *Paradise Lost.* Condemnations of astronomy were not new in poetry and were especially likely to appear in hexamera.[30] Du Bartas and Sir John Davies, for example, blithely point out the absurdity of the idea of an earth in motion and pass on.[31] Milton condemns astronomy in general, not merely the new hypotheses, and devotes several lines to the specific ridiculing of the older astronomy. The dialogue on astronomy in *Paradise Lost* is not merely conventional.

It has points in common with very unconventional passages on astronomy in two other major English works of the seventeenth century, Donne's *First Anniversary* and Burton's *Anatomy of Melancholy,* though there is no solid evidence that Milton had read either of these. Donne and Burton, like Milton, are frustrated and troubled by what they have learned of astronomy—or of the astronomies. Donne finds evidence of the decay of the world in both the "new Philosophy" and the old, and like Milton he has a sardonic perception of the absurdity of the Ptolemaic intricacies. The "various and perplexed" celestial movements which astronomy has recorded have compelled

> Men to finde out so many Eccentrique parts
> Such diuers downe-right lines, such ouerthwarts,
> As disproportion that pure forme. It teares
> The Firmament in eight and fortie sheeres ... (Lines 253-58)

Burton's long and incoherent review of the conflicting theories suggests a bewildered and uneasy incertitude. Donne escapes from his frustration by deciding that knowledge of worldly things is vain, is of no spiritual significance; the good man's soul, on its journey upward from earth after its release from the dungeon of the body, will ignore the meteorological and astronomical phenomena which it might easily be observing *(Second Anniversary,* lines 189-97). Burton eases his anxieties with laughter. Because of his materialistic premises, Milton cannot, like Donne, dismiss knowledge of the heavens as being of no consequence to the pious Christian; and because he is incapable of such a comic view as Burton's, he cannot find relief in amusement at the clamor and confusion of astronomical debate. This is a more consequential matter for Milton than for Donne or for Burton.

Milton never condemns scientific inquiry as curiosity in any other field than in astronomy. He condemns astronomy only in *Paradise Lost.* After *Paradise Lost* astronomy virtually disappears from his writings. There are no significant astronomical details in *Paradise Regained, Samson Agonistes,* or the prose works of the later years.[32] He seems to have given up astronomical questions in defeat.

IV

Milton could not have lived half his lifetime in total ignorance of the new astronomy. Copernicanism was widely understood and discussed among intelligent and well informed men of his time, among just such men as those whom he would have chosen as friends. His Florentine friends included young Carlo Dati, who is said to have been a pupil of Galileo's, and Galileo's own son.[33] His circle of acquaintances in England, both before[34] and after the continental journey, must have included many persons who knew something about the new astronomy and were much inclined to talk about it.

Why then did he remain so ill informed for so long? One can only guess: There were so many interests and duties competing for his time, energy, and eyesight that he was very tardy about updating his astronomy; and being scantily informed, he was very slow in seeing the implications of the new philosophy. He was probably sceptical of it, and scepticism would have made him disinclined to give time or effort to the study of it. For many years I have been coming upon references to extra-sensory perception. To me the idea seems nonsense. But I am completely ignorant of this subject and not at all eager to make the effort to learn. If I ever do inform myself, I shall perhaps have an experience like Milton's astronomical enlightenment— though surely not so painful.

It is likely that, at some time before he went blind, Milton looked at the heavens through a telescope. Many people were doing so. By mid-century telescopes were numerous in England, and telescopic viewing was a popular amusement.[35] If Milton ever looked at the night sky through a glass, what he saw, as Marjorie Nicolson suggested years ago,[36] unquestionably would have remained long in his memory and would have contributed something to the spatial grandeurs of *Paradise Lost.* The references in the poem to Galileo's discoveries have a specificness which suggest actual observation. Milton might have observed the moons of Jupiter and the individual stars of the Milky Way, however, without seeing any good reason to change his mind about astronomical fundamentals. Galileo's discoveries did not prove that the world was sun-centered; they fit the Tychonic theory as well as the Copernican. A layman might easily decide that the revelations of the telescope were not crucial.

Telescopic viewing may have contributed to the descriptive splendors of *Paradise Lost.* It is unlikely that the new astronomical concepts had any similar effect. There is an attractive theory that the grand spaciousness of *Paradise Lost* is due to the stimulation which the vastness of the Copernican universe gave to Milton's imagination.[37] But the influence of Copernican theory seems to have come too late. Some of Milton's very early works, as well as *Paradise Lost,* furthermore, show a love of imaginative self-projection into far spaces—into Ptolemaic spaces.[38] The Ptolemaic universe is vast enough to stretch any man's imagination; Milton would have needed no further imaginative stimulation. I find it as hard to conceive of Al Fargani's 65 million miles as to imagine 65 million light years. There comes a point at which imagination fails and mathematics takes over.

Milton, after all, was not so very far behind the times astronomically. In mid-century the old astronomy was still taught in many schools, sometimes along with the new.[39] In Milton's lifetime Kepler's laws were not yet proved by observation. Though it was the most reasonable hypothesis yet offered, heliocentrism was still a hypothesis, and it remained so until the first successful measurement of a stellar parallax in the nineteenth century.

V

At some time between 1651 and the completion of *Paradise Lost,* Milton for the first time became acutely aware of the reasonableness and the significance of the heliocentric astronomy. This new realization may have been due to a book or books that were read to him.[40] It is not possible to identify any printed source with certainty. There is no good reason to assume, however, that Milton learned what he knew from any book. He exhibits no more knowledge of the new astronomy than he could have gained from conversation with an intelligent informant.

His outline of the Copernican hypothesis and his repudiation of all astronomical theory in the dialogue on astronomy are so much out of harmony with the rest of *Paradise Lost* that it seems unlikely that they were part of the original plan. They do not seem to belong. The Copernican astronomy, though it is very tentatively presented, tends to neutralize the imaginative effect of everything that the poet has to say about the heavens in other parts of the poem. The reader projects himself imaginatively into this thoroughly Ptolemaic set of heavens, imaginatively follows celestial and infernal characters through them, listens to serious discourse about them. Then he is told that the heavens may not be like this at all, that to seek to know more about them than is immediately apparent is impiety, that not even an angel can have real knowledge of them. It may seem especially strange that the angels should be ignorant. When the Son of God rode forth to create the world,

> About his Chariot numberless were pour'd
> Cherub and Seraph, Potentates and Thrones,
> And Virtues, winged Spirits.   (VII, 197-99)

Evidently with divine approval, they watched the Creation. Surely they understood at least a little of what they witnessed. Among them was Uriel, who describes what he saw to Satan. Uriel is now posted in the midst of the superterrestrial heavens as the regent of the sun. Raphael journeys through the spheres from the empyreal Heaven to earth. These two seraphs could hardly avoid knowing whether the earth moved or the sun. Undoubtedly they would know whether there were other inhabited globes besides the earth. But they do not know; at least, so Raphael says. Evidently they perceive only certain illusory Ptolemaic appearances.

It seems unreasonable, moreover, that the starry heavens should be placed beyond the bounds of permitted knowledge when Raphael is commissioned to tell Adam, in relative terms, many things about the empyreal Heaven beyond the world—even more remote from human life than the mundane heavens. This prohibition leaves an illogical blank in the cosmos. Man is permitted a great deal of knowledge of what is immediately about him and a little knowledge, in accommodated form, of God's very distant Heaven, but none at all of what lies between. One would expect knowability to have some relation to proximity.

I offer the conjecture that Milton did not become really well acquainted with or did not see the full significance of the new astronomy until *Paradise Lost* was already in some stage of composition.[41] I believe that he became a reluctant Copernican, possibly without admitting even to himself that he was convinced. If it happened as I am proposing, the physical background of the epic would already have been planned and conceived imaginatively in Ptolemaic forms, and Milton might already have written a great many lines about it. Then came the realization that there was another way to conceive of the organization of the heavens, a way which his candid and logical mind could not fail to see was far more reasonable than the intricate Ptolemaic world.

Copernicanism, he would have to admit, was intellectually more acceptable than his previous beliefs. But acceptance of the heliocentric hypothesis would mean the rejection of astronomical concepts which had been tested through the centuries by the human reason and which were—in a fashion—compatible with Scripture. This last to Milton would be the more significant point. Since the Ptolemaic-Aristotelian astronomy had for generations enjoyed the sanction of Christian theologians, the revolving spheres might seem to a Renaissance mind not altogether separable from revelation. Reflection might show that the Ptolemaic system is not really validated by the Bible. Yet it is not wholly invalidated either. Biblical astronomy is at least geocentric. Copernicanism, on the other hand, is flatly incompatible with Scripture.

Having thought the matter out to this point, a pious man might decide that, although the Copernican theory is nearer the truth, Biblical cosmology and the semi-compatible Ptolemaic astronomy are God's adaption to the limited intellectual capabilities of man. Many of Milton's contemporaries found this a statisfactory solution of the problem. But the doctrine of accommodation would not help Milton. The new astronomy, at the stage which it had reached in the mid-seventeenth century, was simpler and more comprehensible than the Ptolemaic. An accommodation which is more complex and esoteric than the reality is hardly an accommodation. Furthermore, the ancient Semitic conception of the world which appears in the Bible (including a flat earth on foundations) is contradicted by observation and experience. God's reasons for representing himself as man-like in Scripture are understandable. This is accommodation. But why should he represent the world in an over-complicated fashion which human reason can show to be false? The ways of God are indeed beyond understanding.

Milton had a choice between rejecting the very reasonable conclusions of the scientists and abandoning his belief in the infallibility of Scripture. He might have tried to tell himself that the structure of the heavens was an insignificant question, that theories about it had no bearing upon his fundamental religious convictions; but he would soon see that this was not true, for the trustworthiness of revelation was involved. He seems to have found this dilemma frustrating and painful. He did not solve it.

It is possible that he considered revision of his epic, but this is not likely. It would be hard to fit the story—impossible to fit the scriptural Creation —into a Copernican setting. The imaginative adjustment to the newer astronomical concepts, moreover, would be difficult both for him and for his public. Although in one form or another the heliocentric theory had been current for over a century, few readers of the mid-seventeenth century would be really adjusted to it. One discovers from the literature of the sixteenth and seventeenth centuries that among laymen new scientific ideas were accepted slowly. Readers would be ill at ease in a Copernican universe. It is not likely, furthermore, that Milton himself could switch readily from one conviction to another.

More important, to adopt the enormously expanded universe of Kepler and Galileo as background, he would have to rewrite the poem in such fashion as to make the supraterrestrial milieu of the story as undefined as that, for example, of Byron's *Cain.* The physical setting would have lost its meaning. A significant part of the integrated moral structure which Milton has put together in *Paradise Lost* would be missing. In addition, he would have had to sacrifice a great deal of the visual splendor of the poem. *Paradise Lost* would have become a less meaningful and less magnificent poem.

So he compromised. In *Paradise Lost* he represented the world more or less as most men for many generations had imagined the world to be, as he himself in his earlier years had imagined it. But he included reminders— or admissions—that maybe it was not really like this. No one could certainly know how it was. His doubts possibly caused him to be progressively less specific, more evasive, than otherwise he would have been in representing his Ptolemaic heavens. His description of Satan's downward journey through the spheres, for example, is vague (III, 560-76, 739-42); but the account of the friars' upward journey, earlier in the same book, specifically names the spheres (III, 481-83). The latter passage might have been written earlier.

Is it possible that Milton suffered this disturbance of his astronomical beliefs after he had finished the poem and that the references to Copernicanism are patched-in afterthoughts? This could be true. All the material which involves motion of the earth is concentrated in the dialogue of Book VIII and the brief passage which I have quoted from Book IV (592-95). The references to Galileo and the telescope and to the possibility of plural worlds, on the other hand, are scattered through the poem. It is possible that Milton's interest in Galileo's telescope and in the theory of plurality predated his acquaintanceship with the triple motion of the earth. The dialogue on astronomy might be a late insertion; the passage on the "volubil Earth" might have been written in during revision. This, of course, is not at all demonstrable. It seems more likely that Milton's enlightenment occurred while the poem was in progress.

This section has consisted largely of conjecture. What is reasonably certain is that as late as 1651 Milton was a Ptolemaist who believed that astronomy was knowable and that the study of it was laudable. Between 1651 and the completion of *Paradise Lost*, something happened. In *Paradise Lost* the new astronomy appears for the first time (and the last) in Milton's work. For the first time also Milton takes the position that astronomical inquiry is impious curiosity. He is acidly derisive toward Ptolemaic astronomers.

It would be futile to argue that *Paradise Lost* is a better poem because it includes the dialogue on astronomy. This passage has no great poetic power or beauty. Its Copernicanism is likely to confuse the intellectual content of the poem and to disturb its imaginative effects. The reader who is attempting to follow the action imaginatively should ignore the Copernicanism. The discussion of astronomy in Book VIII, however, is one of the more interesting passages in the poem because of its somewhat cloudy revelations concerning the poet's intellectual history.

Chapter VII. THE COSMOS

IF MILTON HAD been insulated a little longer from advanced astronomical theory, there would have been no question in his mind, as he wrote *Paradise Lost*, that his Ptolemaic spheres belonged in the category of literal truth. I believe that it is justifiable, in discussion of the poem, to regard them as belonging in this category. All phenomena which can be perceived by human senses—on earth or in the mundane heavens—can be studied and understood by men and can be literally represented in poetry. But when one reaches the outer shell of the world, he passes beyond the limits of human experience and beyond what men can completely comprehend. Some knowledge of the regions beyond the world is permitted; but it must be communicated to men by beings of a higher order, and it cannot be literal knowledge. What Raphael tells Adam of Heaven and the angels, of the celestial battle, and of the Creation is true, but it falls short of the truth as an angel would understand it. What the poet says in his own person about Heaven, Hell, Chaos, and the activities of superhuman spirits in these regions must likewise be understood an analogic semi-truth.

Milton has constructed a cosmos by the same method which he has followed in writing the story of angelic warfare; that is, he has assembled bits from Biblical revelation and from long-standing Christian tradition and reasoned out something which, he believes, remotely approximates the reality. But he does not pretend to have represented absolute reality. His vision of great spaces and distant regions is indefinite—as it should be. Sometimes, by supplying details, he weakens his effects. The objectives in this chapter will be, first, to put together the picture that Milton sees; and second, to define the meanings that he is attempting to convey through the medium of the setting.

I

Milton has deduced the order in which the various parts of the cosmos came into existence. The angels existed before the world, for at the Creation, "all the sons of God shouted for joy" (Job xxxviii, 7). Milton supports this conviction, perhaps unnecessarily, with patristic authority: "that Angels were long before this visible Creation, was the opinion of many ancient Fathers" (*PL,* I, argument).[1] If there were angels, then the empyreal Heaven must also have existed before the world. Milton accepts the Christian tradition that the human race was created in order to replace the apostate angels. It follows that the rebellion of the angels predated the creation of the world: "it seems even probable, that the apostasy which caused the expulsion of so many thousands from heaven, took place before the foundations of this world were laid."[2] So Hell, created for the punishment of the rebels, must have antedated the world, which was created as a dwelling for those who were to replace them in Heaven. The order of creation, then, was: Heaven, Hell, the world.

From this chronology, something may be deduced concerning the arrangement of the universe. It would surprise no one to be told that Heaven is above the world. But that Hell is beneath the world would be a novel idea to Milton's contemporaries. Hell is traditionally placed in the center of the earth: *"Franciscus Ribera* ... will have Hell a material & local fire in the Center of the earth, 200 *Italian* miles in diameter, as he defines it out of those words, *Exivit sanguis de lacu——per stadia mille sexcenta, &c.* But *Lessius* ... will have this local Hell far less, one *Dutch* mile in Diameter, all filled with fire and brimstone: because, as he there demonstrates, that space cubically multiplied will make a Sphere able to hold eight hundred thousand millions of damned bodies (allowing each body six foot square) which will abundantly suffice."[3]

Evidently Milton feels that he owes the reader of *Paradise Lost* an explanation for his departure from traditional belief. Hell is "describ'd here," he says in the Argument of Book I, *"not in the Centre* [the earth] (for Heaven [the mundane heavens] and Earth may be suppos'd as yet not made, certainly not yet accurst)." Hell could not have been created in a place which was not. So Heaven is above; Hell is far below the world. In this thinking lies an assumption which no one would question: elevation is goodness; lowness is evil. The gulf between Heaven and Hell is Chaos.

In the *Christian Doctrine* Milton argues very similarly that "Hell is situated beyond the limits of this universe [world]," supporting this opinion with Biblical quotation: the "great gulf" of Luke xvi, 26; the "outer darkness" of Matthew viii, 12; the "dogs," of Revelation xxii, 14, 15, that must lie outside the city. As theological support he adds: "This is said [fertur] to have been the opinion of Chrysostom, as likewise of Luther and some later divines."[4] This appeal to authority seems uncharacteristically lame; Milton does not ordinarily depend on hearsay concerning the opinions of important theologians.

St. Chrysostom does, to be sure, express such an opinion in one of his sermons on Romans: "But where, you ask, shall [Hell] be? It is my own belief that it is completely outside this world. For just as the prisons and mines of kings are placed far from them, so Hell shall be outside the world. Let us, then, not inquire where it is, rather how we may escape it."[5] This is preacher's rhetoric, not a reasoned statement on the location of Hell. Chrysostom agrees with Milton, however, that the angels were created before the world.[6] In his commentary on Genesis, Luther repeats from St. Augustine the story of one who asked how God was occupied before the Creation and was "answered to this effect: 'God was making hell ready for those who pried into meddlesome questions.' " This might be the passage that Milton says he has heard of. But obviously neither Luther nor Augustine is expressing a serious opinion. Luther indignantly condemns the "blasphemous" idea that the angels "were created before the beginning," which he associates with the Arian doctrine that the Son is a created being.[7] There remain the "later divines" whom Milton indefinitely mentions. Perhaps there actually is support for him somewhere in the works of Renaissance theologians.

Milton has arrived at his ideas concerning the location of Hell by independent deduction. His argument does not really depend on authority.[8] He seems to feel, however, that authoritative support is needed; he searches his memory and finds nothing there which is definite enough to be really helpful but offers the best that he can. Possibly he could have done better, but probably not much better.

One cannot assert flatly that this or that feature of *Paradise Lost* was unprecedented without risking scornful refutation. It may be that in the future some one will find an earlier version of the vertical construction which Milton has so specifically thought out. But so far, in spite of vigorous combing of Milton's possible sources, no one has come forward with a really close parallel. A passage from Origen's *De Principiis* (II, iii, 6-7) has been quoted as a possible precedent.[9] This describes a paradise located on a sphere beyond the starry sphere which serves as an intermediate habitation for those who are finally to be admitted to Heaven. Origen's demi-paradise, unfortunately, reminds one of Milton's Paradise of Fools. There is really little resemblance between Origen's cosmos and Milton's. No closer analogue has been found. Milton's universe is logical, its spatial relationships are very definite, it is imaginatively represented, and it is, I believe, highly original.

II

If a reader examines this cosmos closely, various mechanical objections may occur to him. Whatever lies within the world seems relatively consistent with human experience; when one leaves the world, incredibilities and inconsistencies begin to appear. We have already noted the difficulty of imagining a "glassy sea" over which blessed souls sail to Heaven and which at the same time encompasses the world and serves as its foundation. Milton's separation of Heaven and Hell from the world, however logical it may be, creates this and various other problems.

Heaven is above the world, Hell lies below. The earth is a stationary sphere with men dwelling all around it. For the inhabitants of large areas, then, the permanent direction of Heaven is downward. In a universe like Dante's, in which Heaven is an enveloping sphere, all men can look upward to Heaven. In Milton's cosmos, however, only the dwellers on the equator in the same longitude as Mesopotamia can do so. The inhabitants of southern Somalia are located at approximately the right point. If Hell is conventionally placed at the center of the earth, then it is beneath the feet of all men, but this is true for only a minority on Milton's earth. For Californians, Hell is approximately overhead.

Probably few readers have noticed these directional difficulties; none have been troubled by them. No one is inclined to object, yet objections can be answered. The concepts and images that we are able to form of the regions beyond the world are only remotely and analogously true. If we could see these regions with an angel's eyes and comprehend them with an angel's mind, everything would be reasonable. It is as if we were trying to understand a four-dimensional or multi-dimensioned reality. Which of us can say what physical and logical principles operate in those regions which, in our present corporeal form, we can never enter or understand. If the glassy sea is wrapped around the world, we may wonder how elected souls can sail on or fly over its surface up to Heaven, but this might be possible although we cannot see how. It might be perfectly possible for Heaven to be above opposite sides of the earth. In the mysterious spaces beyond the shell-of-the-world, our idea of direction might be wholly inapplicable.

When directions are mentioned in *Paradise Lost*,[10] they seem intended to convey symbolic meanings or traditional associations. East is conventionally associated with righteousness and faith, as it is in Donne's "Hymn to God, My God, in My Sickness." In *Paradise Lost* the gate of Paradise is on its eastern side (Genesis iii, 24). The gate of Heaven and the throne of God seem to face east. Lucifer's realm is in the north of Heaven (Isaiah xiv, 13). But Milton says little of points of the compass. Upward and downward are the only directions that really matter.

The incomprehensibility of the regions beyond the world should not discourage attempts at visualization. To the poet they are real, and he tries to convey his sense of their reality in such terms as are humanly meaningful. The images necessarily lack detail, for they represent things "inimitable on Earth / By Model, or by shading Pencil drawn" (III, 508-09). They suggest distances, spaces, grandeurs.

It is a mistake, I believe, to draw pictures of Milton's universe.[11] When one tries, he discovers that he cannot avoid misrepresentation in one way or another and that the more he struggles with the problem, the farther he becomes entangled in absurdities. It is not possible to map the ineffable. It is best simply to think of the empyreal Heaven as a plane area at the top of the cosmos, of the world as a sphere hanging just below Heaven, of Chaos as a vast space between Heaven and Hell through which unorganized matter is diffused, and of Hell as a flat area at the very bottom.

III

In describing Heaven, Milton at times goes more into detail than is proper to description in accommodated language, and at times the details are disenchanting. Yet he contrives to suggest in general a celestial glory reminiscent of the visions of the Apocalypse.

He is uncertain about the shape of Heaven; it is "undetermin'd square or round" (II, 1048). God swears "an Oath / That [shakes] Heav'n's whole circumference" (II, 352-53), yet elsewhere the "Quadrature" of Heaven is contrasted with the "Orbicular World" (X, 381).[12] Heaven, in any case, is a vast but limited area surrounded by a battlemented wall (II, 1049). It has no definite upper limit; there is no sky above it. There are no luminous bodies to light it. Both "light and shade" spring "From that high mount of God" (V, 643). Within the mountain is a cave

> Where light and darkness in perpetual round
> Lodge and dislodge by turns, which makes through Heav'n
> Grateful vicissitude, like Day and Night. (VI, 6-8)

In Heaven "there shall be no night" (Revelation xxi, 25), only a "grateful Twilight" (V, 645) alternating with brightness.[13] The climate of Heaven is invariably temperate.

Milton makes it clear that Heaven does not differ greatly in material character from earth. The soil of Heaven is an "Ethereal mould" (II, 139), an "Ethereous mould" (VI, 473), but these adjectives seem to mean merely "celestial," not "consisting of ether."[14] Raphael suggests that earth may

> Be but the shadow of Heav'n, and things therein
> Each to other like, more than on Earth is thought.
> (V, 575-76)

"Shadow" here, I think, means something like "replica," not "imitation" in the Platonic sense, as it is commonly understood.[15] Satan at least sees a close resemblance:

> O Earth, how like to Heav'n, if not preferr'd
> More justly . . . .
> Terrestrial Heav'n, danc't round by other Heav'ns.
>   (IX, 99-103)

Raphael tells Adam that, if he is obedient, he may, "improv'd by tract of time," dwell either "Here or in Heav'nly Paradises" (V, 498-501), implying that he may choose between two similarly beautiful dwelling places. Only in its brilliance does Heaven (the Empyrean, the "fiery") seem to be markedly different from the prelapsarian earth. The material substance of the earth, however, no longer has the Heaven-like purity that it once had; it has been corrupted by the Original Sin.

Beneath the plain of Heaven, "Deep under ground," are "materials dark and crude, / Of spiritous and fiery spume" (VI, 478-79),[16]

> Th' originals of Nature in thir crude
> Conception; Sulphurous and Nitrous Foam. (VI, 511-12)

During the war in Heaven, Lucifer tells his followers that "the Deep / Shall yield" these materials to them "pregnant with infernal flame" (VI, 382-83); and the rebel angels dig them up for military use. The crude materials which lie beneath the celestial soil are like those which lie hidden within the earth: "nor hath this Earth / Entrails unlike" (VI, 516-17). Milton introduces sulphur and niter (saltpeter) beneath the celestial soil, I believe, simply because he wishes to supply the rebels with the ingredients of gunpowder. The passage as a whole is hard to fit into his scheme of things. The four elements have better claim to the title "originals of Nature" than sulphur and saltpeter. Chaos ("the Deep") does not, according to the description of it in Book II, include such materials, and the fire of Chaos cannot properly be called "infernal." The scientific detail of the passage is more puzzling than poetic.

Nature, the principle of orderly life and activity, operates in Heaven as in the world, adorning Heaven "With Plant, Fruit, Flow'r Ambrosial, Gems and Gold" (VI, 475). Though there is no sun to infuse vital power, the light of Heaven can do so. When "Heav'n's ray" touches and tempers the crude matter, trees and flowers "shoot forth/So beautrous, op'ning to the ambient light" (VI, 480-81) and precious minerals take form. The empyreal soil produces abundant food for the angels:

> in Heav'n the Trees
> Of life ambrosial fruitage bear, and vines
> Yield Nectar . . . from off the boughs each Morn
> [Angels] brush mellifluous Dews, and find the ground
> Cover'd with pearly grain.   (V, 426-30)

The heavenly landscape, of which the earth's is a rough copy, is beautifully varied by irregularities and contrasts, "pleasure situate in Hill and Dale" (VI, 641). During the celestial battle, the loyal angels, to meet the challenge of Satan's newly invented artillery, pluck up "the seated Hills with all thir load, / Rocks, Waters, Woods," and hurl them at the rebels (VI, 644-45). But violent disruption has occurred only this once in the history of Heaven. Normally the "Sons of Light" live in a tranquil and apparently unchanging environment. They form "fellowships of joy" in "blissful Bowers / Of *Amarantin* Shade" and beside celestial waters—"Fountain or Spring" or "the waters of Life" (XI, 77-80).

The beauty of Heaven is due, not only to its natural loveliness, but to its magnificent angel-made constructions. In Heaven there is "many a Tow'red structure high" (I, 733), "Opal Tow'rs" (II, 1049). The pavement is "trodd'n Gold" (I, 682), and it gleams "like a Sea of Jasper" (III, 363). The battlements are adorned with "living Sapphire" (II, 1050). In the wall of Heaven is

> a Kingly Palace Gate
> With Frontispiece of Diamond and Gold
> Imbellisht; thick with sparkling orient Gems
> The Portal [shines].   (III, 505-08)

When Heaven opens its "ever-during Gates," they produce "Harmonious sound" swinging "On golden Hinges" (VII, 206-07). (The gates of Hell fly open with "jarring sound . . . and on their hinges grate / Harsh Thunder," II, 881-83). "A broad and ample road" leads from the "blazing Portals" to "God's Eternal house"; its "dust is Gold / And pavement Stars, as Stars to [men] appear" (VII, 575-78).

The color in Milton's descriptions of Heaven is almost wholly due to his somewhat frequent mention of gold and precious or semi-precious stones. The appearance of these in the poem is doubtless due to the influence, direct or indirect, of the Apocalypse. Before his fall, Mammon admires "The riches of Heav'n's pavement, trodd'n Gold" to the exclusion of all "vision beatific" (I, 682-84). In Hell he finds abundant "Gems and Gold" and proposes to use them to produce a "Magnificence" to rival Heaven's (II, 271-73). Precious metals and stones seem more appropriate to Hell than to Heaven.[17] It is no wonder "That riches grow in Hell; that soil may best / Deserve the precious bane" (I, 691-92). It is fitting that in Hell Satan should sit "High on a Throne of Royal State" which far outshines the *"Barbaric Pearl and Gold"* of Oriental kings (II, 1-4). Heaven should be purely, chastely white; but Milton's Heaven, influenced by Revelation and Christian tradition, seems sometimes to have a golden glitter.

One learns of a few of the geographical features of Heaven: the splendid gate, the road leading inward from it, "God's Eternal house" on the mountain in the center of Heaven, "the Fount of Life" (III, 357). The "river of Bliss through midst of Heav'n / Rolls o'er *Elysian* Flow'rs her Amber stream" (III, 358-59). There is mention also of "The Quarters of the North" (V, 689), Lucifer's domain, and of "The Mountain of the Congregation" (V, 766; Isaiah xiv, 13), upon which Lucifer, before the revolt, enthrones himself in imitation of the state of God.

"In number" the angels are "almost infinite."[18] When God summons them to their annual assembly (annual according to heavenly time), they come "Innumerable before th'Almighty's Throne . . . from all the ends of Heav'n." "Ten thousand thousand Ensigns . . . Stream in the Air," banners which distinguish the "Orders, and Degrees" of the celestial hierarchy or display "Holy Memorials" emblazoned "in thir glittering Tissues" (V, 585-93). On this occasion they engage in activities and enjoy pleasures which seem to be characteristic of the celestial life. After ceremonial "song and dance about the sacred Hill" (V, 619), they feast upon

> Angels' Food, and rubied Nectar flows:
> In Pearl, in Diamond, and massy Gold,
> Fruit of delicious Vines, the growth of Heav'n.
> On flow'rs repos'd, and with fresh flow'rets crown'd,
> They eat, they drink, and in communion sweet
> Quaff immortality and joy.   (V, 633-38)

They wear "Crowns inwove with Amarant and Gold," which rest on "resplendent locks inwreath'd with beams"; "gold'n Harps" hang "Like Quivers" at their sides (III, 352-67). When the angels are engaged in military duty, however, they bear "Celestial" arms, "Shields, Helms, and Spears . . . with Diamond flaming, and with Gold" (IV, 553-54). God has an "Armory . . . between two brazen Mountains" where his "Chariots wing'd" are stored, "Celestial Equipage" (VII, 199-203).

There is a great deal of music in Heaven (and celestial music also in Eden before the Fall, IV, 680-88, 711). The angels carry harps—like the blessed in Revelation—which are "ever tun'd":

> with Preamble sweet
> Of charming symphony they introduce
> Thir sacred Song, and waken raptures high;
> No voice exempt, no voice but well could join
> Melodious part, such concord is in Heav'n.   (III, 366-71)

Choirs of angels sing "Melodious Hymns about the sovran Throne / Alternate all night long" (V, 656-57). Just after the Creation angels celebrate the first Sabbath with harp, "solemn Pipe," dulcimer, and

all Organs of sweet stop,
All sounds on Fret by String or Golden Wire
.... intermixt with Voice
Choral or Unison.   (VII, 594-99)

Not only is there sweet harmony in Heaven but also many sweet odors: clouds of incense "Fuming from Golden Censers" hide God's mount (VII, 600).

It is significant that the joys of Heaven include the pleasures of the senses. All of the senses are delighted. Angels are spatial, temporal, material creatures quite capable of physical enjoyment. Their bodies consist of *spirit*, the same material substance as the spirit of man, an extremely tenuous form of matter.[19] In the persons of the angels (pure spirits) it shines brilliantly. Evidently there are grades of angelic spirit, differences in degree of rarity and brilliance corresponding to the angelic ranks. The degeneration of Lucifer and the other apostate angels shows that this substance is capable of corruption, of becoming gross and carnal.

Milton's descriptions represent the angels as luminously splendid. When Satan approaches Uriel on the Sun,

His back was turn'd, but not his brightness hid;
Of beaming sunny Rays, a golden tiar
Circl'd his Head, nor less his Locks behind
Illustrious on his Shoulders fledge with wings
Lay waving round.   (III, 624-28)

Raphael has three pairs of "gorgeous wings" (V, 250), attached respectively to his shoulders, his waist, and his heels (V, 277-85; Isaiah vi, 2). Milton describes these with glowing imagery. Raphael stands "Like *Maia's* son," and his plumes, when he stirs them, diffuse "Heav'nly fragrance" (V, 285-86). Uriel and Raphael are seraphim, angels of the highest order, and are correspondingly brilliant. Beelzebub, before he was driven from Heaven, was "Cloth'd with transcendent brightness" and outshone "Myriads though bright" (I, 86-87). According to Satan, Beelzebub is a cherub (I, 157), an angel of the second rank. The less glorious myriads supposedly belonged to the seven orders below the cherubim.

When they appear to men, angels sometimes assume a more modest appearance. Michael, when he comes to Paradise to expel Adam and Eve, is a handsome and heroic figure resplendently armed (XI, 238-48). He comes, however, "Not in his shape Celestial, but as Man / Clad to meet Man." But apparently Raphael appears to Adam in "his proper shape" (V, 276), "another Morn / Ris'n on mid-noon" (V, 310-11).

Celestial society has a hierarchal structure with the Son of God at the apex of the social pyramid. The angels are organized in orders, or grades. What Milton says of these is deliberately vague.[20] Like the Protestants of his period in general, he has no faith in the traditional (Roman Catholic) angel lore, for the Bible reveals very little concerning the angels. He does not give the number of the angelic orders; and except for indicating that "The great Seraphic Lords and Cherubim" (I, 794) are the two highest orders, he does not rank them. Yet it is evident that all of Milton's angels are graded and that he is well acquainted with the traditional Dionysian ranking and terminology. He uses the Dionysian terms freely:

> Hear all ye Angels, Progeny of Light,
> Thrones, Dominations, Princedoms, Virtues, Powers.
> (V, 600-01)

The names of all nine of the Dionysian orders or terms very similar to them appear in *Paradise Lost.*

Every angel in Milton's Heaven apparently owes obedience to a specific superior, and every one, except members of the lowest order, governs specific subjects. Heaven is divided into

> the mighty Regencies
> Of Seraphim and Potentates and Thrones
> In thir triple Degrees.   (V, 748-50)

One of these is the province of the seraph Lucifer in the north. When he decides upon rebellion against the government of the Son, Lucifer leads his subjects, one-third of the inhabitants of Heaven, to his northern regency. These angels, "Innumerable as the Stars of Night" (V, 745), seem to constitute a stable political unit under his control.

The heavenly hierarchy, with its specific chain of command, has a military character; and when occasion arises, it functions as a military organization.[21] There is so much angelic military activity in *Paradise Lost* that the reader is likely to forget that the angels normally lead peaceful lives enjoying tranquil pleasures and to think of them as soldiers rather than as citizens. Satan's faction is an army throughout the epic. The higher officers in this army are its seraphim and cherubim, "A thousand Demi-Gods" (I, 796). During the battle in Heaven, Satan's forces are opposed by an equal number of God's "armed Saints" (VI, 47), "bright Legions" (VI, 64) of loyal angels under the command of Michael. At the signal of an "Ethereal Trumpet," they join "in mighty Quadrate" to march against God's enemies (VI, 60-62). Before the Fall, Paradise is (futilely) guarded by a band of angel-warriors under the command of Gabriel (IV, 549 ff.). After the Expulsion, Adam and Eve look back and see the eastern side of Paradise

Wav'd over by that flaming Brand, the Gate
With dreadful Faces throng'd and fiery Arms
(XII, 643-44)

Even though Satan uses artillery, the arms and the tactics of the angel-soldiers seem more classical than Cromwellian.

The geographical center and the spiritual focus of Heaven is the seat of the Eternal God, "a flaming Mount, whose top / Brightness [makes] invisible" (V, 598-99). Before the high throne "golden Lamps . . . burn / Nightly" (V, 713-14), and fumes of incense rise from a "Golden Altar" (XI, 18). The angels frequently celebrate the glory of God by performing song and dance in his presence. At the assembly which ends in Satan's defection, they range themselves three-dimensionally about God the Father "in Orbs / Of circuit inexpressible . . . Orb within Orb" (V, 594-96), apparently in a ceremonial formation. (In Hell Satan's followers also form themselves into a globe around him, II, 511-12.) On the Father's right hand sits the Son "in bliss imbosom'd" (V, 597). For man's sake the Son will leave God's "bosom, and this glory . . . Freely put off" (III, 239-40); but after his death and ascension, he will resume his privileged place "incarnate" (III, 315).

We may assume that God's mount is the highest point in the cosmos, for it is impossible to conceive of anything more exalted than God the Father. Yet to localize an infinite and eternal God on a mountain top is a contradiction. To say that God sits enthroned on his Holy Mount is perhaps a way of expressing an intensity of his presence here above the center of Heaven. The mountain is certainly a physical reality and the Son is a physical presence.

Not many members of the present generation of depraved humanity will envy Milton's angels their dwelling place or their way of life. But every reader will remember the beauty and brilliance of Milton's vision of "the happy Realms of Light" (I, 85). In spite of its lavish golden and jewelled ornamentation, the primary quality of Milton's Heaven is a pure and intense white radiance.

IV

Chaos is a Greek concept.[22] The Christian Fathers, influenced especially by the descriptions of Hesiod and Ovid, adopted it and identified it with "the deep" and "the waters" of Genesis i, 1. In Christian cosmogony Chaos is the material from which God shaped the world. The Chaos of *Paradise Lost* differs from earlier Christian versions in that it is more primitive and more extensive than they are, in that it has furnished the raw material for the creation of Hell (II, 1002-03) and Heaven as well as for the world, and in that it existed long before the world and—somewhat diminished—continues to exist, potential raw material for further creations. It has a quite definite location: it is *"the great Gulf between Hell and Heaven"* (II, argument). In Greek and Latin, *chaos* means "abyss," "gulf." In Milton's cosmos this "gulf" is a tumultuous and enormously extensive ocean, a seething mass of God's "dark materials" (II, 916) for the making of worlds; this is "The Womb of nature and perhaps her Grave" (II, 911).

The primitive matter of Milton's Chaos is composed of atoms, but these are merely "embryon Atoms" (II, 900), atoms not finally formed (see Chap. VIII, sec. ii). They have no permanent character; they are in constant change, becoming indifferently "Light-arm'd or heavy, sharp, smooth, swift or slow" (II, 902). They do not yet have the nature of elements; Chaos is

> neither Sea, nor Shore, nor Air, nor Fire,
> But all these in thir pregnant causes mixt
> Confus'dly.   (II, 912-14)

The pregnant causes are "hot, cold, moist, and dry" (II, 898), qualities or principles which have no substantial being except by association with atoms. There is a distinction in Milton's mind between raw matter and the qualities which give it form and character.[23] In Chaos the qualities are ceaselessly, hostilely, and purposelessly active. In the primeval state, any atom may be drawn into brief adherence to the "Faction" (II, 901) of any one of the four qualities and thus momentarily possesses a single quality. Before earth, water, air, and fire can be, each atom must achieve distinctive character by permanently assuming two of the primary qualities.

The quintessence, as well as the four terrestrial elements, is engendered from the material confusion of Chaos (III, 716-18). There are only four possible pairings of hot, cold, moist, and dry, and these combinations are assigned to the terrestrial elements. Evidently the quintessence, like Aristotle's ether, has no quality which has an opposite. Perhaps there are qualities active in Chaos—of which we know nothing—which were assumed by the quintessential atoms at the time of the Creation and which give them their peculiar character. Or the quintessence may be a sublimation of air and fire or of all four of the elements which we know.[24] Milton reveals only that it is luminous (not necessarily hot) and extremely subtle.

It is not possible to specify the degree of development and definition that matter has in its primitive chaotic form.[25] It seems to have sensuously perceptible characteristics; e.g., sharpness, smoothness (II, 902), solidity, sliminess (X, 286). It is clearly capable of resisting the movement of a material body; Satan pursues his way up through Chaos with great difficulty, "O'er bog or steep, through strait, rough, dense, or rare" (II, 948). On the other hand, because there is nothing in Chaos which can be named or defined, it is said to be empty (before the Creation, says Genesis, "the earth was without form, and void"). Chaos is "the void immense" (II, 829), "the void and formless infinite" (III, 12), "Matter unform'd and void" (VII, 233); or it is said to be "unreal" (X, 471) or "unapparent" (VII, 103). (The heavens and the earth are described as "conspicuous," VII, 63.)

The fierce contention of antithetical forces in Chaos produces appalling confusion and tumult:

> For hot, cold, moist, and dry, four Champions fierce
> Strive here for Maistry, and to Battle bring
> Thir embryon Atoms . . . .
> . . . . To whom these most adhere,
> Hee rules a moment; *Chaos* Umpire sits
> . . . .
> *Chance* governs all.   (II, 898-910)

The uproar is deafening 3 (II, 920-27, 951-54). In the midst of this vast, tumultuous ocean, all sense of "length, breadth, and height, / And time and place" is lost (II, 893-94). This passage cannot be taken literally, as it sometimes has been, to mean that location, duration, and direction do not exist in Chaos. This is simply the expression of the superlative in confusion. Satan has difficulty in finding his way through Chaos, but he proceeds toward an objective, which in time he reaches.

This vast four-cornered battle of opposites proceeds endlessly in complete darkness, for according to Genesis, "darkness was upon the face of the deep." Milton's Chaos seethes in "darkness profound" (VII, 233). It is a "palpable obscure" (II, 406); that is, a darkness which can be felt, which has material substance. Milton once calls it *"utter"* (complete) darkness (I, argument). There is fierce heat as well as fierce cold in Chaos, but in Milton's cosmos heat does not necessarily engender light.

According to Uriel's account of the Creation (III, 708-21), God first segregated "This world's material mould" and stilled the turmoil within it: "Confusion heard his voice, and wild uproar / Stood rul'd." At God's "second bidding darkness fled, / Light shone," and the elements hurried to their proper places. Order sprang from disorder; and matter, now endowed with the power of becoming, assumed forms which would constitute the material of more complex forms. The order which God imposed was *nature* (see Chap. II, sec. i). Nature is the antithesis of Chaos, just as light, nature's concomitant, is the antithesis of darkness. These oppositions are very clear in the poet's description of Satan's emergence from Chaos and his approach to "This pendant world": The light of Heaven

> Shoots far into the bosom of dim Night
> A glimmering dawn; here Nature first begins
> Her fardest verge, and *Chaos* to retire.   (II, 1036-38)

But by far the greater part of Chaos remains in its primitive state. It is presided over—one can hardly say governed—by a divinity, Chaos personified. This person holds court, as he has for uncountable ages, amid clamor and confusion, with his consort "Sable-vested *Night*, eldest of things," enthroned at his side (II, 962).[26] These two are "Ancestors of Nature" (II, 895). They are surrounded by a company of subsidiary personifications, such as Tumult, Discord, *"Orcus* and *Ades*, and ... *Demogorgon"* (II, 964-65), who have no function in the story beyond the suggestions of their names. During his upward journey through "the Reign of *Chaos* and old Night" (I, 543), Satan comes upon this anarchic court. He finds in Chaos a sympathetic ally. Although comparatively he has lost very little, Chaos resents God's diminishing of his empire by the recent building of Hell and the world (earlier Heaven was also subtracted from his realm); and by his nature he is inclined to aid such disruption as Satan intends.

Chaos, Night, and the personifications who attend them seem to me out of place in Milton's cosmos, for they are fictions, "fables," among realities —among phenomena known to men only in accommodated form but still realities. Since he was writing for a generation very familiar with the classics, Milton may have felt that his readers would find pleasure in reminders of Hesiod and other ancient writers. But there are no other characters from classical mythology in *Paradise Lost* (except perhaps Medusa, II, 611). Sin and Death, the only other personifications, are also characters who seem out of proper context. They are concretized abstractions; their father Satan is a real person.

Satan's journey upward through Chaos to the world is an undertaking of enormous difficulty, a heroic achievement. Once the Devil has penetrated the world and seduced mankind, however, travel between the world and Hell becomes very easy, and the way to Heaven becomes correspondingly strait and narrow. To express this moral truth in the physical terms of his cosmos, Milton resorts to mythopoeic invention. He has told the story of the birth of Sin in Heaven and of the birth of Death in Hell. Now he uses this unholy pair to provide an easy means of communication between Hell and the world. Following Satan, Sin and Death pave

> after him a broad and beat'n way
> Over the dark Abyss, whose boiling Gulf
> Tamely endure[s] a Bridge of wondrous length.
>   (II, 1026-29)

The Michigan State University Press

East Lansing, Michigan,

takes pleasure in presenting

this copy for review, and asks that

you send two clippings

of your notice

Title   THE MORAL COSMOS OF
         PARADISE LOST

Author Lawrence Babb

Price $7.50

Publication Date   2/5/71

This stretches from Hellgates to the shell-of-the-world. They accomplish this feat of construction (X, 282-320) by first crowding together great quantities of the indescribable substance of Chaos, "From each side shoaling [crowding it] towards the mouth of Hell." Death smites "The aggregated Soil . . . with his Mace petrific" and renders it firm and hard. The adjacent matter "his look" binds "with *Gorgonian* rigor not to move." Mother and son glue this initial section of the bridge to "the Roots of Hell" "with *Asphaltic* slime." Then they extend "the Mole immense . . . Over the foaming deep high Archt, a Bridge / Of length prodigious." By "wondrous Art / Pontifical" they have constructed "a ridge of pendent Rock / Over the vext Abyss," reaching to

> the outside bare
> Of this round World: with Pins of Adamant
> And Chains they made all fast.

As Satan goes down the new causeway to Hellgate, "Disparted *Chaos*" cries out indignantly and assails "with rebounding surge the bars" (X, 416-17). What bars? Meanwhile the opening just below the heavenly gate in the outer orb of the world diminishes (III, 529); supposedly the golden stairway is, from this time forward, very seldom let down.

When Milton writes of the stairway to Heaven and the crystalline sea beneath it, the reader is conscious of Biblical and traditional sanctions. The bridge across Chaos is wholly the poet's invention, authorized only vaguely by Matthew vii, 13: "wide is the gate, and broad is the way, that leadeth to destruction." Milton presents the stairway and the glassy sea without detail. In the passages concerning the bridge, he becomes unfortunately specific in describing the mechanics of construction. Mechanical particulars are unsuitable in a cosmos described in accommodated language.[27] They provoke the skepticism of literal-minded readers. A bridge is a horizontal thing. How can a bridge be built from a point below to a point above, from the bottom of a sea to its surface? Yet the "high Archt" bridge of Sin and Death extends "Over the foaming deep."[28] How could they have found in Chaos materials suitable for construction? Their formation of stable solids from primitive matter seems to imply creative power. We shall simply have to accept the idea that, as a result of Adam's sin, the world becomes readily accessible to the powers of evil without taking the physical means too seriously.

Milton's rather frequent brief descriptions of Chaos leave the reader with a keen sense of vast and fearsome desolation: "the wasteful Deep . . . monstrous sight" (VI, 862), "th'unreal, vast, unbounded deep / Of horrible confusion" (X, 471-72),

> the hoary deep, a dark
> Illimitable Ocean without bound,
> Without dimension . . . .   (II, 891-93)

The pontifical art of Sin and Death may seem a little trivial. But Chaos is one of the more impressive and memorable features of the physical background of Milton's epic.

V

Hell was created at the bottom of the cosmos as a place of confinement and punishment for the apostate angels and for the eventual punishment of the human damned. Just above it and on all sides of it is Chaos. Milton conceives of it as a tremendous plane area encircled by a wall and covered by an overarching bell, a "huge convex of Fire . . . Ninefold" (II, 434-36), to prevent escape by upward flight. (By God's permissive will, however, the demons escape somewhat easily.) To express the depth of its location—its great distance "from God and light of Heav'n" (I, 73)—Milton calls it "the bottomless pit" (VI, 866; Revelation xx, 1-3), "the utter Deep" (VI, 716). The location of Hell and its fiery bell-like cover seem to be original with Milton. Inside Hell, however, one finds many features derived from Christian literature and the classics.[29]

The principal distinguishing characteristics of Hell are its absolute darkness (Job x, 22; Matthew viii, 12) and, predictably, its superlatively intense heat (Mark ix, 43-48):

> torture without end
> Still urges, and a fiery Deluge, fed
> With ever-burning Sulphur unconsum'd.   (I, 67-69)

Demons "on the wing under the Cope of Hell" hover " 'Twixt upper, nether, and surrounding Fires" (I, 345-46). Hell is a dungeon which, on all sides, flames "As one great Furnace"; and the flames produce, not light, but darkness (I, 61-63).[30] The infernal landscape resembles the side of a volcano after an internal explosion has blown a part of it away, leaving "a singed bottom all involv'd / With stench and smoke" (I, 236-37).

One finds some rather definite geographical details. There is the burning lake (Revelation xx, 10, 14-15) on which the rebel angels, thunderstruck, are floating at the opening of the poem. The lake seems to be at the center of Hell, and Pandaemonium, the capitol building of the rebel host, presumably is built on the burning soil very near it. Into the lake flow four rivers, borrowed from the Greek Hades, Styx, Acheron, Cocytus, and Phlegethon (II, 575-81). At a distance from these, *"Lethe,* the River of Oblivion" (II, 583), also from Greek myth, rolls slowly and silently. Beyond Lethe is a "frozen Continent" (II, 587), which in future times the demons will use to good advantage in the torturing of human souls. Whether Lethe encircles Hell or cuts off a corner or side of it is not clear.

Hell, like Heaven, has a gateway. As he begins his quest for God's newly created World, Satan finds the gates set in the wall—"Hell bounds high reaching to the horrid Roof" (II, 644)—which encircles Hell. (Earlier Satan has said that Hellgates were overhead, II, 436-47.) These are ninefold gates, three folds of brass, three of iron, and three of adamantine rock, "Impenetrable, impal'd with circling fire, / Yet unconsum'd" (II, 645-48). When Sin unlocks them for Satan, they fly open with grating dissonance (II, 880-82).

As *Paradise Lost* opens, both Hell and the world are recent creations. In each case creation was an ordering of confusion, an imposition of the laws of nature. The matter of which Hell consists is an ordered matter behaving as predictably as that of the world. Nature governs in Hell. But this is nature in reverse. In the world, nature is on the whole benign. Before the Fall, it was wholly benign, as it is in Heaven. In Hell it is wholly malignant. The band of demons who explore Hell behold what they find there "With shudd'ring horror pale, and eyes aghast" (II, 616). They pass

> many a Frozen, many a Fiery Alp,
> Rocks, Caves, Lakes, Fens, Bogs, Dens, and shades of death,
> A Universe of death, which God by curse
> Created evil, for evil only good,
> Where all life dies, death lives, and Nature breeds,
> Perverse, all monstrous, all prodigious things,
> Abominable, inutterable, and worse
> Than Fables yet have feign'd, or fear conceiv'd,
> *Gorgons* and *Hydras,* and *Chimeras* dire.   (II, 620-28)

Hell is a region of unmitigated hideousness.

VI

Is Milton's Hell merely a physical metaphor to express extreme torment of mind, or are the pains of Hell a physical reality?[31] There is certainly an internal Hell as well as a "paradise within" (XII, 587). A "hot Hell" always burns in Satan, "Though in mid Heav'n" (IX, 467-68). In his soliloquy of self-revelation in Book IV, Satan shows that he realizes this fully:

> Me miserable! which way shall I fly
> Infinite wrath, and infinite despair?
> Which way I fly is Hell; myself am Hell.   (IV, 73-75)

The greatest pain of all is a mental pain, the sense of exclusion "from God and light of Heav'n"; and God enhances this by punishing "sinne with sinne,"[32] causing the sinner to confirm his own reprobation and to sink himself deeper into hopeless misery, as Satan does. The hard of heart shall

> be hard'n'd, blind be blinded more,
> That they may stumble on, and deeper fall.   (III, 200-01)

Yet mental and physical are never separate in Milton's thinking. The "punishment of the damned," he writes, "seems to consist partly in the loss of the chief good, namely, the favor and protection of God, and the beatific vision of his presence, which is commonly called the punishment of loss; and partly in eternal torment, which is called the punishment of sense."[33] Satan suffers from thoughts "Both of lost happiness and lasting pain" (I, 54-55). His physical pain is as real as his torment of mind. In Hell he walks with "uneasy steps / Over the burning Marl ... and the torrid Clime" tortures him sorely (I, 295-98). Because of our present intellectual limitations, we cannot conceive of Hell as it actually is, but we should understand that the pains of the sense are not metaphoric.

The joys of Heaven are likewise both mental and physical. The angels enjoy not only the love and proximity of God, but also such pleasures of the sense as "vision beatific" (I, 684), the delicious taste of ambrosia, the fragrance of incense, and the sweet harmony of celestial music. Indeed if Milton denied the sensuous pleasures of Heaven or the physical pains of Hell, he would be denying his materialistic ontology. The spirit which is tormented in Hell or rewarded in Heaven is a material thing.

VII

When one tries to express the size of the Ptolemaic world, he uses up his superlatives. Milton's cosmos, of course, is many, many times larger, and Milton tries to give the reader some sense of its grand dimensions.

There are several suggestions of enormous sizes and distances. Raphael, for example, endeavors to convey to Adam an idea of the vastness of Heaven: In comparison with "the mighty Regencies" of Heaven ruled by "Seraphim and Potentates and Thrones,"

All thy Dominion, *Adam*, is no more
Than what this Garden is to all the Earth. (V, 748-52)

In Heaven there is "many a Province wide / Tenfold the length of this terrene" (VI, 77-78). But the hints are never very specific.

The seraph Abdiel, after his courageous defiance of Satan and his host in the Quarters of the North, travels "All night" (VI, 1) to rejoin God and the loyal angels in the center of Heaven. How fast does an angel in a hurry travel? The tremendously rapid spheres, says Raphael, revolve at "speed almost Spiritual" (VIII, 110); an angel, then, moves or can move somewhat faster than the spheres. By taking the speed per hour of the stellar sphere, multiplying by twelve (a twelve-hour night might be assumed), and adding something, one should arrive at the approximate radius of Heaven. But what does "All night" in heavenly time mean in terms of earthly time? All that one learns of celestial time is that the hours, days, and years of Heaven are different from ours, presumably much longer (V, 582-83; VI, 685). Raphael tells Adam that, setting out at "Morning hour," he has accomplished the journey from Heaven to Eden "ere mid-day," a "distance inexpressible / By Numbers that have name" (VIII, 111-14). The distance from Heaven to Earth would be numerically expressible if Raphael had given clock times instead of using such vague phrases as "Morning hour" and "ere mid-day." An error of one hour would make a great difference.

The rebels expelled from Heaven fall nine days before they reach Hell (VI, 871). If one knew how fast spirits would fall through Chaos and if one could be sure that Milton means earth-days, he could compute the distance from heaven to hell, but the essential information is lacking. When Milton says that Hell is as far from Heaven "As from the Center thrice to th'utmost Pole" (I, 73-74), he seems to be giving the distance from top to bottom of his cosmos with uncharacteristic definiteness. Obviously, however, this is far too small a figure. When Satan emerges from Chaos on his journey up from Hell, he sees the world hanging from Heaven "in bigness as a Star / Of smallest Magnitude close by the Moon" (II, 1052-53). If Hell were no farther from Heaven than three times the radius of the world, then it should be visible to Satan just beneath the world, for it would be no farther from the world than the world is from Heaven. But Satan has left Hell far below him. Hell is "distant . . . Worlds between" from the earth (X, 362). "Thrice to th'utmost Pole" must be a thoughtless intensive.[34] Milton uses a comparable expression in a prose work: "deeper from holy blisse than the worlds diameter multiply'd."[35]

Milton's avoidance of specific distances, which is unquestionably deliberate, has prevented us from playing at an intellectual game which was a favorite of the scholastics, whom he despised. If we could, we should map Milton's Heaven, determine the cubic feet available for each of the damned souls in Hell, compute the length of the bridge from Hell to the world and the cubic yards of material required in its construction, etc. Milton, however, gives no definite bases for computation. His purpose is to establish vague images of immensity in his reader's imagination: Heaven is inexpressibly vast; the distance from Heaven to earth is superlatively great; angels travel at an inconceivable speed. Yet heaven, however extensive it may be, is a limited area; it has a "circumference" (II, 353), there are "Empyreal bounds" (X, 380). Angels, because they are material creatures, require time to make a journey, however swift they may be.

The total image is one of magnificent height. One scarcely thinks of lateral dimensions. Milton's cosmos is a vertical stage of three principal levels, Hell, the earth, and Heaven; and the spaces between them are so vast that "Number fails."

VIII

Light[36] is the "Bright effluence of [God's] bright Essence increate"; it is the "Coeternal beam" of the Eternal (III, 2-6). All light emanates from God, who is himself light. It is, then, the physically perceptible evidence of God's presence, or of his influence, or of the exercise of his power. All natural light is "holy Light" (III, 1).[37] The Creation of the world, an exertion of divine power and goodness, was both an ordering of chaotic matter and a glorious illumination of chaotic darkness. At God's command, "Light shone, and order from disorder sprung" (III, 713). Since the Creation, the sun and the lesser luminous bodies of the mundane heavens have diffused the divine influence through the natural world, stimulating and cherishing life. Darkness is absence of light.[38] It is evidence of God's disapproval (in Hell) or of the withholding of his influence (in Chaos).

There are suggestions in Book VII of *Paradise Lost* that light—at least the light which we see in the world—is a physical substance,[39] a "quintessence pure" (VII, 244). Before the creation of the sun it was given temporary residence "spher'd in a radiant Cloud" (VII, 247).[40] When the sun was created, its porous substance drank "the liquid Light" (VII, 362). The divine influence, then, reaches us in the form of a physical entity.[41]

The Eternal God, the fountain of light, is enthroned in Heaven on a flaming mountain. God chooses to be more intensely present on the Holy Mount than anywhere else, and his presence here is manifested by intense luminosity. His radiance is so great ("Dark with excessive bright") that not even the highest of the seraphim could endure to look directly upon it. He consequently wraps himself in cloud, on rare occasions revealing to the angels a fraction of his overwhelming brilliance (III, 375-82). This radiance of unendurable and inconceivable intensity is the concomitant of wisdom, beauty, glory, and goodness which are beyond our comprehension. To say that God is unseeable is a way of saying that he is unknowable, even to the highest angelic intellect. Only the Son of God may see God, may know God (see Chap, VIII, sec. iv).

God imparts his light to his creatures in various degrees. The Son, since he is the most excellent of all finite beings, is the most brilliant of them. Through the visible Son, the Father manifests his nature[42] to angels and to men in so far as they can comprehend it. To the angels also God has imparted something of his radiance, his divinity; they are "Cloth'd with transcendent brightness" (I, 86), each according to his rank in the hierarchy. In a smaller degree, man participates in the divine nature. He is not perceptibly a luminous creature, but he is capable of becoming so. If he perseveres in love and obedience, he will rise on the scale of being and acquire an angelic purity and brightness.

The intensity of light in God's cosmos varies with the distance from the Holy Mount. Heaven is brilliantly luminous. The world is lighted, less intensely, by the sun, moon, and stars. Hell, which is very "far remov'd from God and light of Heav'n," is in "utter darkness" (I, 72-73). *Utter* here means both "outer" (the "outer darkness" of Matthew xxii, 13) and "absolute." The darkness of Hell is due to God's absence and additionally to the alienation from God of those who dwell there. This is an evil darkness. The element of fire is abundantly present in Hell, but the fire of Hell is "Black fire" (II, 67) which throws out "darkness visible" (I, 63). In Milton's cosmos fire does not always give light; heat and dryness are its only inherent qualities.

In the argument of Book I, Milton describes Chaos as *"a place of utter* [absolute] *darkness. "* But in the proem of Book III, Chaos becomes "middle darkness," whereas Hell is "utter" darkness (III, 16). There is a difference between Hell and Chaos. The darkness of Chaos is no evidence of evil. It is simply the absence of God's beneficent influence, of his exerted power. The "dark and crude" materials of Chaos await the creating hand. The Creation is a burst of light; an expression of God's wisdom, creative power, and love; an imparting of order, purpose, and life to raw matter; an infusion of divinity.

In the proem of Book III Milton expresses both his love of light and his sense of loss. Because the holy light of God no longer penetrates his eyes and because wisdom is "at one entrance quite shut out," he prays that a "Celestial light" may "Shine inward" and irradiate his "mind through all her powers" (III, 50-53).[43] This metaphoric use of light suggests that there is another way than through the senses for God's influence to reach men. Yet the poet misses grievously the visual enjoyment of the returning seasons, and of

Day, or the sweet approach of Ev'n or Morn,
Or sight of vernal bloom, or Summer's Rose,
Or flocks, or herds, or human face divine. (III, 42-44)

The "ever-during dark" which surrounds him is very hard to endure.

IX

The vertical dimension of Milton's cosmos is not merely physical; it is also a scale of moral worth.[44] The higher a creature stands, the nearer to God he is. Luminousness is approximately proportional to height and to goodness: Hell is absolutely dark; the world is moderately lighted; Heaven is intensely radiant; God, shrouded on his Holy Mount, is light itself. Rarity, or purity, of substance is also equated with moral excellence. The fallen angels are altogether gross; they have degenerated from a much purer state. Man's body is somewhat gross, but his spirit is a very tenuous substance. Angels consist altogether of subtle spiritual substance. The Son of God and the Holy Spirit are presumably the purest of all material beings. Goodness, then, is the same thing as height-on-the-scale, as luminosity, and as tenuity. Evil is spatial lowness, darkness, grossness. These identifications are logical consequences of Milton's materialism.

They are genuinely identifications. To say that height, or light, or purity of substance *symbolizes* excellence is subtly to misrepresent. Height *is* nobility. Both for rarity of substance and for moral worth Milton uses the word *purity*. Light is not a symbol; it is a quality identical with merit.

Anyone inclined to examine details can find flaws in this scheme of physical-moral gradations. The poem is not consistent with experience and not wholly consistent within itself. Yet unquestionably the poet has, on the whole, succeeded in his attempt to give meaning to substance, position, and luminosity. His cosmos is one of heights and depths, splendors and shadows, which are at the same time physical and moral. The lights and darks are especially striking. The great stage of the narrative—its upper region gloriously radiant, its lower parts totally dark—presents a moral idealism through the medium of an intense chiaroscuro. The blind poet values light as much as righteousness. The two qualities in his mind are the same.

Chapter VIII. SPACE, MATTER, AND TIME

THE COSMIC SETTING of *Paradise Lost* is so vast that the imagination barely succeeds in conceiving it. This is really as much as one can say about its dimensions.

Milton's cosmos, however, has a definite upper limit: the summit of the Holy Mount, upon which God sits in his dazzling splendor "High Thron'd above all highth" (III, 58). There is nothing above the throne of the Eternal Deity, not even any space. The pitch-black floor of Hell is logically the lowest possible point, for one would suppose that God, in banishing the sinful angels from his presence, would drive them as far from him as was spatially possible. Yet Milton twice speaks of Chaos as the "nethermost Abyss" (II, 956, 969), implying that Chaos extends even below Hell. Indeed, though he once refers to the "bottom" of Chaos (VII, 213), he suggests more than once that Chaos (and therefore space) has no lower or lateral limits. It is a "dark unbottom'd infinite Abyss" (II, 405), an "unfounded deep" (II, 829), an "Illimitable Ocean without bound" (II, 892), a "void and formless infinite" (III, 12), "vast infinitude" (III, 711).

God the Father declares that "the Deep" is "Boundless . . . because I am who fill / Infinitude, nor vacuous the space" (VII, 168-69). In its very puzzling context, "Boundless" is apparently not merely a careless superlative. God seems to be saying that he and Chaos are infinitely co-extensive. An infinitude of chaotic matter which has an upper boundary but which extends endlessly downward and outward is a curiously bottom-heavy infinitude. We shall have to assume—with no warrant except the reasonableness of the assumption—that God is referring to potential matter, not to actual Chaos, and that Chaos and space are limited.[1]

God himself is, without question, unlimited, "immensus et infinitus."[2] To say of God that he is *immensus* (not measurable) might mean that he cannot be characterized in any terms which imply extension or occupation of space. This is true of the God of Dante's *Paradiso*. But Milton's God is immeasurable in that he is endlessly extensive; he "fills" infinitude.

Within the limitless extension of God is space, most of it occupied by Chaos. I shall arbitrarily adopt the Aristotelian concept of space, which Milton certainly regarded with respect and probably considered valid. According to Aristotle *(De Caelo,* 279a), space is that within which the presence of a concrete something is possible. It is logical to add: that within which measurement is possible, within which distance and direction exist. If this concept is assumed, space came into existence with matter. No measurement is possible without something to measure. No distance or direction is possible unless there are at least two things to stand in a spatial relation to each other. Matter cannot exist without space, and there is no space without matter.

The reader of *Paradise Lost* need not trouble himself about the bounds or possible boundlessness of Chaos and space. He may think of Chaos as an indefinitely bounded volume of space, incredibly vast, and of total space as the tremendous vertical stretch between the Holy Mount and the floor of Hell. Whatever lies beyond the stage of the poem is unknown to men and angels.

II

The area of Chaos is filled with a material substance, also called Chaos, which seethes uproariously in darkness and confusion. This is primeval matter. But matter once existed in a state even further from concreteness and form. As regards the origin of matter, there are statements in the prose works which sharpen the vagueness of *Paradise Lost.* In the chapter on the Creation in the *Christian Doctrine,* Milton laboriously but "satisfactorily" proves, "under the guidance of Scripture, that God did not produce everything out of nothing," as most theologians have held, "but of himself."[3] Matter is "an efflux of the Deity."[4] In the *Logic,* Milton distinguishes three states of matter: primary matter, remote secondary matter, and proximate secondary matter.[5] The world in which we live consists of proximate secondary matter; remote secondary matter is the matter of Chaos, primeval matter; primary matter is matter as it existed in God before he willed the emanation. Within "the infinite extension of God there existed a passive principle of incorporeal matter," invisible and intangible.[6] Our vocabularly seems to have no more definite a word than "principle" for such an amorphous idea. This is the *materia prima,* the "one first matter" of which Raphael tells Adam (V, 472). The "original matter," says Milton, was not "an evil or trivial thing, but [was] intrinsically good, and the chief productive stock of every subsequent good."[7]

Is God himself material? Evidently he is so in that he contains a material potential. The "material cause" of all things "must be either God, or nothing"; "Nor did St. Paul hesitate to attribute to God something corporeal; Col. ii, 9. 'in him dwelleth all the fulness of the Godhead bodily.' "[8] But materiality is by no means God's only attribute. It is more accurate to say that God includes materiality than that he is material.

Can God have potentialities?[9] Potentiality is contradictory to God's attribute of immutability. Yet the efflux of matter is the realization of a potentiality and a demonstration of mutability. The belief that all things have proceeded from or have been created by an immutable God is paradoxical. Paradox seems to be not wholly avoidable in a theistic religion.

As God willed the emanation of matter from himself, he endowed it with the qualities which are active in Chaos: heat, cold, moisture, and dryness. Or perhaps he endowed it with the semi-forms, or the swiftly transient forms, of the elemental atoms. Matter is now visible, tangible, audible.

The Almighty leaves chaotic matter in its turmoil. He has, paradoxically, withdrawn from a part of his infinite and omnipresent self in the sense that in this part he does not exercise his benevolent power:

> I uncircumscrib'd myself retire,
> And put not forth my goodness, which is free
> To act or not.

He has chosen to be inactive in Chaos; he has left this part of his omnipresence to the government of "Necessity and Chance" (VII, 170-73). Within primitive matter, there is no order, no reasonableness, no light. The Creation is a putting forth of God's goodness.[10]

By willing the emanation of matter and endowing it with the qualities which it has in Chaos, the Almighty has taken the first step toward the realization of a divine idea: the engendering of existences other than himself (and yet not other than himself). Matter is not yet anything, but it is ready to become something. Although it is dark and disordered, it is "intrinsically good" in that it has come from God; it is morally neutral in that it yet has no definable nature. It awaits the creative actions of the Son of God and the assisting Holy Spirit.

The various processes of the Creation (quite distinct from the emergence of matter from God) have been reviewed earlier. The most crucial of these was the penetration of matter by a quickening infusion: "the Spirit of God," says Genesis, "moved upon the face of the waters." The Spirit,[11] accordingly, is active in the Creation as Raphael describes it, infusing matter with a power, a "vital virtue ... and vital warmth" (VII, 236). The *Christian Doctrine* twice refers to the "power of matter."[12] This evidently means the ability to assume those forms which God has willed. Uriel seems to be referring to this power when he says that the quintessence "Flew upward, spirited with various forms" (III, 717).[13]

Matter now receives "embellishment from the accession of forms, which are themselves material."[14] Stimulated by "vital warmth," successive forms become actual, the simpler becoming the material of the more complex and nobler. The first actualized forms evidently were the atoms of the various elements. The last form actualized during the Six Days was man. Nowhere does Milton draw a clear distinction between God's ways of producing inanimate things and of creating animate beings. The "propagation and production of the human form [the soul, the complete man] were analogous to those of other forms, and were the proper effect of that power which had been communicated to matter by the Deity."[15] The story of God's forming man of the dust of the ground is an accommodated truth.

Coincidentally with the miracle of Creation, the Son imposes the law and harmony of nature upon the matter which he has illuminated, ordered, and formed. All inanimate things, all plants, all beasts must obey the law of nature. But the creation of the world, like the creation of Heaven, has produced creatures who are free. Men may disobey God and nature. In man matter and form, although they have "proceeded from God," are in the "power of another party" than God and are subject to "taint and contamination."[16] Only sin may disrupt the orderly and benevolent scheme of things. "If not deprav'd from good," all things will return to the "one Almighty" from whom they have come (V, 469-71).

Heaven and the angels, like the world and man, were created by the Son from the primeval matter of Chaos. This evidently took place aeons before the creation of the world. Hell was created from Chaos shortly before the world.

III

Space is the medium of motion. Matter is that which moves or is moved. Time[17] is "the measure of motion,"[18] that is, of change of any kind. Raphael explains to Adam that

> Time, though in Eternity, appli'd
> To motion, measures all things durable
> By present, past, and future.   (V, 580-82)

All things in God's cosmos are "durable"—that is, they have duration—and are subject to change. Every man and angel lives in a present, remembers a past, and expects a future. All exist in time. Time is *in* eternity.

What is eternity? Most Christian theologians have accepted the meaning given the word by Boethius and before him by St. Augustine. The expression "God is ever," says Boethius, "denotes a single Present, summing up His continual presence in all the past, in all the present—however that term may be used—and in all the future.... He is ever, because 'ever' is with Him a term of present time.... God's present ... [is] eternity."[19] God does not experience duration. His knowledge of things past is not memory; his knowledge of things to come is not foreknowledge. All things are simultaneously present to him.

Milton seems to have rejected this idea of eternity or to have grasped it imperfectly. He uses the adjective *eternal* very frequently. In most cases he obviously means "everlasting," "enduring forever" (the most common usage); sometimes he means no more than "continuous" ("Led on th'Eternal Spring," *PL*, IV, 268). In the *Christian Doctrine* he writes that "nothing is eternal, strictly speaking, but what has neither beginning nor end."[20] In the *Logic* he says that "to God everlastingness or eternity, not time, is generally attributed, but what properly is everlastingness except eternal duration."[21] I have found no instance in his works in which *eternal* clearly means "timeless," "not subject to duration." In at least one passage of *Paradise Lost*, he seems to approach the concept of God's eternal present: "from his prospect high," God beholds "past, present, future" at one view (III, 77-78). In the next line, however, he speaks of God's "foreseeing." Milton conceives of the Eternal God as a being whose existence reaches limitlessly back into the past and will extend limitlessly into the future, a being who is temporally unlimited just as he is spatially unbounded.

Milton nevertheless distinguishes between eternity and time. Time is that minute segment of eternity in which there is motion, change. He distinguishes also between God's mode of existence and the mode of existence of the active and mutable creatures of his material cosmos. Among God's attributes are immutability and quiescence; he is in a state of "holy Rest / Through all Eternity" (*PL*, VII, 91-92).

Time had a beginning and will have an end. The beginnings of both time and space correspond logically with the effluence of matter from God, when "things durable" first came into being.[22] In the absence of matter there could be nothing which could be located, no distance, no directions; therefore no space. There could be no motion, no change; therefore no time. Matter, space, and time came into being simultaneously. After the purposes for which God willed this cosmos have been fulfilled, there will come "the World's great period" (XII, 467). Time will end in the world and in Heaven; evidently matter, in the form in which we know it, will cease to be; and space will cease to have meaning.

IV

In the beginning, God generated or emitted from himself a space-time-matter cosmos, which at first consisted altogether of semi-matter. From this, in a sense, he withdrew. Within it he might choose to put forth his power or choose not to. He has chosen to do so on at least three notable occasions, the creation of Heaven and the angels, the creation of Hell, and the creation of the world and man.

To create is to perform an action. An infinite, immutable, and quiescent being, although he may be characterized as pure act (i.e., a being without potentiality), does not act, is not capable of local exertion. God must, therefore, engender an agent to carry out his will in the temporal and spatial cosmos. This agent is God the Son, the Word, the Logos. "In the beginning was the Word," says St. John, and Milton paraphrases him: "the Son existed in the beginning, under the name of logos or word."[23] The Son, he believes, is a creature and was the first of all creatures; and to support this belief, he quotes several texts, including: "the first born of every creature" (Colossians i, 15) and "the beginning of the creation of God" (Revelation iii, 14).[24] The begetting of the Son logically would be simultaneous with the flowing forth of matter and God's withdrawal.

Since the Son is himself the Creator, his coming-into-being could not be like that of other existences. Milton prefers the noun *generatio* and the verbs *gigno* and *genero* (instead of *creatio* and *creo*) in referring to the engendering of the Son.[25] Yet *generation*, like *creation*, seems to be an act, an exercise of *"external efficiency,"*[26] and therefore to be contrary to the nature of the Eternal God. Possibly Milton distinguishes causation by will from production by action.

It has been repeatedly suggested, first by David Masson[27] in the last century, that Milton's trinitarian doctrine distinguishes different stages in the existence of the Second Person. One version of this theory traces Milton's ideas to early Neoplatonists and to certain pre-Nicene Fathers who had developed a modified, Christian Neoplatonism: The Logos is the word, the wisdom, the thought of God, corresponding to the *mind (nous)* of the Neoplatonists. The Logos, the first stage of existence, is intrinsic in God and is eternal. Responding to the will of the Father, the Logos externalizes himself and becomes a separate entity, the Son.[28] The Father's exaltation, or "begetting," of the Son in *Paradise Lost* (V, 600-15) is the externalization of the Logos. This theory at least explains the somewhat astonishing fact that, up to the time of the exaltation, the angels have apparently been unconscious of the Son's existence although he has existed for many ages.

It is quite possible that Milton believes that the Son has had different stages of existence. He has read authors in whom he would have found this doctrine. But if this is his belief, he is remarkably reluctant to say so. What he says concerning the origin of the Son in the *Christian Doctrine* shows a humble awareness of his human limitations: God, he says, "imparted to the Son as much as he pleased of the divine nature, nay of the divine substance itself.... This is the whole that is revealed concerning the generation of the Son of God." He is scornful of theologians who, wishing to know more of this subject than men can know, become "entangled in the deceit-

fulness of vain philosophy, or rather of sophistry, and involved in darkness."[29] He never explicitly distinguishes between *Logos* and *Son.* It is true
that in the *Christian Doctrine* he writes that God is said "to have begotten
the Son in a double sense, the one literal, with reference to the production
of the Son, the other metaphorical, with reference to his exaltation." The
context indicates, however, that this metaphorical begetting was the Son's
"resuscitation from the dead" or "his unction to the mediatorial office."[30]
The passage refers neither to externalization of the Logos nor to the Son's
elevation to the regency of Heaven. The exaltation of Book V of *Paradise
Lost* is best explained, I think, as an episode which the poet has developed
from Psalms ii, 6-7, to supply an immediate and dramatic motivation for
Satan's rebellion (see Chap. II, sec. v).

Milton has found no clear revelations in the Bible concerning how the
Son came to be. But he has read that the Son "is the image of the invisible
God ... by him were all things created, that are in heaven, and that are in
earth, visible and invisible ... all things were created by him, and for him"
(Colossians i, 15-16); God has "spoken unto us by his Son, whom he hath
appointed heir of all things, by whom also he made the worlds ... the
brightness of his glory, and the express image of his person" (Hebrews i,
2-3). The *Christian Doctrine* echoes Scripture: the Son is "the brightness of
[the Father's] glory, and the express image of his person"; by the Son "all
other things were made both in heaven and earth."[31]

The Son is God in time and space. He "was begotten of the Father ...
within the limits of time"[32] ("in tempore genuit Deus Filium"). He is
everlasting, not eternal, for he had a beginning. He has a "visible"[32] material
body; he is capable of motion. He is "the image ... by which we see God,
[and] the word by which we hear him ... whom no one can see or hear,"[33]
the sensible manifestation of the Father to angels and men:

> Divine Similitude,
> In whose conspicuous count'nance without cloud
> Made visible, th'Almighty Father shines,
> Whom else no Creature can behold.   (III, 384-87)

He is the agent through whom the Father gives effect to his will in time
and space, the Father's "word ... wisdom, and effectual might" (III, 170),
"Heir of all [the Father's] might" (V, 720), a "high collateral glory" (X, 86),
a "Second Omnipotence" in that, as the Father says, he performs concretely "what by Decree I do" (VI, 683-84). Performing the will of the
Father, he has created the "Heav'n of Heavens" (III, 390), the angels,
presumably also Hell; and in *Paradise Lost* we see the Son, "th'Omnific
Word" (VII, 217), ride forth at the Father's command to create the world—
to actualize the Father's "great Idea."

The Son is also Christ, "the anointed," the ruler over God's temporal realm, "Viceregent Son" (X, 56). He was so appointed on the occasion of the exaltation: "to him shall bow / All knees in Heav'n, and shall confess him Lord" (V, 607-08). He is soon called upon to exercise the powers of regency, for the exaltation provokes the rebellion of Satan and his legions. It is the Son who defeats and punishes the rebels: by him God "threw down / Th'aspiring Dominations" (III, 391-92). After the Fall of man, the Son pronounces sentence on Adam and Eve. In time to come he will sit in judgment on all men (III, 330-32).

Through the Son, furthermore, the Father expresses his love and extends his mercy:

> in him all his Father shone
> Substantially express'd, and in his face
> Divine compassion visibly appear'd,
> Love without end, and without measure Grace.
>
> (III, 139-42)

As Jesus he becomes incarnate—assumes human flesh—to take upon himself the penalty of man's disobedience, and he dies an extremely painful death to redeem humanity. In his self-immolation, he shows his abounding love and goodness; he is found Son of God "By Merit more than Birthright" (III, 309). After the Ascension,

> thy Humiliation shall exalt
> With thee thy Manhood also to this Throne;
> Here shalt thou sit incarnate, here shalt Reign
> Both God and Man, Son both of God and Man,
> Anointed universal King.   (III, 313-17)

The Incarnation does not degrade the Son; instead it ennobles man.

In *Paradise Lost* the poet does not always keep the natures of Father and Son distinguished. The Father speaks "audibly" to the Son (VII, 518). God the Son tells Adam that he has been "alone / From all Eternity" (VIII, 405-06). A possible explanation for this reversal of characters is that Father and Son "speak and act with unanimity."[34] A better explanation is that Milton did not write the poem to stand such close examination as some of us give it.

God the Son is a person numerically distinct from the Father. Although he speaks and acts as the Father wills, he is free. He may obey or disobey. He may choose to die for man or choose not to; he offers "Freely" to "put off" his heavenly glory to become a man (III, 240). The "Merit" which exalts him above all of God's other creatures consists in the perfection of his loving obedience, manifested most clearly in his self-sacrifice for the redemption of man.

He is the only creature (except possibly the Holy Spirit) who can endure the Father's full glory. When the Father directed the Son to go forth to battle with the rebel host, he infused divine power into him by shining on him "with Rays direct," and the Son then

> all his Father full exprest
> Ineffably into his face receiv'd.   (VI, 719-21)

Just before the Son's descent to judge Adam and Eve in the Garden, the Father

> on the Son
> Blaz'd forth unclouded Deity; he full
> Resplendent all his Father manifest
> Express'd.   (X, 64-67)

That the Son can see God seems to mean that he can know God as he is. The angels, who cannot behold the unshrouded Deity, see the Father's glory and goodness reflected in the Son, the "radiant image" of the Father (III, 63).

The Son is the most exalted of all God's creatures, but still he is a *creature.* He is not, like the Father, omnipresent, or omniscient, or omnipotent.[35] His powers and his knowledge are endowments from the Father. He is not co-essential with the Father, and he is not eternal. Most Christians of most periods of history would regard this conception of the Son as heresy. Orthodox belief concerning the Trinity is identified with the decisions of the Council of Nicaea (A.D. 325). This council declared that the Son was *"begotten not made, of one substance* [essence] *with the Father";* it condemned the assertions of the heresiarch Arius: that there was a time when the Son " 'was not'; saying also that the Son of God, in virtue of his free-will, is capable of evil and good, and calling him a creature and a work. All these utterances the holy Synod anathematized."[36] So Milton is an *Arian,* or perhaps more precisely, a *subordinationist.*[37] It is my impression that *Paradise Lost* gives the Son a greater degree of power and glory than one would expect from a reading of the *Christian Doctrine.* Yet if one looks for it, one can find evidence in *Paradise Lost* that the author is a subordinationist-Arian:[38] the Son was "of all Creation first"; he is the "Divine Similitude" (III, 383-84).

Discussion of Milton's heterodoxy, or of the degree of it, is of little value to the reader of *Paradise Lost,* although the subject has been much debated. The trinitarian heresy is very inobtrusive in the poem. In the *Christian Doctrine,* on the other hand, Milton states his unorthodox beliefs clearly and bluntly. Until the publication of the *Christian Doctrine* in 1825, no one seems to have noticed the Arianism in *Paradise Lost,* yet the poem had been widely read by pious Christians for one hundred and fifty years. It is quite sufficient for the reader to understand that the Son in *Paradise Lost* is manifestation, creator, governor, judge, redeemer. These offices are attributed to him by the most orthodox and are firmly based on Biblical authority. Milton does not display his heterodoxy in his Christian epic. This is a poem for all Christians—at least for all Protestants.

Belief in the co-essentiality of Father and Son would not have prevented Milton from presenting an anthropomorphic Son. It had not prevented other Christian writers from doing so. Yet because of his conception of the Son as a finite and material creature, he attributes to him a degree of concretenesss and immediacy which more orthodox thinking might have discouraged. The Son of *Paradise Lost* is a person who moves and acts, who is visible and audible, who is moved by pity and love, who has freedom of will. Milton conveys the feeling of his physical proximity in the Garden of Eden. On the first day of Adam's life, God appears to him "among the Trees ... Presence Divine" (VIII, 313-14). In the judgment scene he is "the sovran Presence" (X, 144), who approaches, again through the trees, calling to Adam aloud. He is "the mild Judge and Intercessor both" (X, 96), unyieldingly just yet compassionate. Milton wisely declines to describe his visible glory, but relying on Scripture, he gives his audible words.

The substance of the Son is a spiritual matter, brilliantly luminous. In the future he will assume the gross flesh of humankind in order that he may die as a man dies; and thus, as Jesus, he will redeem the sin of Adam.

V

Milton finds the third member of the Trinity a difficult subject, for as he says in the *Christian Doctrine*, Scripture reveals very little about the Holy Spirit, although it uses the word *spirit* many times and in many senses.[39] He seems a little irritated at having to deal with the matter. The text on which belief in the Spirit is principally based (I John v, 7) is "in the opinion of many ... suspicious [corrupt?]; and yet it is on the authority of this text, almost exclusively, that the whole doctrine of the Trinity has been hastily adopted."[40] The *Christian Doctrine* nevertheless includes a somewhat perplexed and uncertain discussion of the Holy Spirit, based on New Testament texts. The Spirit, says Milton, "is a minister of God, and therefore a creature ... created or produced of the substance of God ... probably before the foundations of the world were laid, but later than the Son, and far inferior to him."[40] The fact that the Father "promised that he would put his Spirit" upon the Son[41] indicates that the Spirit is an emanation from the Father, not a creation of the Son, but Milton declines to say how he originated. He asserts, at any rate, that the Spirit is a "creature"; this seems to mean a limited temporal-spatial-material being. He is "a minister of God," the agent by whom God enters the hearts of men to inspire, direct, enlighten, comfort, and sanctify. He is God's immediate influence upon—or within—the truly faithful. Unlike the Son, he has never been visible to men. He seems to have been active only since the advent of the Son; he is the gift of the Son to those who believe. During the baptism of Jesus, the Spirit appeared "under the appropriate image of a dove." The "symbol" of the personal Holy Spirit is the dove.[42] Because the Spirit is a gift which one implores of God, he cannot himself be "an object of invocation."[43]

According to the *Christian Doctrine*, the Old Testament never refers to the personal Spirit. The spirit which moved upon the waters during the Creation was God's "divine power, rather than any person";[44] that is, it was the power with which God endowed the creating Son, or was the Son himself.

What *Paradise Lost* says of the Holy Spirit, however, does not altogether agree with what one reads in the *Christian Doctrine*. In his prophecy of the future, Michael refers twice to the Spirit. He assures Adam that Christ will send "a Comforter" to his persecuted followers of the future:

> The promise of the Father, who shall dwell
> His Spirit within them, and the Law of Faith
> Working through love, upon thir hearts shall write.
> (XII, 486-89)

This is the Holy Spirit as conceived in the *Christian Doctrine*, the Spirit who is God-in-the-hearts-of-men. Scripture, says Michael, again speaking of the future Christian era, will be understood only through the aid of "the Spirit" (XII, 514). In the invocation at the opening of the epic, the poet himself addresses the "Dove-like" Spirit who prefers "Before all Temples th'upright heart and pure" (I, 21, 18), praying for instruction and illumination.[45] Milton has said in the *Christian Doctrine* that the personal Spirit may not be invoked. Both the function of private inspiration and the symbolic dove-form, however, show that he is here invoking the Third Person of the Trinity. Furthermore, he identifies this Spirit from whom he is seeking support and inner enlightenment with the Spirit that moved upon the waters and took part in the Creation:

> Thou from the first
> Wast present, and with mighty wings outspread
> Dove-like satst brooding on the vast Abyss
> And mad'st it pregnant.　　(I, 19-22)

In Book VII, as the Son rides forth into Chaos to create the world, the Father sends with him "My overshadowing Spirit and might" (VII, 165). Spreading "His brooding wings" over the "fluid Mass" of Chaos, the Spirit impregnates it with life, with "vital virtue ... and vital warmth" (VII, 235-37). The "brooding wings" once more suggest the dove-symbol. In the Nicene Creed the Spirit is called "the Lord and the Life-giver."[46]

In *Paradise Lost* the personal Holy Spirit has two not obviously related roles: He is God's enlightener and comforter in men's hearts, and he is God's quickening and hatching power, an auxilliary agent who assists the Son in creation. Milton has fused two concepts here which he keeps separate in the *Christian Doctrine.* In general Milton's thinking on this perplexing subject is cloudy and uncertain. But he makes it clear at least that, like the Son, the Spirit is an instrument through whom the Eternal God operates in time and space and that both are creatures of and in God's material universe.

Milton avows his dependence on the Holy Spirit in the preamble to the *Christian Doctrine,* in the initial invocation of *Paradise Lost,* and in the opening lines of *Paradise Regained.*

VI

The chronological beginning of the story of *Paradise Lost* is Raphael's narrative of the celestial rebellion in Books V and VI.[47] The earliest event recorded in the poem is God's exaltation of the Son. This occurred at an assembly of all the angels "on such day / As Heav'n's great Year brings forth" (V, 582-83), apparently an annual occasion. *Great Year* sometimes is used to mean the period of the precession of the equinoxes (25,800 years) and sometimes to mean the Platonic Year (49,000 years). Milton probably means simply an enormously long recurrent period, in comparison with which a year of earthly time seems momentary. One feels in reading these lines that the angels who answer God's call have done so many times before, that they have existed through many, many celestial years—incalculable aeons of bliss, which have been uneventful except for "Grateful vicissitude."

With the exaltation of the Son, however, things begin to happen. During the night which follows the Father's significant announcement, Sin is born (II, 749-58) and Lucifer plots rebellion with his subordinate seraphim. The battle of the angels begins on the following day and for two days continues inconclusively. On the third day the Son of God, single-handed, defeats the rebels disastrously and drives them from Heaven. They fall nine days through Chaos to Hell (VI, 871), which supposedly has been newly created to receive them.[48] Raphael's chronology seems as definite as one could ask of a historian. But how long is a heavenly day? No man knows. It must be incomparably longer than an earthly day. Were the nine days of the apostates' fall through Chaos angel-days or man-days?

After the apostate angels have lain "confounded" on the burning lake of Hell "Nine times the Space that measures Day and Night / To mortal men" (I, 50-51), the represented action of the poem begins as Satan rouses himself from his burning couch, flies to shore with Beelzebub, and assembles his host on the burning land. Shortly thereafter certain fallen angels build Pandaemonium, and the chieftains of the infernal army hold a council therein. These events evidently occupy little time (Pandaemonium "Rose like an Exhalation," I, 711), but we are not told how much. Satan now struggles upward through Chaos, finds God's newly created world, and penetrates it. The time which he spends on his journey is not specified.

Except for the fact that the rebels' stupefaction lasts for nine earth-days, one learns nothing which is at all definite about the duration of the events which precede Satan's arrival on the earth. The poet cannot be precise, for he is dealing with supra-human events in regions beyond man's comprehension. He gives the impression, however, that, in terms of angel-time, the celestial rebellion occurred rather shortly before the temptation of man. At some unspecified time during the vague period following the rebels' expulsion from Heaven, God created the world and man.

When Satan reaches the earth, the time-schedule immediately becomes quite definite; and because the setting is terrestrial, "hour" and "day" have a definite and familiar meaning for us. Satan alights on Mount Niphates at noon (IV, 29-30)[49] and soon afterward enters Paradise. During the night which follows (the night before Raphael's visit), he is discovered at Eve's ear by the angelic guardians. They drive him from the Garden at dawn (IV, 1015). He then hides from them for seven days and nights, dodging around the earth to stay on the dark side of it. He returns on the eighth night (IX, 62-69). He inveigles Eve into eating the fruit at noon on the next day, just nine days from his arrival. The judgment in the Garden occurs on the evening of the day of the Fall, and Adam and Eve are expelled from Paradise on the following day. The action which takes place in the Garden occupies ten days.

How long have Adam and Eve been alive when the reader first sees them? Milton is indefinite, but he gives the impression that they have lived in Paradise for some time, certainly for weeks, perhaps for months.[50] They have become quite accustomed to each other and to their environment. They have made a home and have established a daily routine of labor and worship. They offer prayers "each Morning" in "various style" (V, 145-46). God has made several visits (IX, 1080-82; X, 103-04, 119; XI, 317-22). Adam refers to the angelic singing which they have "often" heard at night in the Garden (IV, 680-82). Eve speaks of her storing of such foods as gain "firmness" by drying (V, 324-25). Eve has grown a flower garden (XI, 273-79).

A recurrent idea in early Christian literature is that "Adam 'stayed not one night in Paradise,' that he was 'formed and deformed' in one day. By analogy with the passion of Christ, many of the fathers held that man was created in the first hour, put in Paradise in the third, ate the fruit in the sixth, and was judged and ejected from Paradise in the ninth."[51] Milton allows our first parents a much longer period of happiness than this, but he declines to give a figure. However long the Age of Innocence may have been, it was tragically brief.

The story does not end with the Expulsion. Michael's revelations to Adam in Books XI and XII extend it far into the future. This long prophetic narrative deals at some length with events recorded in Genesis (with Michael making appropriate moral comment), hurries through the rest of Old Testament history, predicts and explains the Incarnation and the Redemption, sketchily reviews the history of the Christian Church, and closes with an account of the end of the world. Michael's review of human events has stretched from the Fall to the end of time,[52] when God's purposes will have been fulfilled. Many readers have found the final books of *Paradise Lost* less interesting and moving than those which precede. There is nevertheless good reason for the two historical books: they give the narrative a temporal sweep corresponding with the grand dimensions of the setting.

To deal with his subject—the condition of man and the reasons for it—Milton must review the whole history of God's universe. The time-span of his story is all time. Through the use of flashbacks and of prophecy, he takes us back toward the beginning—as far back as human knowledge may go—and forward to the final consummation. These interpolations constitute nearly half of the poem. There is an intense focus, however, on the events in Paradise which determined the course of human history. These occupy an inexpressibly small fraction of the entire temporal stretch. Just as the time-span is all knowable time, so the setting is all knowable space. Just as the temporal focus is on an eye-blink of time, so the spatial focus is on the minute area, Paradise, where the tragic determination of human destiny occurred. Pivoting on these miniscule points, the story moves temporally backward and forward through the ages and spatially through Hell, Chaos, and Heaven.

The time of the action in Paradise is ten days. Although every reader is conscious of its brevity, none would know just how long the action lasts without consciously making the effort to pick out the temporal clues. In his absorption in the poet's grand vision, the reader is scarcely conscious of the passage of time in Eden. There is a timeless, static quality about *Paradise Lost*. And because past and future are introduced by narrative interpolations, there is a side-by-sideness of events rather than a beforeness-and-afterness. The reader has the God-like privilege, as Isabel MacCaffrey says,[53] of seeing all time at one view.

VII

Milton's conception of history was "linear" rather than "cyclic." He believed that human events reveal a progression toward fulfillment of the divine purposes. In spite of the pessimism of his later years, he retained the "providential" view of history which the Renaissance had learned from early Christian writers and from the Old Testament prophets. As "the Chain of Being upheld a vertical unity in the universe, so the world history affirmed a horizontal unity throughout history, from its inception upon the act of creation to its termination upon the Last Judgment." "For Milton, as for his great predecessors, human events constituted a record of God's constant intervention in the affairs of the world."[54] In 1641 the "providential purpose" seemed to Milton "on the point of fulfillment." But in his later years "he no longer had the confidence that he could see" the unfolding of the divine plan. "He never lost his faith in the eternal principles which gave ultimate meaning to history—Truth, Justice, Righteousness." Yet in human history he saw "no general advance toward a discernible goal." The senseless and malignant conflicts of pride and passion would continue "until the final decisive act of judgment should destroy time and history with it."[55] Something of Milton's disillusionment seems to have crept into *Paradise Lost*. After reviewing some of the future results of human ambition, greed, and stupidity, Michael comments:

> so shall the World go on,
> To good malignant, to bad men benign,
> Under her own weight groaning.   (XII, 537-39)

The brighter future must have seemed to Milton very distant indeed.

VIII

The sorry spectacle of human history will ultimately end, and at the end God will gather to him the righteous and reject the wicked. In four principal passages of *Paradise Lost*[56] Milton describes the final events. In an hour which no man can predict, the Son of God, still in his human incarnation, will appear in the sky "attended gloriously" (III, 323). A great fire will now envelop the world and will "purge all things new" (XI, 900; see II Peter iii). The angels attending the Second Coming will proclaim the "dread Tribunal," and the living and the dead will be summoned to judgment before the Son of God (III, 324-32). The dead will be reconstituted, body, spirit, and soul, the various material particles of the former self brought once more together from their wide dispersal;[57] and the whole man will stand before the judgment seat. Those alive at the time of the Second Coming will undergo "a sudden change."[58] "For this corruptible must put on incorruption, and this mortal must put on immortality" (I Corinthians xv, 53). The "faithful" will be received "into bliss" (XII, 462) purified and glorified. Wicked men will be condemned to "The fourth and last degree of death ... *death eternal.*"[59] After the Last Judgment, the Son will lay down his "regal Sceptre" (III, 339), for there will no longer be need of government or judgment.

From the ashes of the great conflagration which is to destroy the world there will spring

> New Heav'n and Earth, wherein the just shall dwell
> And after all thir tribulations long
> See golden days, fruitful of golden deeds,
> With Joy and Love triumphing, and fair Truth.   (III, 335-38)

The world, now cleansed of the corruption and evil arising from Adam's sin, "Shall all be Paradise," and the blessed apparently will be allowed to enjoy their bliss either "in Heav'n or Earth" (XII, 463-64; cf. V, 500).

The eschatology of *Paradise Lost* is very clearly based on the New Testament.[60] In fact, what the poem says on the subject is a succinct and relatively complete review of scriptural revelations concerning last things. Milton, however, seems to omit the Millenium[61] predicted in Revelation xx, the thousand golden years intervening between the Second Coming and the Judgment, when Christ and his saints will reign on earth. In the *Christian Doctrine* he affirms that "The second advent of Christ will be followed by the resurrection of the dead and the last judgment"[62] and solves the problem of the thousand years intervening between the Coming and the ultimate fire by supposing that the "day" (i.e. period) of judgment will be coincident with "that glorious reign of Christ on earth with his saints."[63] The Apocalypse is hard to accept without interpretive modification.

By the final conflagration and the Last Judgment the Son will complete the cleansing of his Father's material cosmos. Already the sinful angels will have been consigned to Hell, whose substance is evil. At the Judgment sinful men will be sentenced to punishment in Hell. While the elect are glorified, those rejected will become gross and dark like the apostate angels. Since the Fall of man, Sin and Death have roamed the Earth as God's scavengers,

> Hell-hounds, to lick up the draff and filth
> Which man's polluting Sin with taint hath shed
> On what was pure.   (X, 630-32)

After the Judgment the Son will hurl "Both *Sin,* and *Death* ... Through *Chaos*" to

> obstruct the mouth of Hell
> For ever, and seal up his ravenous Jaws.
> Then Heav'n and Earth renew'd shall be made pure
> To sanctity that shall receive no stain.   (X, 635-39)

Hell, "her numbers full," will be finally sealed (III, 332-33). At the end of time, then, all of the evil in God's cosmos will be segregated in a capsule very remote from the throne of God. Yet since God includes all, paradoxically there remains a cyst of evil within God.

Paradise Lost has now

> Measur'd this transient World, the Race of time,
> Till time stand fixt: beyond is all abyss,
> Eternity, whose end no eye can reach.   (XII, 554-56)

What will be the nature of existence for the blessed in eternity? Milton wisely does not try to answer this question. But he says at least, in the *Christian Doctrine,* that what God has created, "after having been governed in divers manners for a few thousand years," will finally "be received into an immutable state within himself, or ... rejected from his presence for all eternity."[64] In the eternal life to come, time will "stand fixt." Neither the angels nor the human elect will lead a temporal life in a spatial environment. How or whether they will retain their physical natures is difficult to say. All change and motion will have ceased. The Son says to the Father that, "in the end," he will gladly resign the "sceptre and Power" which the Father has given him:

> Thou shalt be All in All, and I in thee
> For ever, and in mee all whom thou lov'st.   (VI, 730-33)

The Son, and with him the faithful (who as the Church dwell in him), will somehow be reabsorbed into the Eternal God, from whom they came. Their happiness will consist in union with him. God's infinitude, modified in some fashion by the temporary cosmos, will resume its homogeneity and quietude. Just how God's reassimilation of his creatures can be reconciled with personal immortality—in which Milton certainly believed—is not clear. The end of time is the utmost bound of human thought. It is certain, at least, that, as St. Paul predicts, God will be "all in all" (I Corinthians xv, 28).

IX

One may wonder with Adam

> what cause
> Mov'd the Creator in his holy Rest
> Through all Eternity so late to build
> In *Chaos.* (VII, 90-93)

Certainly God's cosmos is a teleological universe, but what is its purpose? The answer that Milton gives in the *Christian Doctrine* is that *"God the Father produced every thing that exists by his Word and Spirit, that is, by his will, for the manifestation of the glory of his power and goodness."*[65] Among various other texts he quotes Romans xi, 36: "of him, and through him, and to him, are all things: to whom be glory for ever." In *Paradise Lost* the Son says that God has made the world for his "glory," as a manifestation of his "goodness" and "greatness" (III, 164-65).

That God should create simply to demonstrate his power and manifest his glory is not a very good answer. Why should he demonstrate his power? He himself understands its full extent, and no other being could comprehend it. What satisfaction could he get from provoking, by a manifestation of his glory, the admiration of his creatures, who are so far inferior to him? Can God need or enjoy admiration?

Perhaps a desire to exercise his goodness was God's principal motive. Jesus says in *Paradise Regained:*

> his word all things produc'd,
> Though chiefly not for glory as prime end,
> But to show forth his goodness, and impart
> His good communicable to every soul
> Freely; of whom what could he less expect
> Than glory and benediction, that is thanks.
> (III, 122-27)

The purpose of God's creative acts, then, might have been to give being to creatures whom he might love and cherish, and who in return might love, revere, and obey him. So long as there is only God, his goodness and love remain passive, unexerted. Though the divine motivation cannot be fully expressed in human concepts, at least this much of it a man can understand.

If God's love and beneficence are to be just, they must be directed only toward those creatures who in some degree approximate the purity and goodness of God himself. They must be virtuous. So it is necessary that they be endowed with mind and free will, given the opportunity of evil, and

judged as morally responsible beings. For unless one *chooses* good in prefer-
ence to an alternative evil, his virtue is only a blank virtue. He is not
deserving. Because God has endowed angels and men with will, he loses
some of them. Some choose evil and become permanently corrupted. God
cannot justly intervene. At the end of time, these are locked in Hell, where
all evil is segregated, walled off eternally. God did not will evil. Evil was
a contingent and necessary result of the actualization of his great idea. Hell
and its contents are the unavoidable waste.

Two paradoxes remain: the paradox of a God to whom there can be no
addition who yet desires and creates addition; and the paradox of a Deity
perfectly good whose infinite being nevertheless generates and includes
evil.

Chapter *IX*. SUMMARY AND CONCLUSION

IN CREATING A MILIEU for his story, Milton has drawn freely from the traditional sciences and has done some independent thinking. His physics of the four elements, his geology, meteorology, physiology, and psychology did not seem novel to any seventeenth-century reader. They would not have seemed novel to a well informed fourteenth-century reader. The mundane heavens of *Paradise Lost* are basically Ptolemaic, likewise traditional and familiar. The areas beyond the outermost sphere, however, are peculiarly Miltonic. Milton has reasoned out a plan for God's cosmos which he regards as essentially true but which has little likeness to earlier conceptions.

He seems to have no doubt of the literal truth of his information about the earth and man. He very probably would have considered his Ptolemaic astronomy literally true if his belief in it had not been disturbed by his becoming acquainted, somewhat late, with Copernicanism. But having some knowledge of both systems and perceiving their utter irreconcilability, he has decided that the truth about the starry heavens cannot be known and that God disapproves of inquiry. What he believes he knows of the cosmos beyond the world—Heaven, the angels, Hell, Chaos—he regards as relative knowledge, knowledge accommodated to human intelligence.

Milton's thought is unusual, though not unique, in its materialism; that is, in its premise that every form of existence in the cosmos has material substance. He believes also that excellence and dignity are not merely abstractions but material qualities, purity as opposed to grossness, luminousness as opposed to darkness. Spiritual elevation is literally height. Thus the religious and ethical content of *Paradise Lost* is presented, not at all abstractly, but concretely in images which have moral meaning. Unlike the amoral universe of modern times, Milton's cosmos is morally significant throughout. The study of Milton's "science" and ontology, then, should contribute more toward the understanding of the poem than merely explanatory notes concerning bits of curious and forgotten lore. The physical milieu is an integrated part of a complex medium of poetic expression.

Many minds have contributed to the cosmos of *Paradise Lost.* There are precedents, more or less remote, for even its unconventional features. In its combination of ideas it is original, but it is nevertheless an eclectic construction. It is the product of the author's study of books and his reflection upon them, not of any observation of nature. The book on which Milton has depended most of all is the Bible, which, he believes, he has read with a mind illuminated by the Holy Spirit. He is confident that he has had divine aid and inspiration. What he has to say of the history and substance of God's cosmos is truth, not opinion. He makes no assertions concerning matters which lie beyond the limits of God's revelations.

II

Neither human documents nor divine guidance, however, have led Milton to the truth concerning the physical universe as we see it. His error, by our scientifically influenced modern standards, consists not so much in the falsity of his concepts as in the invalidity of the kind of thinking which has produced them. His deductive and authoritarian thinking has devised a cosmos which, to our twentieth-century minds, is totally and fantastically unreal.

Criticism distinguishes fictional time from clock time, fictional space from surveyor's space. These distinctions are undoubtedly useful in critical discussion of *Beowulf*, or *The Canterbury Tales*, or *The Faerie Queene*, or *Hamlet*, *Othello*, and *King Lear*. But their applicability to *Paradise Lost* is questionable. In justice to any poet, we should try to understand the poem as he intends it to be understood. Shakespeare does not regard the times and places of *King Lear* as actual or possible, and he does not expect his audience to regard them as realistic. To Milton, however, the events, times, spaces, objects, and localities of his epic correspond to an objective reality. They are not his own poetic creation; he has deduced them from divine revelation. In many cases, he realizes, they are only a remote and simplified approximation, but they represent the reality as closely as it is possible for the human mind to approach it. A *Paradise Lost* written by an angel for angels would come much closer to absolute reality.

If a twentieth-century reader is asked to accept *Paradise Lost* as a representation of things-as-they-really-are, he cannot do so. A seventeenth-century reader would have had much less difficulty in reconciling Milton's cosmos with reality as he understood it. But in our time we must read *Paradise Lost* with a suspension of disbelief, with a poetic faith of a kind which Milton would have repudiated. We think of the spaces of *Paradise Lost* as fictional, but they were not so to the poet.

Poetic faith, however, is surprisingly effective. We forget that up and down, high and low, are locational expressions which imply the action of gravity and that there could be no gravity in the spaces between Milton's Heaven and Hell. We are willing to believe that Heaven is spatially and spiritually "high," that Hell is spatially and spiritually "low," even though there are no heights or depths or moral qualities in the universe as our science represents it. Just as we accept Milton's physical cosmos, so we accept his moral and religious assumptions. For the time at least, we accept *high* and *low, bright* and *dark* as ethical terms. Though our poetic faith may become rather faint, we are even willing to believe that Milton's God is loving and giving and that Adam's decision, when he must choose between loyalty to Eve and obedience to God, is heinously wrong.

III

Milton believed that he was writing a work which posterity would not willingly let die. It never occurred to him, I am sure, that his small but fit audience of three centuries in the future would be as pagan as it is. If he had known, he might not have been so confident of the longevity of his epic. But even though there are few of us whom Milton would consider Christians, we do not let his poem die. Readers of the twentieth century do undoubtedly react to it. I have seen the reaction over and over among students: the somewhat startled discovery that *Paradise Lost*, the ponderously formidable work of the austere Puritan, is an exhilarating poem.

The principal reason why we in our time read *Paradise Lost* with pleasure is unquestionably its magnificence. With this inadequate word, I mean to suggest the poet's success in conveying the miraculous forces, the vastnesses, the glooms, and the brilliances which are appropriate to his story—in conveying all of these through the sensuous medium of imagery. This means that the appeal of *Paradise Lost* is due in very large part to Milton's creation of a milieu whose grandeur can be sensed, can be seen in imagination. In imagination, also, the reader hears, even smells and tastes. The effect of the imagery is heightened by the musical resonance of the verse. The primary excellences of the poem are just those which are most peculiarly poetic.

Milton does not, obviously, excel in the painting of detailed pictures. There are vivid images in "L'Allegro," "Il Penseroso," and *Comus*, but there is nothing in Milton's verse like the tufted wart on the end of Chaucer's Miller's nose. He does not attempt the precisely particular kind of image that one finds so abundantly in nineteenth century poetry, for example, in Coleridge's "Dejection":

> For lo! the New-moon winter-bright!
> And overspread with phantom light
> (With swimming phantom light o'erspread,
> But rimmed and circled by a silver thread),
> I see the old Moon in her lap . . .

Or in Browning's "Two in the Campagna":

> one small orange cup amassed
> Five beetles—blind and green they grope
> Among the honey-meal . . .

Readers of Milton's period did not demand sharp-edged imagery of its poets and seldom got it. If Milton had any aptitude for this kind of description, he did not develop it. He had no need of such an ability in the composition of *Paradise Lost*. Distinctness and detail would not be appropriate in the presentation of places and persons that cannot really be described, "inimitable" in the medium of any human art (III, 508). The poet must stimulate the reader's imagination without drawing the picture.

Milton represents Paradise with vivid but general imagery:

> Another side, umbrageous Grots and Caves
> Of cool recess, o'er which the mantling Vine
> Lays forth her purple Grape, and gently creeps
> Luxuriant; meanwhile murmuring waters fall . . .
> The Birds thir quire apply; airs, vernal airs,
> Breathing the smell of field and grove, attune
> The trembling leaves.   (IV, 257-66)

This is not a description of a specific landscape, and there is no reference to particular grottoes, vines, or birds. The poet has assembled generic images of sight, sound, and odor which collectively call up a vision of natural luxuriance and profusion, beautiful beyond anything which we can ever hope to see but which could have been when the world was young. Above Paradise the heavenly bodies glow with a splendor which is suggested rather than described. The sun is a "great Palace" of light, "Regent of Day" (VII, 363, 371). The bright moon, "mirror" of the sun, revolves

> on Heav'n's great Axle, and her Reign
> With thousand lesser Lights dividual holds,
> With thousand thousand Stars . . . . . .
> Spangling the Hemisphere.   (VII, 377-84)

Milton's Hell is a huge and murky furnace, indefinitely horrible. Its flames produce, not light, but visible darkness, which discovers "sights of woe / Regions of sorrow, doleful shades" whose character is not specified (I, 64-65). Chaos is by its nature indescribable, yet Milton contrives images which convey its character indistinctly yet imaginably:

> the vast immeasurable Abyss
> Outrageous as a Sea, dark, wasteful, wild,
> Up from the bottom turn'd by furious winds
> And surging waves, as Mountains to assault
> Heav'n's highth.   (VII, 211-15)

The vast miracle of the Creation becomes dimly visible: At the voice of God, the light of Heaven, "as with a Mantle," invests

> The rising world of waters dark and deep,
> Won from the void and formless infinite.   (III, 10-12)

Heaven shines brilliantly, adorned with "Opal Tow'rs and Battlements . . . Of living Sapphire" (II, 1049-50). Only one of the lustrous buildings of Heaven is specifically mentioned:

> High on a Hill, far blazing, as a Mount
> Rais'd on a Mount, with Pyramids and Tow'rs
> From Diamond Quarries hewn, and Rocks of Gold,
> The Palace of great *Lucifer*.   (V, 757-60)

One sees heights piled on heights and a golden and jewelled splendor which is a little more splended that it should be, nothing more definite. The solemn troops and sweet societies of angels, with their golden crowns and harps, express their ardor and beatitude very concretely: Gathered "thick as Stars" (III, 61) about the throne of God, the sons of light give exultant testimony of their faith and love; Heaven rings

> with a shout
> Loud as from numbers without number, sweet
> As from blest voices, uttering joy.   (III, 345-47)

There is intensity in all of these celestial images, but there are no outlines and no specifics.

The inexpressible glory of God himself presents the greatest possible challenge to the poet's powers:

> Fountain of Light, thyself invisible
> Amidst the glorious brightness where thou sit'st
> Thron'd inaccessible, but when thou shad'st
> The full blaze of thy beams, and through a cloud
> Drawn round about thee like a radiant Shrine,
> Dark with excessive bright thy skirts appear,

Yet dazzle Heav'n, that brightest Seraphim
Approach not, but with both wings veil thir eyes.
(III, 375-82)

Language could hardly come closer to saying what cannot be said. The light-dark imagery of *Paradise Lost* is its most memorable and beautiful stylistic feature. There are many images of absolute blackness, yet the poem as a whole is radiantly luminous.

IV

Milton would consider all this faint praise. He has not created imagery for its own sake. *Paradise Lost* is a statement of religious and ethical truth. The images, the dramatic story telling, the resonant verse are all means to the moral end. The poem is not didactic in the sense that it attempts to teach the reader something that he does not know or to convince him of something with which he would be likely to disagree. Milton assumes that his reader is a Christian and that he knows quite well the difference between right and wrong. It is the poet's obligation, he writes in *The Reason of Church-Government*, to use his God-given powers in the presentation of "whatsoever in religion is holy and sublime, in virtu amiable, or grave, whatsoever hath passion or admiration." By illustrative example, he should teach, in a manner which gives delight, "the whole book of sanctity and virtu ... to those especially ... who will not so much as look upon Truth herselfe, unless they see her elegantly drest." If the poem does no more than stimulate the imagination, it has failed.

Milton is endeavoring to deepen his reader's understanding of religious and moral truths and to give him an emotional and imaginative awareness of them. Specifically what truths? It would be inappropriate for me to offer a thoroughgoing exposition of the doctrinal content of *Paradise Lost*. But the doctrine which seems to me the primary idea of the poem is clearly related to the subject of this study. This is a very general and not at all abstruse idea which appears in many forms: that all created existence is beneficently conceived and directed. The world and life are good. God's ways to men are not only just but loving.

His gifts to men are manifold. He has given them the earth and all its beauties and pleasures, and these men may and should enjoy (but not immoderately). He has given them bodies and psychological faculties of wonderful complexity and capability. He has, moreover, given to every man the great gift of freedom, the power of intelligent choice. This carries with it a moral responsibility, and it might therefore be considered a burden. But to Milton freedom is an opportunity and a privilege, for the capability of sin is only the obverse of the capability of virtue—that is, the capability of pleasing God by love and obedience freely given. Freedom of the will gives man a very high place among God's creatures. He is not ignominiously controlled by any power external to himself, not even by God. He is not merely artificial like the Adam of the motions. If he wins salvation, it will be by his own reasonable choice and righteous effort to think, and feel, and act in God's way. It will be his own achievement, and he will have earned a just reward.

Paradise Lost is an assertion not only of the goodness of life and the world but also of the author's pride in his humanity. Man was the final and crowning work of the Six Days, a creature marvelously endowed, made in God's own image. He is very little lower on God's scale of being than the angels, and he has the God-given opportunity of winning a place beside them. Man's worth and pre-eminence lie in his freedom.

Although in his later years his hopes for humanity declined, Milton's thought is confidently optimistic. He is quite well aware of the sin and folly which men commit and of the pain which they consequently suffer. For these things men themselves are responsible. Those who turn from God do so by their own free decision. God does not will that any man should be lost. In spite of human depravity and weakness, every man, if he so wills, may win salvation. Some men do so.

Some of us who are students of the history of ideas find Milton's theology interesting for what it reveals concerning the intellectual past. But to almost all of us, there seems to be little truth in it. Possibly we can nevertheless subscribe to his moral optimism, broadly understood, and to his confidence in the nature of man. His poetry may serve as a corrective for the moral relativism, the pessimism, and the low evaluation of human nature which we have absorbed from our twentieth-century environment. If we read Milton as he wished to be read, we must respond with more than the merely temporary adjustments of suspended disbelief, and we must value his poem for more than the excitement and glamor of its narrative, its verbal music, and the imaginative stimulation of its imagery. The poet is offering us truth "elegantly drest." If we will allow him to do so, he can perhaps, through the emotional power and imaginative vividness of his story, soften our stony hearts and make us sharply and deeply aware of truths in which we believe only hazily and sluggishly or not at all.

We are not impervious to moral statements, but our men of letters are disinclined to give them to us. Perhaps they could not do so with conviction. As Douglas Bush has said so well in *Paradise Lost in Our Time,* the work of a poet who truly sees a difference between right and wrong, to whom good and evil are realities, is salutary reading for a period in which moral distinctions have become so greatly blurred.

Paradise Lost had greater impact in the seventeenth century than it can have in our time. But only a little of its glory has departed, and its moral ideas, if not its theology and metaphysics, still have value. These are presented through a story of human failure and divine grace and through a poetic medium which stirs the feelings and the imagination. It is a deeply moving drama enacted upon the grandest imaginable stage.

NOTES

ABBREVIATIONS:

CD	*Christian Doctrine*
DDD	*Doctrine and Discipline of Divorce*
HTR	*Harvard Theological Review*
JEGP	*Journal of English and Germanic Philology*
JHI	*Journal of the History of Ideas*
MLQ	*Modern Language Quarterly*
PL	*Paradise Lost*
PMLA	*Publications of the Modern Language Association*
PQ	*Philological Quarterly*
PR	*Paradise Regained*
SA	*Samson Agonistes*
SP	*Studies in Philology*
Works	*The Works of John Milton*, ed. Frank A. Patterson, 18 vols., New York, 1931-38 (Columbia Milton)
Yale Milton	*Complete Prose Works of John Milton*, ed. Don M. Wolfe, 8 vols., New Haven, 1953—

Dates within brackets are dates of original publication.

CHAPTER II: KNOWLEDGE

[1]See Harris Fletcher, *Milton's Rabbinical Readings* (Urbana, 1930), pp. 187-205; Arnold Williams, *The Common Expositor* (Chapel Hill, 1948), pp. 81-84.

[2]*CD, Works*, XV, 115-17.

[3]*Of Education, Works*, IV, 277.

[4]*CD, Works*, XIV, 25. Christian writers distinguish a primary law of nature (that which was given to Adam) and a secondary law of nature (that given to fallen man). Among the commentaries on Milton's use of this concept: Arthur E. Barker, *Milton and the Puritan Dilemma* (Toronto, 1942), *passim;* C. A. Patrides, *Milton and the Christian Tradition* (Oxford, 1966), pp. 79-88; William J. Grace, preface to *A Defence of the People of England*, Yale Milton, IV (1966), 285-94.

[5]*CD, Works*, XVI, 101.

[6]*Ibid.*, XV, 93.

[7]*Ibid.*, XIV, 27. William G. Madsen discusses Milton's use of various concepts of nature: *The Idea of Nature in Milton's Poetry*, in *Three Studies in the Renaissance* (New Haven, 1958), pp. 181-283.

[8]*CD, Works*, XIV, 31.

[9]*Ibid.*, XV, 35.

[10]*Ibid.*, XV, 37-39. See Patrides, *Christian Tradition*, pp. 49-51, for some of the senses (including Milton's) in which "made in his image" was understood.

[11]*CD, Works*, XIV, 37.

[12]*Ibid.*, XIV, 31-33. See also p. 37.

[13]Christian writers sometimes say that God has adapted his message to vulgar understanding, sometimes to human understanding in general. See St. Thomas Aquinas, *Summa*

Theologica, I, lxviii, 3; Robert Burton, *The Anatomy of Melancholy*, ed. A. R. Shilleto (London, 1926-27), II, 64.

There has been a considerable use of the concept of accommodation in Milton commentary: e.g., Roland M. Frye, *God, Man, and Satan* (Princeton, 1960), pp. 7-13; C. A. Patrides, *"Paradise Lost* and the Theory of Accommodation," *Texas Studies in Literature and Language*, V (1963), 58-63. There has been no attempt, however, to distinguish specifically between those parts of *PL* to which it is applicable and those to which it is not.

[14] *DDD, Works*, III, 440.

[15] *CD, Works*, XV, 275.

[16] *Ibid.*, XV, 273. Cf. XIV, 193.

[17] *Ibid.*, XV, 107.

[18] *Ibid.*, XIV, 317.

[19] Howard Schultz, in *Milton and Forbidden Knowledge* (New York, 1955), has capably reviewed Renaissance thinking on this subject. See especially Chap. I. See also Paul H. Kocher, *Science and Religion in Elizabethan England* (San Marino, 1953). One learns from Kocher (Chap. IV) that, in England at least, scientific investigation was not greatly impeded by outcries against curiosity. Typical and lively attacks on curiosity appear in Burton's *Anatomy*, I, 420-22; II, 67-69.

[20] *DDD, Works*, III, 371.

[21] *Works*, XV, 113-15. This explanation was not unusual; see Williams, *Common Expositor*, p. 107. Various modern expositors have struggled with this problem: e.g., Basil Willey, *The Seventeenth Century Background* (Garden City, N.Y., 1953 [1934]), pp. 243-58; John S. Diekhoff, *Milton's Paradise Lost: A Commentary on the Argument* (New York, 1953 [1946]), pp. 45-47; J. M. Evans, *Paradise Lost and the Genesis Tradition* (Oxford, 1968), Chap. IX.

[22] *Works*, IV, 310-11.

[23] Arnold Stein, *Answerable Style* (Minneapolis, 1953), p. 17. Paradise, says Stein, is "a metaphor," "an image of the archetype . . . a symbolic image" (p. 53). Helen Gardner, somewhat more exactly, calls *Paradise Lost* "a vast simile . . . it is like but yet not like the things of which it tells us."—*A Reading of Paradise Lost* (Oxford, 1965), p. 51.

[24] "Milton definitely conceived his celestial battle as representing events which were none the less actual for surmounting the reach of human sense."—Merritt Y. Hughes, "Milton's Celestial Battle and the Theogonies," in *Studies in Honor of T. W. Baldwin*, ed. Allen (Urbana, 1958), p. 238.

[25] See S. I. Hayakawa, *Language in Action* (New York, 1941), pp. 19-23. René Wellek and Austin Warren *(Theory of Literature*, Penguin Books, 1963 [1949], p. 189) say that, in literary criticism, *symbol* is best used in the sense of "an object which refers to another object but which demands attention also in its own right." *Symbol* differs from *image* and *metaphor* "Primarily . . . in the recurrence and persistence of the 'symbol.' " They accept the common distinction "between the 'private symbolism' of the modern poet and the widely intelligible symbolism of past poets." Milton's symbols, in his time, were widely intelligible.

[26] See George W. Whiting, *Milton's Literary Milieu* (New York, 1964 [1939]), p. 152; Whiting, *Milton and This Pendant World* (Austin, Texas, 1958), pp. 59-87; C. A. Patrides, "Renaissance Interpretations of Jacob's Ladder," *Theologische Zeitschrift*, XVIII (1962), 411-18.

[27] See J. H. Adamson, "The War in Heaven: Milton's Version of the *Merkabah, " JEGP*, LVII (1958), 690-703.

[28] C. A. Patrides, *"Paradise Lost* and the Language of Theology," in *Language and Style in Paradise Lost*, ed. Emma and Shawcross (New York, 1967), p. 108. The quoted phrase is from I. T. Ramsey's *Models and Mystery*.

[29] *CD, Works*, XVI, 263.

[30] William G. Madsen's *From Shadowy Types to Truth: Studies in Milton's Symbolism* (New Haven, 1968) is a thoroughgoing treatment of Milton's typology. Madsen possibly finds more typology in *Paradise Lost* than Milton intended.

[31] J. M. Evans, in *Paradise Lost and the Genesis Tradition*, shows the relationship between Milton's poem and its background of Christian writings, points out various judicious choices which Milton has made among different interpretations of Genesis, and identifies various instances of Milton's elaboration and invention. See also Arnold Williams, "The Motivation of Satan's Rebellion in *Paradise Lost, " SP*, XLII (1945), 253-68.

[32]See Evans, *Genesis Tradition*, pp. 224-27; Maurice Kelley, *This Great Argument* (Princeton, 1941), pp. 94-101. This begetting cannot be the "metaphorical" begetting which Milton distinguishes in *CD* from the actual generation of the Son. See Chap. VIII, sec. iv.

[33]John M. Steadman defends Milton's allegory on the basis of Aristotelian principles adopted by Italian Renaissance critics: "Allegory and Verisimilitude in *Paradise Lost:* The Problem of the 'Impossible Credible,' " *PMLA*, LXXVIII (1963), 36-39. See also Joseph H. Summers, *The Muse's Method* (Cambridge, Mass., 1962), pp. 39 ff.

[34]Pierre Charron, *Of Wisdom. Three Books* [1601], tr. George Stanhope (London, 1729), p. 180.

[35]*Works*, IV, 19.

[36]*Works*, XIV, 9. "Mihi certe hanc rationem ineundo ita satisfactum est, ut quid credendum in sacris, quid duntaxat opinandum sit, percepisse nunc non diffiderem."

CHAPTER III: MILTON AND SCIENCE

[1]*Works*, XII, 169-71.

[2]*Works*, XII, 255-65.

[3]See Douglas Bush, "The Date of Milton's *Ad Patrem,*" *Modern Philology*, LXI (1964), 204-08.

[4]Merritt Y. Hughes' translation: *Complete Poems and Major Prose* (New York, 1957), p. 85.

[5]Hughes' translations: *Paradise Regained, the Minor Poems, and Samson Agonistes* (New York, 1937), pp. 9, 13.

[6]*Of Education, Works*, IV, 283-84.

[7]*Ibid.*, IV, 290.

[8]This justification of scientific study was commonplace during the Renaissance, as various scholars have pointed out. See, for example, Kocher, *Science and Religion*, pp. 42-44; Patrides, *Christian Tradition*, pp. 68-71.

[9]*Works*, XII, 255-57.

[10]*Works*, XIV, 25-27.

[11]The concept of nature as the book of God appears frequently in Renaissance documents: e.g., Sir Thomas Browne, *Religio Medici, Works*, ed. Keynes (London, 1928-30), I, 21. Among modern treatments of the idea: Williams, *Common Expositor*, pp. 174-75; Patrides, *Christian Tradition*, pp. 68-71.

[12]Robert B. Hinman, in *Abraham Cowley's World of Order* (Cambridge, Mass., 1960), gives a good deal of space to the scientific ideas and attitudes in Cowley's poetry. See especially Chaps. VI-VIII. He points out many specific likenesses between Cowley's and Milton's scientific and ontological ideas.

[13]Kester Svendsen, *Milton and Science* (Cambridge, Mass., 1956), pp. 43, 234-48.

[14]*Ibid.*, pp. 3-4, 27-42, *et passim.*

[15]For an exception, see below, note 24.

[16]See Balachandra Rajan, " 'Simple, Sensuous, and Passionate,' " *Review of English Studies*, XXI (1945), 290-93; William R. Parker, "Education: Milton's Idea and Ours," *College English*, XXIV (1962), 1-14.

[17]*Of Education, Works*, IV, 277.

[18]*Ibid.*, pp. 282-84. Donald C. Dorian's notes for *Of Education* in the Yale Milton (II, 388-96) supply some information about these authors and their works.

[19]See Robert R. Cawley, *Milton and the Literature of Travel* (Princeton, 1951), Chaps. V and VI.

[20]See the preface to *A Brief History of Muscovy, Works*, X, 327.

[21]Merritt Y. Hughes, *Complete Poems and Major Prose*, pp. 1029-30.

[22]I assume that, both in *Of Education* and in Phillips' biography, "Hesiod" refers to the *Works and Days* rather than to the *Theogony.*

[23]Allan H. Gilbert, in "Milton's Textbook of Astronomy," *PMLA*, XXXVIII (1923), 297-307, has characterized a typical Renaissance edition with its commentaries and notes. See also Grant McColley, "The Astronomy of *Paradise Lost,*" *SP*, XXXIV (1937), 223-24. It is not possible to identify the edition that Milton used.

[24]It is evident, however, that Milton had read Aratus very closely. See Maurice Kelley and Samuel D. Atkins, "Milton's Annotations of Aratus," *PMLA*, LXX (1955), 1090-1106 (especially

p. 1105). Milton's copy of Aratus, purchased in 1631, includes both the *Phaenomena* and the *Diosemeia*, actually a single poem.

²⁵See William T. Costello, *The Scholastic Curriculum at Early Seventeenth-Century Cambridge* (Cambridge, Mass., 1958), especially Chap. III. Mark H. Curtis, in *Oxford and Cambridge in Transition: 1558-1642* (Oxford, 1959), shows that Oxford was somewhat more receptive to new scientific ideas than Cambridge in the early decades of the seventeenth century. He tries—not too successfully, I think—to show that there was a significant degree of scientific curiosity at Cambridge also. See Chap. IX.

²⁶R. T. Gunther, *Early Science at Cambridge* (Oxford, 1937), p. 155. Gunther lists other contributions which Horrox made to astronomy. Horrox died in 1641 at about the age of twenty-five.

²⁷See George W. Whiting, "Milton and Bacon," in *Milton's Literary Milieu*, pp. 267-81.

²⁸*Works*, III, 294. But in the *Areopagitica* Milton writes that "To sequester out of the world into *Atlantick* and *Eutopian* polities, which never can be drawn into use, will not mend our condition."—*Works*, IV, 318.

²⁹*Works*, XI, 25.

³⁰*Works*, XII, 171-73.

³¹See Paul H. Kocher, "Paracelsan Medicine in England: The First Thirty Years (ca. 1570-1600)," *Journal of the History of Medicine and Allied Sciences*, II (1947), 451-80.

³²George N. Conklin has discussed at length Milton's reliance on and use of the Bible: *Biblical Criticism and Heresy in Milton* (New York, 1949); see especially pp. 24-40.

³³*CD, Works*, XVI, 277-79.

³⁴*Ibid.*, XVI, 259.

³⁵*Ibid.*, XIV, 3. See Harry F. Robins, *If This Be Heresy: A Study of Milton and Origen* (Urbana, 1963), pp. 12-16.

CHAPTER IV: EARTH, MEN, AND ANGELS

¹See S. K. Heninger, Jr., *A Handbook of Renaissance Meteorology* (Durham, N.C., 1960), especially pp. 37-46.

²Kester Svendsen, in *Milton and Science*, Chaps. III and IV, covers much of the ground covered in the first section of this chapter. He deals with some subjects in much greater detail than I do, and gives point to a great many lines and passages in *PL*.

³See Chap. V, note 16.

⁴I find no reference anywhere in Milton's works to the sphere of fire. The "Spheres of watchful fire" of the "Vacation Exercise" (line 40) are the stars and planets.

⁵Gerhard Mercator describes the atmosphere and the spheres above it as a continuum whose substance (air) becomes purer with increasing distance from the earth: *Atlas*, tr. Henry Hexham (Amsterdam, 1636; facsimile reprint, Amsterdam, 1968), pp. 13, 17. Sir Walter Raleigh refers to the sphere of fire as if it were merely a supposition: *Works* (Oxford, 1829), II, 15. See also Burton, *Anatomy*, II, 57-58.

⁶See *PL*, IV, 940, and *PR*, I, 39-47; II, 117-18.

⁷See William B. Hunter, Jr., "Milton's Materialistic Life Principle," *JEGP*, XLV (1946), 71-73; Svendsen, pp. 66-67; Walter Clyde Curry, *Milton's Ontology, Cosmogony, and Physics* (Lexington, Ky., 1957), pp. 135-43. Joseph A. Mazzeo reviews medieval doctrines of solar and stellar influence which resemble Milton's: "Light Metaphysics, Dante's 'Convivio' and the Letter to Can Grande Della Scala," *Traditio*, XIV (1958), pp. 191-229.

⁸Svendsen discusses this question, pp. 79-84. Theodore H. Banks decides, on the basis of passages in the prose works, that Milton's attitude toward astrology was sceptical: *Milton's Imagery* (New York, 1950), pp. 173-75. Milton's horoscope is reproduced in *Works*, XVIII, 348.

⁹*Works*, XI, 89.

¹⁰Edgar H. Duncan explains the processes involved in detail: "The Natural History of Metals and Minerals in the Universe of Milton's *Paradise Lost,*" *Osiris*, XI (1954), 386-421.

¹¹See Duncan, pp. 391 ff.; William B. Hunter, Jr., "Milton and Thrice Great Hermes," *JEGP*, XLV (1946), 327-36; Svendsen, pp. 123-25; Curry, pp. 125-31, 139-42. Banks has assembled Milton's alchemical images: *Milton's Imagery*, pp. 175-76. Milton, he believes, was contemptuous of alchemy.

[12]Duncan, p. 405. A. B. Chambers argues plausibly that "Proteus" is a mythographical name for the prime matter: "Milton's Proteus and Satan's Visit to the Sun," *JEGP,* LXII (1963), 280-87.

[13]There are many classical precedents for the idea of cyclic transmutation; e.g., Aristotle, *De Generatione et Corruptione,* 331; Seneca, *Quaestiones Naturales,* III, x; IV, xvi. A. B. Chambers gives a list of them: "Chaos in *Paradise Lost,*" *JHI,* XXIV (1963), pp. 57-58 (note). Concerning the sources of Milton's idea of progressive transmutation, see note 32 below.

[14]The idea was a commonplace. See Svendsen, pp. 53, 65-66; Curry, p. 124.

[15]*De Anima,* 413-15; St. Thomas Aquinas, *Summa Theologica,* I, lxxvi, 3; I, lxxviii, 1, 2.

[16]Milton's scale of being has often been expounded, recently by Patrides, *Christian Tradition,* pp. 59-68.

[17]In this passage J. H. Adamson sees the influence of the Neoplatonic doctrine of "egressus-regressus," emanation from and return to God: "Milton and the Creation," *JEGP,* LXI (1962), 771-73.

[18]A great deal has been written about Milton's Paradise. Williams' *Common Expositor* shows its relation to exegetical tradition (Chap. V). Similar material appears in Grant McColley's *Paradise Lost: An Account of Its Growth and Major Origins* (New York, 1963 [1940]), pp. 142-57, and in Sister Mary I. Corcoran's *Milton's Paradise with Reference to the Hexameral Background* (Washington, 1945), especially Chap. II. Evert M. Clark traces several details to geographers' and travellers' accounts of Mount Amara: "Milton's Abyssinian Paradise," *University of Texas Studies in English,* XXIX (1950), 129-50. A. Bartlett Giamatti devotes a chapter of *The Earthly Paradise and the Renaissance Epic* (Princeton, 1956) to Milton (pp. 295-351) and shows that Milton's Paradise had precedents in literary works.

[19]Ann Gossman ("The Use of the Tree of Life in *Paradise Lost,*" *JEGP,* LXV [1966], 680-87) defines the symbolism of this tree. Evidently the fruit of the Tree of Life was not forbidden before the Fall (*PL,* XI, 57-61, 93-96).

[20]Joseph Summers has developed this idea. See Chap. VII, note 13.

[21]See Michael Macklem, *The Anatomy of the World* (Minneapolis, 1958), Chap. I. According to this theory, the pristine earth was encrusted by a smooth sphere of the element earth, beneath which lay a spherical zone of water. This arrangement was disrupted during the Flood.

[22]John R. Knott, Jr., outlines the daily routine and associates it with the shepherds' daily schedule in pastoral poetry: "The Pastoral Day in *Paradise Lost,*" *MLQ,* XXIX (1968), 168-82. He emphasizes the fact that the paradisiac rhythm of life is rudely and finally disrupted by the Fall.

[23]See Banks, *Milton's Imagery,* pp. 53-60.

[24]Aristotle, *Parva Naturalia,* 466a, 469b.

[25]Juan Huarte, *Examen de Ingenios,* tr. R. Carew (London, 1594), p. 59.

[26]Philipp Melanchthon, *Liber de Anima,* in *Opera,* ed. Bretschneider (Halle, 1834-60), XIII, 88. The theory of the spirits was derived ultimately from the Stoics, more immediately from Galen.

[27]Pierre de la Primaudaye, *The French Academie,* tr. T. B. C. (London, 1618), p. 564. Cf. Melanchthon, *Opera,* XIII, 88.

[28]Timothy Bright, *A Treatise of Melancholie* (London, 1586; facsimile reprint, New York, 1940), p. 52.

[29]Thomas Walkington, *The Optick Glasse of Humors* (London, 1664 [1607]), pp. 96-97.

[30]*Areopagitica, Works,* IV, 344.

[31]Milton uses *spirit (spirits, spiritus)* in several senses, not always clearly distinguished. His primary meaning seems to be "that which animates." Among the subsidiary meanings: 1) the life-infusing breath of God, Father or Son, 2) the Holy Spirit (see Chap. VIII, sec. v), 3) the rarefied material substance which performs physiological and psychological functions in the human body and brain and which in its purest form constitutes the bodies of the angels. Since angels are "pure intelligential spirits" (as men are not), they are properly called "spirits."

Sometimes Milton equates *spirit* and *soul* (e. g. *Works,* XV, 229), but usually he reserves *soul* for the Aristotelian sense discussed below. He avoids *sensible soul* and *vegetable soul,* terms often used by Renaissance authorities to refer to the sub-rational faculties, substituting such phrases as "the sentient and vegetative faculty" *(CD, Works,* XV, 25), "substance individual, animated, sensitive, and rational" *(ibid.,* p. 41).

When I had nearly completed this study, I procured a copy of Willard C. Moser's unpublished doctoral dissertation: *The Meaning of "Soul" and "Spirit" in the Later Works of John Milton* (Tulane, 1968). Moser's treatment of Milton's concept of *soul* and of its philosophical background is very informative. He finds six meanings of *spirit* in Milton's works (two of them closely related). The dissertation includes a competent review of the matter-spirit continuum. Moser apparently would not agree with my proposal that, in Milton's material continuum, the spirit of man in its highest form consists of the same substance as the angels.

[32]Numerous analogues and possible sources have been suggested: e.g., in A. S. P. Woodhouse, "Notes on Milton's Views of the Creation: The Initial Phases," *PQ* XXVIII (1949), 221; Curry, pp. 158 ff.; Adamson, "Milton and the Creation," pp. 767 ff.

[33]Burton's brief exposition *(Anatomy,* I, 170) is typical. P. Ansell Robin comments on the flower-spirit passage: Milton "makes no mention of natural spirits, but adds an intellectual kind, presumably more refined than animal spirits. This may be Milton's own invention (for I know of no support for it in any other author)."—"The Old Physiological Doctrine of Spirits as Reflected in English Literature," *Englische Studien,* XL (1909), 336.

[34]See St. Thomas, *Summa,* I, lviii, 4; I, lxxix, 10. To St. Thomas, angels are non-material, "spiritual."

[35]*Avicenna's Psychology,* tr. Rahman (London, 1952), p. 31. See also St. Thomas, *Summa,* I, lxxviii, 4.

[36]St. Thomas explains this difference. But the discursive (rational) process, he says, is not actually distinct from the intellectual (intuitive) process. The two differ only as acquisition from possession, imperfection from perfection. The angels, he believes, always acquire their knowledge intuitively; men are permitted a small degree of "intellectual light." After death the (immaterial) human soul retains, of its psychological powers, only intellect and will. Angels possess no other psychological faculties. See *Summa,* I, lviii, 4; I, lxxix, 4, 8.

[37]Robert H. West, in *Milton and the Angels* (Athens, Ga., 1955), reviews the earlier beliefs concerning angels (Chap. I) and the ideas and controversies of Milton's own time (Chap. II). A great many discussions of angels were published in England between 1640 and 1665, the period when Milton was planning and composing *Paradise Lost.* West finds similarities between Milton's ideas and those of some of his contemporaries, notably Robert Fludd and Henry More (pp. 73-90). He shows, in fact, that although Milton's angelology is unconventional, few if any of his ideas are unique. He finds no close parallels, however, for Milton's belief that angels may eat human food or for the physical consummation of angelic loves (see pp. 162-64).

[38]John E. Parish argues that it was only before the Fall, before the earth and its fruits were cursed, that angels could eat terrestrial food: "Milton and the Well-Fed Angel," *English Miscellany,* XVIII (1967), 87-109.

[39]*CD, Works,* XV, 25. In the same chapter Milton refers to the "secondary faculties" of the spirit, "the vital or sensitive faculty for instance."—p. 41.

[40]See also VI, 361-62, 393-95, 435-55.

[41]These words are said to have been inscribed above the portals of the Temple of Apollo at Delphi. The Greeks understood them as a reminder to men of their humanity and as, therefore, an exhortation to humility. To the Renaissance they meant that men, if they are to be virtuous and happy, must know their own bodies and minds. Albert W. Fields sketches the history of the phrase, deals with its Renaissance meanings, and lists the occurrences of the idea in Milton's works: "Milton and Self-Knowledge," *PMLA,* LXXXIII (1968), 392-99.

[42]*Works,* XII, 171.

[43]*De Anima,* 412b (tr. Smith, in Vol. III of *Works,* ed. Ross, Oxford, 1908-31).

[44]Willey, *Seventeenth Century Background,* p. 239.

[45]*CD, Works,* XIV, 29.

[46]Svendsen *(Milton and Science,* pp. 36-38, 182-83) discusses the psychology of dreams. The belief that the Devil practiced upon men's minds by disturbing the humors and natural organs was common; see Kocher, *Science and Religion,* pp. 125-29; Burton, *Anatomy,* I, 227-30; III, 452-56, 490.

[47]Cf. *PR,* IV, 131-45; *SA,* lines 268-71.

[48]See Fields, "Milton and Self-Knowledge," pp. 396-98. Arnold Stein's perceptive essay on the Fall *(Answerable Style,* pp. 75-118) emphasizes the psychology and ethics involved.

[49]*Paradise Lost and Its Critics* (Cambridge, 1947), p. 54.

[50]*Works,* XV, 215-17.

[51] *Ibid.*, XV, 251.

[52] *Ibid.*, XV, 239.

[53] *Ibid.*, XV, 25.

[54] See Patrides, *Christian Tradition*, pp. 274-76.

[55] *CD, Works,* XV, 41.

[56] See George Williamson, "Milton and the Mortalist Heresy" [1935], in *Seventeenth Century Contexts* (London, 1960), pp. 148-77; Kelley, *This Great Argument*, pp. 153-55; George N. Conklin, *Biblical Criticism*, Chap. VI; Nathaniel H. Henry, "Milton and Hobbes: Mortalism and the Intermediate State," *SP*, XLVIII (1951), 234-49; Leonard N. Wright, "Christian Mortalism: A Prospectus," in *The Great Torch Race*, ed. Osborne (Austin, Tex., 1961), pp. 35-44; Robins, *If This Be Heresy*, pp. 58, 145-46; Patrides, *Christian Tradition*, pp. 264-66; Virginia R. Mollenkott, "Milton's Mortalism: Treatise vs. Poetry," *Seventeenth-Century News*, Autumn 1968, pp. 51-52. D. P. Walker supplies valuable background information in *The Decline of Hell* (Chicago, 1954), Chaps. I-III. In his dissertation on Milton's use of *soul* and *spirit* (see note 31), Moser emphasizes the fact that mortalism is a logical consequence of Milton's Aristotelian ("hylomorphic") concept of the soul.

[57] *The History of the Church*, tr. Williamson (Penguin Books, 1965), p. 272 (Book VI, 37).

[58] According to Patrides, psychopannychism was a mild form of mortalism and was the most common form during the Rennaissance: " 'Paradise Lost' and the Mortalist Heresy," *Notes and Queries*, CCII (1957), 250-51; "Psychopannychism in Renaissance Europe," *SP*, LX (1963), 227-29.

[59] Including John Donne. See Helen Gardner's essay on "Donne's Views on the State of the Soul After Death" in her edition of Donne's *Divine Poems* (Oxford, 1959), pp. 114-17.

[60] *Works,* XV, 219.

[61] *Works,* XV, 27.

[62] Woodhouse, "Milton's Views of the Creation," p. 212.

CHAPTER V: THE SUPRALUNAR WORLD

[1] For the first section of this chapter, I have drawn generously from J. L. E. Dreyer, *A History of Astronomy from Thales to Kepler* (New York, 1953 [1905]) and from Thomas S. Kuhn, *The Copernican Revolution* (Cambridge, Mass., 1957). Other works which I have found very helpful: Francis R. Johnson, *Astronomical Thought in Renaissance England* (Baltimore, 1937); Alexandre Koyré, *From the Closed World to the Infinite Universe* (Baltimore, 1957); and James A. Coleman, *Early Theories of the Universe* (New York, 1967).

[2] Coleman, pp. 46-47.

[3] Herakliedes may have been anticipated by two early Pythagoreans, Ekphantus and Hiketas (Dreyer, pp. 50-51). The idea of a rotating earth was widely known, though not widely accepted, in the ancient world. See, for example, Cicero, *Academica*, II, xxxix; Seneca, *Quaestiones Naturales*, VII, ii. Grant McColley has outlined the history of the idea: "The Theory of the Diurnal Rotation of the Earth," *Isis*, XXVI (1937), 392-402.

[4] *De Mundo*, 391-93; *De Caelo*, 269-70. See Kuhn, p. 78.

[5] *De Re Publica*, tr. Keyes (Loeb Classical Library, 1928), pp. 271-73. Aristotle explains the theory rather fully but rejects it (*De Caelo*, 290b-291a).

[6] Dreyer (p. 257) gives a table of the distances as computed by three Arabian astronomers, including Al Fargani, in terms of semidiameters of the earth. Al Fargani's figure for the semidiameter is 3250 miles, about six hundred miles too low. See also Kuhn, pp. 80-81.

[7] Burton, *Anatomy*, II, 60-61.

[8] Johnson traces the progress of astronomical learning in England in the sixteenth century and gives a great deal of information about the available books and their authors: *Astronomical Thought*, Chaps. III, V, VI.

[9] Burton, *Anatomy*, II, 58.

[10] This is the opinion of Allan Gilbert: "The Outside Shell of Milton's World," *SP*, XX (1923), 444-47, and of Svendsen, pp. 53-54. McColley (*Growth and Origins*, p. 129) lists some analogues of Milton's protective shell.

[11] See Harry F. Robins, "That Unnecessary Shell of Milton's World," in *Studies in Honor of T. W. Baldwin*, ed. Allen (Urbana, 1958), pp. 215-17.

[12] *Paradiso*, xxviii ff. Beyond the *primum mobile*, says La Primaudaye, "our deuines do yet

declare to be a tenth heaven, which they call Empyreall. . . . But this heaven and the throne of God, cannot properly bee reckoned with the other nine. For they bee mooueable, but this is stable and immooueable, they be of one substance onely, and this of another."—*French Academie*, 1618 edition, p. 679. La Primaudaye denies the existence of the crystalline sphere.

[13] See Chap. II, note 26. Don C. Allen suggests that the golden chain and the ladder are the same thing: "Two Notes on *Paradise Lost,*" *Modern Language Notes*, LXVIII (1953), 360.

[14] Burton, *Anatomy*, II, 57.

[15] See above, note 4.

[16] *Ethereal* occurs rather frequently, twenty times in *PL*. It seems to mean nothing more definite than "heavenly." *Ethereous* occurs once *(PL,* VI, 473). *Quintessence* appears one other time in *PL*: "Light / Ethereal . . . quintessence pure" (VII, 243-44). This obviously is not a reference to the fifth element.

[17] This idea was a Renaissance commonplace. It occurs in Plato's *Timaeus*, 40. Plato's Great Year (49,000 years) is the period required for the completion of the stellar dance figure *(Timaeus,* 39d).

[18] *The Jewish Encyclopedia* (New York, 1901-05), article on "Cosmology." The articles on "Gehenna" and "Heaven" are informative.

[19] Louis Ginzberg, *The Legends of the Jews,* 7 vols. (Philadelphia, 1911-38), I, 13.

[20] Joseph Gaer, *The Lore of the Old Testament* (Boston, 1951), pp. 25-26.

[21] *Anatomy*, II, 64.

[22] *Ibid.,* II, 59-60.

[23] See Williams, *Common Expositor*, pp. 54-55. St. Thomas decides that the waters above the heavens are the transparent bodies above the firmament, in whatever sense the word may be used *(Summa,* I, lxviii, 2-3). Mercator identifies the upper waters with the Empyrean *(Atlas,* p. 17). Raleigh believes that they are vapors in the distant upper air *(Works,* II, 21-23).

[24] Harry F. Robins agrees with me in placing the upper waters outside of Milton's world: "The Crystalline Sphere and the 'Waters Above' in *Paradise Lost,*" *PMLA,* LXIX (1954), 903-14. Whiting reviews Christian commentary on the glassy sea. He believes that in *PL* it has a symbolic significance: "in its clarity the pure Word of God, a revelation of the divine mind and will," "the order, the peace, the clearness of the created universe."—*This Pendent World,* pp. 104, 106.

[25] In *Comus* he refers to the "pillar'd firmament . . . And earth's base" (lines 598-99) and in *PR* to "the pillar'd frame of Heaven" and "the Earth's dark basis underneath" (IV, 455-56). The foundations of the world appear in the "Nativity Ode" (line 123) and in "Ad Patrem" (line 47).

[26] Some of the many commentaries on Milton's account of the Creation: Fletcher, *Milton's Rabbinical Readings,* Chap. V; Whiting, *Milton's Literary Milieu,* Chap. I; Kelley, *This Great Argument,* pp. 122-30; Conklin, *Biblical Criticism,* Chap. V; Woodhouse, "Milton's Views of the Creation"; Curry, *Milton's Ontology,* Chap. IV; Adamson, "Milton and the Creation"; Patrides, *Christian Tradition,* Chap. II.

[27] See McColley, *Growth and Origins,* Chap. III; Williams, *Common Expositor,* Chap. III.

[28] Whiting discusses the precedents and background of this image in Christian literature and art: *This Pendent World,* pp. 104-20.

[29] See David Daiches, "The Opening of *Paradise Lost,*" in *The Living Milton,* ed. Kermode (London, 1960), p. 66. From Luther's commentary on the Creation: "As a hen broods her eggs, keeping them warm in order to hatch her chicks . . . to bring them to life through heat, so Scripture says that the Holy Spirit brooded, as it were, on the waters to bring to life those substances which were to be quickened and adorned. For it is the office of the Holy Spirit to make alive."—*Works* (St. Louis, 1958-67), I, 9.

[30] Robins *(op. cit.* in note 24, pp. 910-11) has made a laudable attempt to explain this not altogether lucid passage in detail. I doubt that Milton meant to say, as Robins believes he did, that God inflated the world like a bubble. A. B. Chambers suggests the two stages of the sorting out of matter: "Chaos," p. 80.

[31] The currency of this idea has often been pointed out. Kocher *(Science and Religion,* pp. 76-88) and Patrides *(Christian Tradition,* pp. 271-72) discuss the subject informatively.

[32] See Victor Harris, *All Coherence Gone* (Chicago, 1949), especially Chaps. II, III.

[33] See Joseph A. Bryant, Jr., "Milton's Views on Universal and Civil Decay," in *SAMLA*

Studies in Milton, ed. Patrick (Gainesville, Fla., 1953), pp. 1-8, and C. A. Patrides, "Renaissance and Modern Thought on the Last Things," *HTR,* LI (1958), 170.

[34]Letter to Gill, *Works,* XII, 11.

[35]*Works,* XII, 279.

[36]*Works,* III, 237. Milton's reference to the possible disadvantage of English climate shows that he is acquainted with the Renaissance theory of the influence of climate on mind and character. See Zera S. Fink, "Milton and the Theory of Climatic Influence," *MLQ,* II (1941), 67-80. Other references to this theory occur in *Defensio Secunda, Works,* VIII, 107, and in *Paradise Lost,* IX, 44-45. It seems unlikely that Milton seriously believed it.

[37]*CD, Works,* XV, 91.

[38]*Works,* XVI, 339. The "King" is "shortly-expected."—*Of Reformation, Works,* III, 78.

[39]*CD, Works,* XV, 3.

CHAPTER VI: THE NEW ASTRONOMY

[1]Dreyer, *Thales to Kepler,* p. 343. Much of the material in this section I have drawn from Dreyer, from Kuhn's *Copernican Revolution,* and from Johnson's *Astronomical Thought.*

[2]"The Astronomy of *Paradise Lost,*" *SP,* XXXIV (1937), 209-47; "Nicholas Reymers and the Fourth System of the World," *Popular Astronomy,* XLVI (1938), 25-31.

[3]Burton, *Anatomy,* II, 65-66. This is a small but representative fraction of a long and disorderly discourse which illustrates the state of astronomical theory as it would look to a layman.

[4]Apparently Thomas Harriot was simultaneously engaged in telescopic observations (Johnson, pp. 226-29). Thomas Digges may have anticipated both Galileo and Harriot (p. 174).

[5]See Grant McColley, "The Seventeenth-Century Doctrine of a Plurality of Worlds," *Annals of Science,* I (1936), 385-430.

[6]See Marjorie Nicolson, *Voyages to the Moon* (New York, 1960 [1948]). According to Miss Nicolson, the most widely read of the seventeenth-century books concerning extra-terrestrial life were Kepler's *Somnium* (written 1608, published 1634), an account of a flight to the moon and of the people whom the author found there; Francis Godwin's *The Man in the Moone* (see note 10), a similar science fantasy; and John Wilkins' *The Discovery of a New World* (1638), a work of serious speculation concerning the character of the moon and its possible inhabitants. She discusses these in detail (pp. 41-52, 71-85, 93-98).

[7]*Anatomy,* I, 344; II, 64. Burton is paraphrasing Kepler: see *Kepler's Conversation with Galileo's Sidereal Messenger* [1610], tr. Edward Rosen (New York, 1965), p. 43. What Kepler says about plural inhabited worlds in this document is somewhat ambiguous, but he thinks that Jupiter at least is probably inhabited.

[8]Pp. 213, 220, 249.

[9]See *Anatomy,* II, 61. Robert M. Browne has studied the additions to and revisions of the long passage on astronomy in Burton's successive editions: "Robert Burton and the New Cosmology," *MLQ,* XIII (1952), 131-48.

[10]*The Anchor Anthology of Short Fiction of the Seventeenth Century,* ed. Charles C. Mish (Garden City, N.Y., 1963), pp. 257-59. Godwin's fantasy was published in 1638 but had been written some years earlier.

[11]Galileo Galilei, *Dialogue Concerning the Two Chief World Systems,* tr. Stillman Drake (Berkeley, 1962), pp. 379-80, 398-99. Copernicus' third motion, says Galileo, is really "a motionlessness and a conservation of the [angle of the earth's axis] unchanged" (p. 399). Dreyer (pp. 328-30) and Kuhn (pp. 163-64) make the matter clearer.

Modern astronomy explains precession by a third motion, a slight and extremely slow wobble of the axis of the earth, but this is not the same thing as Copernicus' third motion. Copernicus explained precession by assuming a slight retardation of the earth's axial spin.

[12]*Works,* XII, 171.

[13]*Ibid.,* p. 257.

[14]M. Y. Hughes' translations in his edition of *Paradise Regained, The Minor Poems, and Samson Agonistes* (New York, 1937), pp. 9, 13.

[15]*Works,* IV, 329-30.

[16]Banks *(Milton's Imagery,* pp. 111-18) discusses Milton's astronomical images.

[17]For this and the following quotation I have used Hughes' translations, *Poems and Major*

Prose, pp. 34, 147. There is a reference to the *primum mobile* also in "On the Death of a Fair Infant," line 39.

[18] *Works*, IV, 348.

[19] *Ibid.*, IV, 190.

[20] *Works*, V, 271.

[21] *Works*, III, 389. The passage does not appear in the first edition.

[22] See Kuhn, *Copernican Revolution*, p. 187.

[23] *Works*, VII, 67.

[24] *Ibid.*, p. 481.

[25] The spots on the moon are mentioned twice (V, 419; VIII, 145) in passages referring to what Adam can see, not to telescopic observations.

[26] There are references to the Milky Way in early poems ("Elegy I," line 58; "In Obitum Praesulis Eliensis," line 60), but these show no consciousness of the fact that the Milky Way is composed of stars.

[27] The passages in question are: I, 650; II, 916; III, 566-70; VII, 191; VII, 209; VII, 621-22. Some doubtful instances: III, 668-70; V, 259, 268.

[28] Arthur O. Lovejoy considers Milton's God "A singularly detestable being" for setting up a cosmic riddle so that he may laugh at astronomers: "Milton's Dialogue on Astronomy," in *Reason and Imagination*, ed. Mazzeo (New York, 1962), p. 140. Milton's attitude is "an obscurantist ultilitarianism hostile to all disinterested intellectual curiosity" (p. 142).

[29] Svendsen (*Milton and Science*, pp. 233, 244-45) believes that Milton was not greatly concerned about astronomical truth. Cosmology, he says, was for Milton "a quarry of images, not a formal statement of scientific theory" (p. 43).

[30] McColley regards Milton's condemnation as conventional: *Growth and Origins*, pp. 92-97.

[31] *Bartas His Divine Weekes and Works* [1605], tr. Joshua Sylvester (Scholars' Facsimiles & Reprints, 1965), pp. 120-21; Sir John Davies, *Orchestra* [1596], *Complete Poems*, ed. Grosart (Fuller Worthies' Library, 1869), p. 196.

[32] In *PR* Milton incorporates the old meteorological idea of the zones of air and refers to the pillars of Heaven and the foundations of the earth (IV, 455-56). I am assuming that *PR* and *SA* were written later than *PL*.

[33] Concerning Dati, see James H. Hanford, *John Milton, Englishman* (New York, 1949), p. 79; William R. Parker, *Milton: A Biography* (Oxford, 1968), I, 178. Vincenzo Galilei was among those who sent "affectionate salutations" to Milton through Dati in Dati's letter of December 1648. See J. Milton French, *The Life Records of John Milton* (New Brunswick, N.J., 1949-58), II, 224.

[34] Sir Henry Wotton, for example, had at one time been much excited about Galileo's discoveries. See Marjorie Nicolson, "The 'New Astronomy' and English Imagination" [1935], in *Science and Imagination* (Ithaca, N.Y., 1956), pp. 35-36. Milton's personal contact with Wotten, however, was slight.

[35] See Nicolson, "The 'New Astronomy,'" pp. 38-39; Kuhn, *Copernican Revolution*, p. 225.

[36] "Milton and the Telescope" [1935], *Science and Imagination*, pp. 80-109. In this essay (p. 83) Miss Nicolson notes an apparent punning reference to the telescope ("Prospective Glass") in Milton's "Vacation Exercise," line 71.

[37] Miss Nicolson apparently believes that abstract theory as well as telescopic viewing stimulated Milton's spatial imagination. See *The Breaking of the Circle* (New York, 1960 [1950]), pp. 182-88. She does not, however, think that Milton became a Copernican: "Milton the artist felt aesthetic gratification in the new vastness which as metaphysician he did not accept."—p. 188. See also Miss Nicolson's *Mountain Gloom and Mountain Glory* (New York, 1959), pp. 273-76.

[38] For example: the passages quoted above (sec. iii) from the Third and Seventh Prolusions; "In Obitum Praesulis Eliensis," lines 47-64; "Naturam Non Pati Senium," lines 33-50.

[39] See Kuhn, *Copernican Revolution*, p. 227.

[40] Allan Gilbert proposes Galileo's *Dialogue* as the source of most of Milton's knowledge of the new astronomy: "Milton and Galileo," *SP*, XIX (1922), 152-85. Johnson (*Astronomical Thought*, 286-87) agrees with him and explains Milton's apparent ignorance of the Tychonic theory by the fact that Galileo says nothing of it. It is hard to believe that Milton could have been acquainted with Galileo's argument against life on the moon (*Dialogue*, pp. 63, 99-101) and yet have written Raphael's suggestion that there might be rain on the moon which would

"produce / Fruits in her soft'n'd Soil" (VIII, 146-47). McColley *(Growth and Origins,* pp. 217 ff.) has tried to show that nearly all of Milton's dialogue on astronomy was drawn from the debate on Copernicanism of Wilkins and Ross. Of all people McColley should know better than to name specific sources.

⁴¹John T. Shawcross, in "The Chronology of Milton's Major Poems," *PMLA,* LXXVI (1961), 345-58, has tried to demonstrate that the composition of *Paradise Lost* extended over several years, that considerable sections of it were written in the 1640's. It seems to me likely that this is true, though I have doubts about the details of Shawcross' chronology.

CHAPTER VII: THE COSMOS

¹The same appeal to the authority of the Fathers appears in *CD, Works,* XV, 33. In neither place does Milton name his authorities. Grant McColley is happy to supply the deficiency *(Growth and Origins,* p. 29).

²*CD, Works,* XV, 35.

³.Burton, *Anatomy,* II, 49.

⁴*Works,* XVI, 375. He suggests also in *DDD* that Hell lies outside the world: *Works,* III, 442.

⁵"Sed quonam in loco, inquies, erit? Extra mundum hunc totum, ut ego puto. Quemadmodum enim regum carceres et metalla procul posita sunt, ita extra mundum hunc erit gehenna. Non ergo quaeramus ubinam sit, sed quomodo illam fugiamus."—*Patrologia Graeca,* LX, 674.

⁶*Ibid.,* XLVII, 427.

⁷*Luther's Works* (St. Louis, 1958-67), I, 10. The story is in St. Augustine's *Confessions,* XI, 12.

⁸McColley writes that, in placing Hell in Chaos, Milton had "the example of various theologians and poets."—*Growth and Origins,* p. 99. He does not name the theologians and poets. According to Allan Gilbert, Milton's "assignment of hell to a place beyond the limits of the world . . . has backing in the writings of the Fathers."—"The Outside Shell," *SP,* XX (1923), p. 445. He names no Fathers. Robert H. West believes that Milton's placing Hell outside the world was "Against almost everybody."—*Milton and the Angels,* p. 125. It is Curry's opinion that "the arrangement of contents in Milton's total universe is different essentially from that of all others conceived."—*Milton's Ontology,* p. 184.

⁹Robins, *If This be Heresy,* pp. 103-04. McColley *(Growth and Origins,* pp. 131-32) quotes the same passage as an analogue for Milton's outer shell. He quotes also, from Chapter XXXVII of *The Book of Enoch,* a description of a fiery Hell located in "a place chaotic and horrible" *(ibid.,* p. 100). There is a remote resemblance to Milton's Hell within Chaos.

¹⁰Robins attempts to work out the directions suggested in the text of *Paradise Lost* and their symbolic meanings: "Satan's Journey: Direction in *Paradise Lost,*" *JEGP,* LX (1961), 699-711. Although he may have found more directional significances in the poem than Milton intended, his article is revealing. See also Curry, *Milton's Ontology,* pp. 147 ff. Robins says that Heaven's gate faces east; Curry says west.

¹¹William Fairfield Warren, in *The Universe as Pictured in Milton's Paradise Lost* (New York, 1915), reproduces earlier scholars' diagrams of Milton's universe and adds his own (pp. 23, 27). B. A. Wright deplores the diagrams: "Masson's Diagram of Milton's Spaces," *Review of English Studies,* XXI (1945), 42-44. "Milton's spaces," he says, "are infinitely better" (p. 44).

¹²Robins believes that Milton's Heaven is square ("Satan's Journey," pp. 700-01). Circularity seems more in keeping with Renaissance symbolism. But as Robins points out, Revelation xxi, 16, supports the idea of a square shape.

¹³Joseph Summers, in his essay on "Grateful Vicissitude" *(The Muse's Method,* pp. 71-86), sees in this alternation of light and shadow an illustration of the "change, variety, movement . . . vitality and joy characteristic of both the divine and the human master artist's work" (p. 71) —characteristic, that is, both of God's universe and of the poem in which Milton celebrates it.

¹⁴See Chap. V, notes 4, 16.

¹⁵William G. Madsen denies the Platonic sense and argues that the war in Heaven is typological, a foreshadowing of the coming tribulations of humanity, to be relieved by the Son of God: *From Shadowy Types,* pp. 87-88, 111.

¹⁶Edgar H. Duncan, in his article on "Minerals and Metals," comments on the mineralogy and chemistry of this passage (pp. 411-12).

¹⁷The "value of gold or any other material thing depends on one's attitude toward it."— Madsen, *Nature*, p. 232. This may be Milton's belief. Yet Jesus asserts in *PR* that riches are "the toil of Fools, / The wise man's cumbrance if not snare" (II, 453-54). Helen Gardner believes that the oriental splendor of the imagery of Revelation was an "obstacle" preventing Milton "from exercising his power to suggest."—*A Reading of Paradise Lost*, p. 55.

¹⁸*CD, Works*, XV, 35.

¹⁹West writes that materially Milton's angels consist of "what the age called *ether* or the *empyrean* or *heavenly fire;* Milton repeatedly refers to them as 'Ethereal substance' (VI, 330), 'Empyreal substance' (I, 118), 'Empyreal forme' (VI, 433)."—*Milton and the Angels*, p. 141. The terms are so vague that I do not know whether I have disagreed with West or not. Curry (p. 162) believes that the substance of both Heaven and the angels is "ether," or quintessence. He does not identify Milton's fifth essence, however, with Aristotle's ether. See Chap. V, note 16.

²⁰See West, pp. 131-35.

²¹James H. Hanford has reviewed Milton's military studies and his use of military terms and concepts in *PL* and *PR*: "Milton and the Art of War" [1921], in Hanford's *John Milton: Poet and Humanist* (Cleveland, 1966), pp. 185-233.

²²A. B. Chambers deals with the history of Chaos in classical and Christian literature and with the nature of Milton's Chaos and its unusual features: "Chaos in *Paradise Lost,*" *JHI*, XXIV (1963), 55-84. This is an unusually competent and enlightening article. In another article Chambers explains why Milton, appropriately, calls the non-watery Chaos a sea: "The Sea of Matter in *Paradise Lost,*" *Modern Language Notes,*" LXXVI (1961), 693-95.

²³Though he does not follow Aristotle, Milton's characterization of chaotic matter seems to owe something to what Aristotle says about primary qualities ("contraries") and the "simple bodies" with which they associate themselves: *De Generatione et Corruptione*, 229-30.

²⁴This is Curry's idea *(Milton's Ontology*, p. 162).

²⁵Curry believes that Milton's atoms are very transiently earthy, airy, etc. (pp. 79-80). According to Chambers, matter in Chaos is "partially endowed with form" ("Chaos," p. 74).

²⁶Chambers *(ibid.,* pp. 75-76) identifies Night with the primal matter. Curry (pp. 48-73) believes that Milton's Chaos and Night represent Neoplatonic concepts.

²⁷E. M. W. Tillyard considers this passage "one of the grandest and most elaborate in *Paradise Lost.*"—"The Causeway from Hell to the World in the Tenth Book of *Paradise Lost,*" *SP*, XXXVIII (1941), 266.

²⁸Curry prints an ingenious sketch (p. 156) showing a vertical tube leading from Hellgates to the surface of Chaos and a horizontal bridge stretching across the surface of Chaos from the top of the tube to the world. There is no mention of a tube in Milton's lines.

²⁹John E. Hankins deals with the traditional Christian features of Milton's hell: "The Pains of the Afterworld: Fire, Wind, and Ice in Milton and Shakespeare," *PMLA*, LXXI (1956), 482-95. Marjorie Nicolson thinks it likely that Milton's recollection of a volcanic area near Naples has contributed to his description of the region around Pandaemonium: "Milton's Hell and the Phlegraean Fields," *University of Toronto Quarterly*, VII (1938), 500-13. Rebecca W. Smith relates Milton's representation of Pandaemonium with his memories of the Church of St. Peter in Rome: "The Source of Milton's Pandemonium," *MP*, XXIX (1931), 187-98. Irene Samuel, in *Dante and Milton* (Ithaca, N.Y., 1966), points out similarities between Milton's and Dante's conceptions of Hell (see Chap. IV, especially pp. 69-84). The similarities are not very striking. J. B. Broadbent, in Chap. II of *Some Graver Subject* (London, 1960), comments on the aesthetic and emotional effects of Milton's description of Hell.

³⁰John M. Steadman presents documentation from seventeenth-century writers and from Basil, Ambrose, and Gregory the Great to show that lightless fire was traditional and conventional: "Milton and the Patristic Tradition: The Quality of Hell-fire," *Anglia*, LXXVI (1958), 116-28.

³¹Roland M. Frye regards the torments of Milton's Hell as symbolic: *God, Man, and Satan*, pp. 39, 40. Joseph E. Duncan analyzes Milton's ideas concerning God's punishments, physical and mental: "Milton's Four-in-One Hell," *Huntington Library Quarterly*, XX (1957), 127-36. Ernest Schanzer points out the correspondency between the mental state of the damned sinner and his infernal environment: "Milton's Hell Revisited," *University of Toronto Quarterly*,

XXIV (1955), 136-45. C. A. Patrides reviews Renaissance discussion of the pains, physical and psychological, which the damned must suffer: "Renaissance and Modern Views on Hell," *HTR*, LVII (1964), pp. 217-36.

[32] *DDD, Works*, III, 442.

[33] *CD, Works*, XVI, 371.

[34] As B. A. Wright puts it, this is "an intensive, or rather idefinitely extensive, not a computative expression."—"Masson's Diagram" (see note 11), p. 43.

[35] *DDD, Works*, III, 442.

[36] Merritt Y. Hughes surveys the abundant critical writing on Milton's concept of light and adds some ideas of his own: "Milton and the Symbol of Light," *Studies in English Literature*, IV (1964), 1-33.

[37] The "holy Light" which Milton addresses at the opening of Book III has been identified with the Son of God: William B. Hunter, Jr., "Holy Light in *Paradise Lost*," *Rice Institute Pamphlet*, XLVI (Jan. 1960), 1-14; J. H. Adamson, "Milton's Arianism," *HTR*, LIII (1960), 269-76; Albert R. Cirillo, " 'Hail Holy Light' and Divine Time in *Paradise Lost*," *JEGP*, LXVIII (1969), 45-56. I do not believe that this was Milton's meaning. It is not possible to argue this complex question briefly. I shall simply say that, because the Son (before as well as after the Incarnation) is a creature, he can hardly be a "Coeternal beam." See Chap. VIII, sec. iv.

[38] In commenting on Isaiah xlv, 7 ("I form the light, and create darkness"), Milton says in *CD (Works*, XV, 17) that darkness is a created thing. In *PR*, however, he writes concerning darkness and night that they are "unsubstantial both, / Privation mere of light and absent day" (IV, 399-400).

[39] There is no evidence in Milton's works, as there is in Cowley's, of knowledge of contemporary developments in the science of optics. Yet light has much the same religious significance to both of them. See Hinman, *Cowley's World*, pp. 299-315.

[40] See Williams, *Common Expositor*, pp. 52-54, for exegetical opinions concerning the light that shone in the world before the creation of the sun.

[41] Don Cameron Allen finds clarification in a doctrine of Ficino's: The divine light ("essential" light) is incorporeal; "but as it descends from the fountain of light, it assumes materiality, it becomes clouded and shadowy."—*The Harmonious Vision* (Baltimore, 1954), p. 101. Joseph A. Mazzeo reviews doctrines concerning light which appear in the works of Neoplatonists and of Christian writers under Neoplatonic influence: "Light Metaphysics," *Traditio*, XIV (1958), 191-229. This is an excellent study. Although it concerns Dante, not Milton, it expounds various ideas which could readily be read into *Paradise Lost*, such as the idea of the emanation of divine light downward through a hierarchy of forms of being, or the idea of the diffusion of vivifying divine influence in the physical world through the luminous heavenly bodies.

[42] David Dickson shows that the language which Milton uses in reference to the Son would have suggested to a seventeenth-century reader the "metaphor of divine Light reflecting divine Light," which Christian writers had often used in explaining the relation of the Son to the Father: "Milton's 'Son of God,': A Study in Imagery and Orthodoxy," *Papers of the Michigan Academy*, XXXVI (1950), 275-81. See also the articles by Hunter and Adamson cited above, note 37.

[43] A. B. Chambers points out the traditional belief that the loss of physical sight enhances the inner vision: "Wisdom at One Entrance Quite Shut Out," *PQ*, XLII (1963), 114-19.

[44] Isabel MacCaffrey develops the idea that place and direction have moral meanings: *Paradise Lost as "Myth"* (Cambridge, Mass., 1959), pp. 64-73.

CHAPTER VIII: SPACE, MATTER, AND TIME

[1] It is Marjorie Nicolson's opinion that "to Milton, God, not Space, was infinite."—"Milton and the Telescope," *Science and Imagination*, p. 107. The universe of *PL*, she says, "is not infinite, yet it is indefinite, immense, and majestic."—*Breaking of the Circle*, p. 188. Curry's idea that Milton's space "is curved, closed but boundless, and finite," that it is a "tiny bubble" within God's infinity is not really supported by anything that Milton himself says (*Milton's Ontology*, pp. 20, 43, 145).

[2] *CD, Works*, XIV, 42.

[3] *Ibid.*, XV, 27. Patrides (*Christian Tradition*, pp. 29-33) reviews the *creatio-ex-nihilo* versus

creatio-ex-Deo controversy. Adamson believes that Milton misunderstood the *creatio-ex-Deo* theory ("Milton and the Creation," pp. 757-58). If this is true, many Milton commentators have also misunderstood it.

⁴ *Works*, XV, 23.

⁵ *Works*, XI, 53. Milton undoubtedly knew of Aristotle's distinction between the material substrate and sensible matter: *De Physica*, 191a, 192a; *De Generatione et Corruptione*, 329. Costello's *Scholastic Curriculum* includes a useful explanation of the Aristotelian concept of matter (pp. 74-75).

⁶Chambers, "Chaos," p. 81. Curry (*Milton's Ontology*, p. 36) and Robins (*If This Be Heresy*, pp. 47, 76-78) interpret Milton similarly. Robins believes that Milton might have derived the idea from Origen. Woodhouse ("Milton's Views of the Creation," p. 221) names Stoic sources from which Milton might have derived his "theistic monism."

⁷ *CD, Works*, XV, 23.

⁸ *Ibid.*, XV, 21, 25. John Reesing discusses this difficult question: "The Materiality of God in Milton's De Doctrina Christiana," *HTR*, L (1957), 159-73. See also Woodhouse, p. 222.

⁹Woodhouse believes that God, as Milton conceives him, necessarily has potentiality (p. 223). See also Reesing, p. 171 (note).

¹⁰My understanding of these much disputed lines agrees substantially with Kelley's (*This Great Argument*, p. 211), with Woodhouse's (pp. 226-28), and with Summers' (*The Muse's Method*, pp. 138-39).

¹¹According to *CD*, the spirit that moved on the waters—"that divine breath or influence by which every thing is created and nourished"—refers to the Son, the Creator (*Works*, XIV, 359). Elsewhere he speaks of God's (the Son's?) breathing "the breath of life into [all] living beings" (XV, 53). In *PL* the Spirit that took part in the Creation seems to be the personal Holy Spirit. See below, sec. v.

¹² *Works*, XV, 49, 53.

¹³Curry (pp. 33-37, 105-06, 116) and Chambers ("Chaos," pp. 77-79) believe that in Milton's universe God plants the "seeds" of forms in matter. The theory of the seeds (*rationes seminales*) which God has implanted in the material world was widely known in the seventeenth century. William B. Hunter, Jr., deals informatively with this concept and its seventeenth-century modifications: "The Seventeenth Century Doctrine of Plastic Nature," *HTR*, XLIII (1950), 197-213. Its origin was classical; it received Christian sanction from Augustine and Aquinas. In another article Hunter denies that Milton subscribes to this doctrine, pointing out the fact that he never specifically mentions it: "Milton's Power of Matter," *JHI*, XIII (1952), 551-62. One can only guess at what Milton means by "that power . . . communicated to matter by the Deity" (*CD, Works*, XV, 53). But it seems unlikely that he could have adopted the seminal theory without occasionally using its characteristic vocabulary: *seeds, spermatikoi, rationes seminales.*

¹⁴ *CD, Works*, XV, 23.

¹⁵ *Ibid.*, XV, 53.

¹⁶ *Ibid.*, XV, 25.

¹⁷Laurence Stapleton reviews what Milton has to say on this subject in *CD*: "Milton's Conception of Time in *The Christian Doctrine*," *HTR*, LVII (1964), 9-21. In a later article he traces the chronology of events in *PL* and comments on Milton's artistry in the handling of the time element: "Perspectives of Time in *Paradise Lost*," *PQ*, LXV (1966), 734-48. Other discussions of time in *PL*: MacCaffrey, *Paradise Lost as "Myth*," pp. 73-81; Rosalie L. Colie, *Paradoxia Epidemica* (Princeton, 1966), Chap. V; Jackson I. Cope, *The Metaphorical Structure of Paradise Lost* (Baltimore, 1962), Chap. III; Albert R. Cirillo, "Noon-Midnight and the Temporal Structure of *Paradise Lost*," *Journal of English Literary History*, XXIX (1962), 372-95; Cirillo's article on "Holy Light" (see Chap. VII, note 37).

¹⁸ *CD, Works*, XV, 35. See also p. 241. This is a commonplace derived from Plato's *Timaeus*, 37-38, and from Aristotle's *De Caelo*, 279a, and *Metaphysics*, 1017b.

¹⁹ *De Trinitate*, in *Boethius*, tr. Stewart and Rand (Loeb Classical Library, 1926), p. 21. St. Augustine's reflections on eternity are in Book XI of the Confessions. See also Plato's *Timaeus*, 37-38. This is still orthodox Roman Catholic doctrine; see Romano Guardini, *The Last Things*, tr. Forsythe and Branham (South Bend, Ind., 1965), pp. 102, 104.

²⁰ *Works*, XIV, 43.

²¹ *Works*, XI, 93-95. Milton goes even further: "all times are not present to God, as is popularly

supposed, for he is able to change the present but not the past."—*ibid.*, p. 309.

[22]Milton's belief that time began before the Creation of the world was a minority view; see Arnold Williams, "Renaissance Commentaries on 'Genesis' and Some Elements of the Theology of *Paradise Lost,*" *PMLA*, LVI (1941), p. 156.

[23]*CD, Works*, XIV, 181.

[24]*Ibid.*, XIV, 191.

[25]Hunter points out a passage in *CD* in which Milton uses three different verbs for the Father's engendering of the Son: "Milton's Arianism Reconsidered," *HTR*, LII (1959), 22-23. In the passage in question ("Deus Filium . . . creavit sive generavit aut produxit," *Works*, XIV, 192) Milton is commenting on Colossians i, 15, and Revelation iii, 14, and is trying to reconcile the phrases occurring in these texts ("rei creatae," "principium creationis Dei") with his own terminology. He is fairly consistent in avoiding *creatio* and *creo* in connection with the Son. He believes "spiritum sanctum . . . creatum, id est, productum fuisse."—*ibid.*, p. 402.

[26]*Ibid.*, XIV, 179.

[27]*The Poetical Works of John Milton* (London, 1890), III, 473. In *This Great Argument* (pp. 94-101) Kelley reviews the somewhat voluminous literature concerning this subject up to 1940. He rejects the emergence theory.

[28]See William B. Hunter's "Milton's Arianism Reconsidered" and his article on "Holy Light." J. H. Adamson ("Milton's Arianism") supports Hunter but has somewhat different ideas concerning sources. Another recent version of the stages-of-existence theory is that of Harry F. Robins: *If This Be Heresy*, pp. 48-53, 98-100, 115-18.

[29]*Works*, XIV, 193.

[30]*Ibid.*, XIV, 181, 183.

[31]*Ibid.*, XIV, 341, 181.

[32]*Ibid.*, XIV, 189.

[33]*Ibid.*, XIV, 401.

[34]*Ibid.*, XIV, 211. C. A. Patrides believes that, although Father and Son are distinct persons during the heavenly dialogues, they become one in the terrestrial scenes: "The Godhead in *Paradise Lost*: Dogma or Drama?" *JEGP*, LXIV (1965), 29-34. He finds good support in *PL*, VIII, 405-07. But there are many objections.

[35]*CD, Works*, XIV, 315-21.

[36]*Documents of the Christian Church*, selected and edited by Henry Bettenson (London, 1963), pp. 37, 57-58.

[37]Hunter has made it clear that *subordinationist* is the more accurate term: "Milton's Arianism Reconsidered." Adamson supports him in his article on "Milton's Arianism." Maurice Kelley makes it equally clear that, as the term is ordinarily and imprecisely used, Milton is an Arian: "Milton's Arianism Again Considered," *HTR*, LIV (1961), 195-205; "Milton and 'Arian,'" *Seventeenth-Century News*, Spring-Summer, 1965, pp. 2-3, and Spring 1969, p. 5. Barbara Lewalski's discussion of the subject *(Milton's Brief Epic*, Providence, R.I., 1966, pp. 138 ff.) seems to me sane and well informed. There are many others.

[38]Patrides finds contrary evidence and insists that, although there is heterodoxy in *CD, PL* is orthodox: "Milton and Arianism," *JHI*, XXV (1964), 423-29. Stella Purce Revard argues that, as the Father endows the Son with various powers during the poem, he is progressively raising him toward equality ("all Power / I give thee," III, 317-18): "The Dramatic Function of the Son in *Paradise Lost*: A Commentary on Milton's 'Trinitarianism,'" *JEGP*, LXVI (1967), 45-58. The Son, then, receives equality by gift, is not equal by nature. The argument seems very reasonable.

[39]Milton himself uses the word in various senses. See Chap. IV, note 31.

[40]*Works*, XIV, 403.

[41]*Ibid.*, XIV, 341.

[42]*Ibid.*, XIV, 367, 369.

[43]*Ibid.*, XIV, 395.

[44]*Ibid.*, XV, 13. Cf. XIV, 361.

[45]Some commentators regard the Spirit and the Heavenly Muse of the invocation as the same person. John M. Steadman reviews the various opinions and adds his own: "Spirit and Muse: A Reconsideration of Milton's Urania," *Archiv für das Studium der Neueren Sprachen und Literaturen*, CC (1964), 353-57. Steadman believes that, at the opening of *PL*, Milton is address-

ing two persons: Urania, who personifies the power of appropriate utterance, and the Holy Spirit, from whom he hopes to receive inner illumination. This opinion, I believe, is valid.

⁴⁶Bettenson, *Documents*, p. 37. Luther believes that the Holy Spirit, brooding bird-like over the waters, infused life into lifeless and chaotic matter. See Chap. V, note 29.

⁴⁷McColley (*Growth and Origins*, pp. 16-17, 159-61), Stapleton (*op. cit.* in note 17), and Gardner (*A Reading of Paradise Lost*, pp. 37-39) have worked out chronological schedules for *PL*, all of them differing somewhat from mine.

⁴⁸Yet just before the battle, there are references to Hell as a place already existing (VI, 53-55, 183). The rebellious angels seem to have had prior knowledge of the creation of the world and man (I, 650-54; II, 345-49).

⁴⁹Albert R. Cirillo, in his article on "Noon-Midnight" (see note 17), points out that all important events in the poem happen at noon or midnight (also a noon). Noon is "the image of eternity" (p. 375). So events are happening both in time and eternity.

⁵⁰McColley (*Growth and Origins*, p. 160) is under the impression that Satan first sees Adam and Eve on the day of their creation. Harris Fletcher says that Adam "had had at most but a few hours or a day and a night" before Raphael's visit (*Milton's Rabbinical Readings*, p. 190). No such brief period is specified or implied anywhere in Milton's lines.

⁵¹Williams, *Common Expositor*, p. 137.

⁵²H. R. MacCallum ("Milton and Sacred History: Books XI and XII of *Paradise Lost,*" in *Essays . . . Presented to A. S. P. Woodhouse*, ed. MacLure and Watt, Toronto, 1964, pp. 149-68) shows a correspondency between Michael's review of history and the traditional six ages of the world. He also traces the considerable element of typology in these two books. See also Whiting, "The Pattern of Time and Eternity," in *Milton and This Pendant World*, pp. 169-200.

⁵³*Paradise Lost as "Myth,"* p. 53. *PL* "is meant to be seen, is only rightly seen, as a great *structure.*" The poem is not static. But the poet "provides a medium in which motion can take place without the awareness of temporal process . . . the design is dynamic as architecture is." —pp. 50-51.

⁵⁴C. A. Patrides, *The Phoenix and the Ladder: The Rise and Decline of the Christian View of History* (Berkeley, 1964), pp. 36, 59. Joseph A. Bryant ("Milton's Views on Decay," pp. 8-9) shows the development of a cyclic theory of history in Milton's works prior to 1645.

⁵⁵French R. Fogle, "Milton as Historian," in *Milton and Clarenden* (Los Angeles: Clark Library, 1965), pp. 15-16.

⁵⁶*PL*, III, 313-41; X, 630-39; XII, 451-65, 545-51. Patrides deals very adequately with Milton's eschatology and its relation to tradition (*Christian Tradition*, pp. 264-79). See also Robins, *If This Be Heresy*, pp. 151-56.

⁵⁷*CD, Works*, XV, 239. See Chap. IV, sec. v.

⁵⁸*Ibid.*, XVI, 353.

⁵⁹*Ibid.*, XV, 251.

⁶⁰Especially on Matthew xxiv, xxv; Mark xiii, 24-37; Luke xvii, 20-36; xxi, 8-28; II Peter iii; Revelation xx, xxi, 1.

⁶¹D. P. Walker (*The Decline of Hell*, p. 35) says that Christian writers, finding the passage on the Millenium awkward, tended to ignore it. Robins (*If This Be Heresy*, pp. 54, 59, 155) says that Milton was a millenarian. Patrides (*Christian Tradition*, pp. 278-79) says that Milton abandoned belief in millenarianism. The pertinent passage in *CD (Works*, XVI, 359-65) seems to me a compromise.

There are suggestions of Christ's warfare with Satan toward the end of time in *PL* (III, 250-61; XII, 451-55), but just where this belongs in Milton's eschatological sequence is not clear.

⁶²*Works*, XVI, 349.

⁶³*Ibid.*, XVI, 363, 359.

⁶⁴*Ibid.*, XV, 3-5.

⁶⁵*Ibid.*, XV, 5.

BIBLIOGRAPHY

J. H. Adamson. "Milton's Arianism," *HTR*, LIII (1960), 269-76.
————"Milton and the Creation," *JEGP*, LXI (1962), 756-78.
Theodore H. Banks. *Milton's Imagery.* New York, 1950.
Joseph A. Bryant, Jr. "Milton's Views on Universal and Civil Decay," in *SAMLA Studies in Milton,* ed. J. Max Patrick (Gainesville, Fla., 1953), pp. 1-19.
Robert Burton. *The Anatomy of Melancholy.* Ed. A. R. Shilleto. Three vols. London, 1926-27.
A. B. Chambers, "Chaos in *Paradise Lost,*" *JHI*, XXIV (1963), 55-84.
George N. Conklin. *Biblical Criticism and Heresy in Milton.* New York, 1949.
William T. Costello, S. J. *The Scholastic Curriculum at Early Seventeenth-Century Cambridge.* Cambridge, Mass., 1958.
Walter Clyde Curry. *Milton's Ontology, Cosmogony, and Physics.* Lexington, Ky., 1957.
J. L. E. Dreyer. *A History of Astronomy from Thales to Kepler.* New York, 1953 [1905].
Edgar H. Duncan. "The Natural History of Metals and Minerals in the Universe of Milton's *Paradise Lost,*" *Osiris,* XI (1954), 386-421.
J. M. Evans. *Paradise Lost and the Genesis Tradition.* Oxford, 1968.
Harris F. Fletcher. *Milton's Rabbinical Readings.* Urbana, 1930.
Helen Gardner. *A Reading of Paradise Lost.* Oxford, 1965.
S. K. Heninger, Jr. *A Handbook of Renaissance Meteorology.* Durham, N.C., 1960.
Robert B. Hinman. *Abraham Cowley's World of Order.* Cambridge, Mass., 1960.
William B. Hunter, Jr. "Milton's Materialistic Life Principle,"*JEGP,* XLV (1946), 68-76.
————"The Seventeenth Century Doctrine of Plastic Nature,"*HTR,* XLIII (1950), 197-213.
————"Milton's Power of Matter," *JHI,* XIII (1952), 551-62.
————"Milton's Arianism Reconsidered," *HTR,* LII (1959), 9-35.
————"Holy Light in *Paradise Lost,*" *Rice Institute Pamphlet,* XLVI (Jan. 1960), 1-14.
Francis R. Johnson. *Astronomical Thought in Renaissance England.* Baltimore, 1937.
Maurice Kelley. *This Great Argument: A Study of Milton's De Doctrina Christiana as a Gloss upon Paradise Lost.* Princeton, 1941.
Paul H. Kocher. *Science and Religion in Elizabethan England.* San Marino, 1953.
Thomas S. Kuhn. *The Copernican Revolution: Planetary Astronomy in the Development of Western Thought.* Cambridge, Mass., 1957.
Isabel G. MacCaffrey. *Paradise Lost as "Myth."* Cambridge, Mass., 1959.
William G. Madsen. *The Idea of Nature in Milton's Poetry,* in *Three Studies in the Renaissance* (New Haven, 1958), pp. 181-283.
————*From Shadowy Types to Truth: Studies in Milton's Symbolism.* New Haven, 1968.
Joseph A. Mazzeo. "Light Metaphysics, Dante's 'Convivio,' and the Letter to Can Grande Della Scala," *Traditio,* XIV (1958), 191-229.
Grant McColley. *Paradise Lost: An Account of Its Growth and Major Origins.* New York, 1963 [1940].
Marjorie Nicolson. *Science and Imagination.* Ithaca, N.Y., 1956.
C. A. Patrides. *Milton and the Christian Tradition.* Oxford, 1966.
Harry F. Robins. *If This Be Heresy: A Study of Milton and Origen.* Urbana, 1963.
Denis Saurat. *Milton: Man and Thinker.* London, 1944 [1925].
Arnold Stein. *Answerable Style: Essays on Paradise Lost.* Mineapolis, 1953.
Joseph H. Summers. *The Muse's Method: An Introduction to Paradise Lost.* Cambridge, Mass., 1962.

BIBLIOGRAPHY

Kester Svendsen. *Milton and Science*. Cambridge, Mass., 1956.

Robert H. West. *Milton and the Angels*. Athens, Ga., 1955.

George W. Whiting. *Milton's Literary Milieu*. New York, 1964 [1939].

————*Milton and This Pendant World*. Austin, Texas, 1958.

Basil Willey. *The Seventeenth Century Background*. Garden City, N.Y., 1953 [1934].

Arnold Williams. *The Common Expositor: An Account of the Commentaries on Genesis, 1527-1633*. Chapel Hill, 1948.

A. S. P. Woodhouse. "Notes on Milton's Views of the Creation: The Initial Phases," *PQ* XXVIII (1949), 211-36.

INDEX